THOMAS BEECHAM:
AN INDEPENDENT BIOGRAPHY

THOMAS BEECHAM

An Independent Biography

by

CHARLES REID

READERS UNION
VICTOR GOLLANCZ LTD
LONDON 1962

This RU edition was produced in 1962 for sale to
its members only by Readers Union Ltd at Aldine
House, 10-13 Bedford Street, London W.C.2 and
at Letchworth Garden City, Herts. Full details of
membership may be obtained from our London address.
The book is set in 11 point Bembo type leaded and
has been reprinted by The Camelot Press Ltd, Southampton. It was first published by Victor Gollancz Ltd.

*To those hundreds of musicians who, during half
a century, played in Thomas Beecham's three great
English orchestras, making the world resound with
his gifts—and their own*

PART I

CONTENTS

INTRODUCTORY

A WORD ABOUT THE proportions of this book.

The life of Sir Thomas Beecham Bart, C.H., was crowded, combative and loquacious to a degree which has no parallel whatsoever in English musical history and few parallels in any other field or country. So many things happened to him—and he, in turn, happened to so many things and to so many people—that a readable volume could be written about each decade of his career from 1899 on. Such a scale would yield six volumes in all. Instead of six, here is one.

The processes of winnowing and selection have perforce been rigorous. A more detailed picture will be found in these pages of the young Beecham and his environment than of the accepted and enthroned master. This duality of scale was adopted for two principal reasons.

Firstly, the Beecham who exploded upon London music and London society under Edward VII was, in relation to his milieu, a more startling phenomenon than the Beecham who railed and quipped and generally applied himself to the business of stirring people up under succeeding reigns. Secondly, the magnitude and excitement of his pre-1915 achievements, whether in the concert hall or at Covent Garden and Drury Lane, have been without counterpart or similitude from that time to this. In short, the Beecham of the early battles or girding himself for them is, on the whole, the most rewarding Beecham of the six to read about.

Much of the present narrative traverses the period covered by Beecham's first volume of autobiography. For this the author makes no apology. *A Mingled Chime* was remarkable even more for what its author left out than for what he put in. Certain of his omissions were dictated by modesty, others by prudence. An attempt is made in the first sections of this book to fill some of the gaps.

A further word as to sources. This account is based in part on conversations with many who, during sixty years, worked for Beecham; with members of his family; and, not least, with Beecham himself whom the writer first met, as a musical journalist, nearly thirty years ago. For the rest use has been made of a vast accumulation of printed or written material, including diaries, memoirs and millions of words of newsprint.

Hampstead, June 1961.   C.R.

CHAPTER ONE

THE MAYOR'S CONCERT

(1)

At FIFTY-ONE, Joseph Beecham, father of Thomas, had greying hair and a reddish drooping moustache. His manner with strangers was diffident or shrewd according to the business in hand. The more intimate of his critics said he was capable of harshness, even of cruelty. For reasons of their own, these critics reckoned his income, based on the million pills a day he was selling, at £85,000. When cornered Joseph put his earnings at £20,000 a year, not a penny more. He appears to have arrived at this sum by an ingenious whittling-down process which was more cogent to himself than to the outside world.

Unostentatious by long habit, he dressed on ordinary occasions less like a pill-making millionaire than a solid senior clerk in one of his own counting houses. Wednesday December 6th, 1899, was no ordinary occasion, however. For his reinstallation as Mayor of St. Helens, Lancashire, and for the Mayor's concert which, conducted by his son Tom, was to follow, he had ordered from Edes of London, robemakers to the Queen, a robe of state whose opulent like the town had not seen or suspected before. It was of corded crimson silk, with a white silk lining and black velvet trimmings, the whole edged with sable fur. With the robe went a gilt-looped hat in black silk.

The grandeur of these trappings must have struck many who had watched Joseph grow up as out of keeping with his retiring nature. In many male lives the age of fifty is a crucial divide. The truth seems to be that Joseph's nature was in the process of change. He was sloughing old skins and uncovering a new self. The new self, as will appear, was enterprisingly, even scandalously amorous. On Sundays now and then he still went to the Congregational church and listened approvingly to the sermons of his confidant and counsellor, the Reverend Alfred Carter, *éminence noire* of the Ewanville household. Afterwards he would fumblingly play hymns on the electrically-blown organ which had replaced the old hand-pumped one in the billiard room at Ewanville, his mansion outside St. Helens. These were habits of the old Joseph. They lingered on to the end, surviving the new Joseph's dream and feats of public glory.

With the Mayor's concert, a sumptuous innovation for St. Helens, he was entering upon a career of patronage which culminated fifteen years later in various bewildering things: pattings on the back from the fabulous Diaghilev; a baronetcy piled on top of a knighthood and the Order of Saint Stanislaus (conferred by Czar Nicholas II) piled on top of that; and a wholly improbable night at the Theatre Royal, Drury Lane, when, after a performance of *Petrushka*, he was hauled on to the stage and given a gilded laurel wreath which he didn't know how to get rid of. Against the garish scenery of Admiralty Square, St. Petersburg, *circa* 1830, with its showman's booth and hucksters' stalls, he cut a pallid and sheepish figure. There was a tumult of clapping and cheers that night from an effervescent, fashionable audience and from respectful Russian dancers, who came crowding on from the wings still in their costumes and greasepaint.

This was a startling apotheosis for a man who once said, "Although I am one of the biggest advertisers in the world, I do not like advertising myself. I have a strong aversion to the limelight, and I never allow a photograph of myself to be published."

(2)

While attendants were getting Joseph into his robe in a Town Hall antechamber, intent preparations were going on outside. At the Fleece Hotel in Church Street, the landlord, Mr. Bennett, and his womenfolk were preparing mountains of sandwiches and rivers of lemonade and claret cup. The sandwich varieties were tabulated on frilly-edged menu cards: shrimp, lobster, *foie gras*, beef, chicken and ham. Gardeners brought palm trees, rare ferns and drayloads of chrysanthemums from the municipal greenhouses and from the Mayor's own conservatories at Ewanville to adorn the Town Hall corridors and the platform in the adjoining assembly room. In the square before the Town Hall men on mobile towers were rigging arc lamps in globes netted with wire to enhance the brilliance of an occasion which, like Joseph's robe, was unmatched in the town's history. The traditional Mayor's reception had been tea and buns for a handful of duty guests, cronies and wives. Instead of a handful Joseph had invited between eight and nine hundred. As well as claret cup and *foie gras* he was giving his guests Beethoven, Wagner and Tchaikovsky.

As he looked himself over in the anteroom mirror he had only one immediate worry. During the morning Miss Blauvelt, who was down on the programme for soprano numbers from *Roméo et Juliette* and *I Vespri Siciliani*, had sent a message that she was unwell and could not sing. Making the most of his new-found buoyancy, the Mayor had talked Miss Blauvelt out of her indisposition; but there was some doubt as to whether she would be able to turn up for the rehearsal with the Hallé Orchestra during the afternoon. Lillian Blauvelt, a twenty-five year-old American, was highly considered by a rising young conductor, Henry J. Wood (later Sir Henry) for whom she sang at the Albert Hall. Looking back after forty years Wood bracketed Blauvelt ("a happy and fascinating personality") with Busoni, Kreisler and Casals, among others, in a short list of the finest artists with whom he ever collaborated. Tom Beecham (who later had different views on the subject) thought highly of Mr. Wood's judgments and all his musical works. The question which gnawed the Mayor was whether Tom, with an unrehearsed Blauvelt on his hands, might not come a humiliating cropper.

At one minute to two the Mayor, preceded by his mace bearer, entered the council chamber, rapped with his gavel and hoped the members would get through the business quickly, as the Hallé band had a rehearsal in the contiguous assembly room at 3 p.m.—"and I am afraid if we are not through by then we shall either disturb them or they will disturb us." There was a tendency to browse over the minutes of the sewage committee, and passions were threatened by paving and street lighting. By judicious driving the Mayor rounded these and other danger points. The Council rose at 2.50 p.m.

(3)

Already the Hallé Orchestra, seventy-five strong, had come in from Manchester and were waiting for the Mayor's son on the bedizened assembly room platform.

When he first arranged the concert—and undertook to pay for it— the Mayor understood that it would be conducted by the celebrated Dr. Hans Richter, whilom protégé of Richard Wagner. Richter's patriarchal beard, spectacles, frock coat and billycock hat were to be a cultural portent in and around Manchester's Free Trade Hall for a full decade. He was shortly to take over as the Hallé's permanent conductor. Richter has not been revered quite as much in retrospect as he was in life.

"These damned foreign importations!" Beecham exclaimed to me more than half a century later. "Take Richter. He could conduct five works, no more. I was at a concert where he broke down in the *Peer Gynt* suite. Next morning I read, 'Never has this great man asserted his dominance over the orchestra so completely'!"

There was to be no Richterian dominance on this occasion, however.

Some days before the concert news came to Ewanville that other engagements would prevent Richter's conducting for the Mayor. Joseph announced the calamity to his assembled family. According to one who was present, Tom immediately said, "If Richter can't conduct, I will." Except for Joseph the entire family laughed derisively.

Tom persisted. "Why shouldn't I conduct?" he challenged. "I know most of the scores by heart."

Joseph, who already stood in some awe of his dynamic son, pondered for a moment, then decreed: "Well, yes, have a try."

When Joseph's whim—for it must have appeared no less to outsiders—was conveyed to Manchester, the Hallé players went purple in the face. Risegari, the principal violinist, who had hoped to conduct the concert himself, refused to play under Tom, and the entire orchestra threatened to strike. To the recalcitrant leader Joseph said, "You're not going to play? Well then, damn you, stay away!" To the Hallé management he said, "If your orchestra don't want to play I'll go to London for one." Before this intransigence the players recanted. Apart, apparently, from a second bassoon who got drunk—"he had partaken too liberally of my father's hospitality", as Beecham orotundly explained later—they gave of their best at the rehearsal. Thomas had them for a mere hour and a half and was able to go through "one or two pieces" only. Miss Blauvelt did not put in an appearance at this session. Joseph's anxiety about the accompaniments to her arias must have been fully shared by his son.

For a beginner the programme was exacting. It was as follows:

Overture	*Die Meistersinger*	Wagner
Song, "Je veux vivre" (*Roméo et Juliette*)		Gounod
	Miss Lillian Blauvelt	
Symphony No. 5 in C minor		Beethoven
Symphonie Pathétique (3rd movement)		Tchaikovsky
Songs:	(a) "Pourquoi?"	Delibes
	(b) "The Sicilian Vespers" (*sic*)	Verdi
Introduction to Act III, *Lohengrin*		Wagner
Hungarian March		Berlioz

Under the blue sputter of arc lamps the guests began to arrive at 7 p.m. Wearing his chain of office, Joseph, stationed in the vestibule, shook them by the hand. At his side, wearing her jewel of office, stood the Mayoress. For Mayoress Joseph had chosen his second daughter, Josephine, known to the family as Josie, a slim girl of eighteen, whose dark prettiness was set off by a flounced and fringed gown of cream silk. As her elder sister Emily was away in America, studying medicine, Josie had been brought in to substitute her ailing and absent mother. For ten years Joseph Beecham's wife had been increasingly subject to a nerve malady, a mild form of epilepsy, apparently, which unfitted her to cope with Ewanville and its swarm of growing or grown-up children. Two of the ten children she had borne Joseph had died young. Of the surviving eight, Emily, the eldest, was twenty-five and Christine, the youngest, five years old at the time of the Mayor's concert.

(4)

Shortly before eight o'clock Tom Beecham took his place on the assembly room rostrum and plunged into the National Anthem. Beethoven's C minor Symphony—and "one of two other pieces" which the local reporters failed to identify—he conducted without score, a fashion which, although familiar enough in Central Europe, thanks to Hans von Bülow's practice, left St. Helens in a state of staring incredulity. The accompaniments to Miss Blauvelt's arias, although unrehearsed, greatly pleased the lady herself; so, at any rate, she told Beecham when the concert was over. Beecham's own account in *A Mingled Chime* says the programme went off "without any of the hitches expected in most quarters and hoped for in some." Beecham does not tell us who his ill-wishers were. They are not likely to have been the Hallé players. To ascribe the concert's success after meagre rehearsal solely to the genius of a boy who had appeared on a public rostrum only once before is post-hoc hysteria. Most of the pieces heard that night were in the Hallé repertory. Clearly, the young man relied as much upon the players' familiarity with the notes as upon his own. The Hallé men, despite their initial moment of revolt, must have been well disposed towards him.

Tom's dynamism and intuition impressed professionals from the start. On the morrow of the concert a reporter from *The St. Helens Newspaper* sought out the leading professional of the region, J. T. Elliott, the veteran conductor of the St. Helens Choral Society. The reporter asked Mr. Elliott if he didn't think the previous night's music had been rather above the heads of the audience.

"I don't think so," replied Elliott. "Ordinarily I would be almost afraid of a dull half-hour with [Beethoven's C minor] Symphony, but last night I was interested from the first."

"Can you criticise any part of the performance?"

"Well, I thought at first that the brass preponderated, and the strings were scarcely heavy enough. That was in the [*Meistersinger*]

Overture. The brasses sounded too loud for the hall, and the themes could hardly be distinguished with the clarity which should characterise a performance in a large hall. But as we got accustomed to that the disadvantage disappeared somewhat. . . ."

"What about the conductor? Was it not a somewhat daring thing for a young conductor like Mr. Beecham to undertake the leading of such an orchestra and for such an orchestra to put itself in the hands of so young and comparatively untried a man?"

"Perhaps. But some of the members of the band must have known him. I think he impressed his personality on the performance. His work was very clever indeed. It was more than a merely concert interpretation of the music; he put energy and life into his conducting. His memory must have been wonderful to go through the Symphony without the music. . . . His method of conducting is such as to convey to the performers what he wants—and he gets it."

"Were there any slight faults in the performance that were due to him?"

"I think there was a slight exaggeration in the *sforzandi*, perhaps due to over-enthusiasm. . . . But he conducted most ably."

There is just one sour note on the record. A long-defunct weekly called *The Musical News* in its issue for December 1899 reported the Mayor's concert and the circumstances attending it without naming either the town or the parties involved.

The writer reproached Joseph for "stipulating" that the concert should be conducted by his son, argued that a conductor "of the highest attainments" should have been engaged, and alleged that Thomas began the Beethoven symphony "with a down beat instead of an up-beat", which illustrated the risks that had been run. He grudgingly admitted that the concert passed off without disaster but added that such "experiments" were not to be recommended.

The writer's point about the opening of the C minor Symphony suggests a jaundiced or slovenly eye. It means, if anything at all, that Beecham treated the opening notes of the Symphony (i.e., the famous 'Fate' motif) as a triplet starting on the second beat of a 2/4 time bar. It is clear, however, that the young man knew the musical rudiments —and his scores—well enough to avoid any such elementary solecism. Since the slip, if there was one, had no consequences it was niggling in the writer to mention it at all. In any case *The Musical News* was an obscure sheet. Many years later it was suggested in Beecham circles that the article had been mischievously "inspired" by the disappointed Risegari.

(5)

Beecham's own reflections on the concert were tranquil, almost lordly. He was buttonholed a few days later by the admirable *St. Helens Newspaper* interviewer. Their conversation carries much seed of the mature Beecham. How had the audience acquitted itself? he was asked.

"On the whole", he replied, "I was very well satisfied. . . . Notwithstanding that the programme was classical and a little too much for some, they were quiet and attentive."

"What about the band?"

"The band played excellently, the more so when you consider they had only one short rehearsal."

"Do you mean you had only one rehearsal with the orchestra?"

"Yes, for an hour and a half on the Wednesday afternoon. We were able to go through only one or two pieces. . . ."

"May I ask where you learned your music, Mr. Beecham?"

"Well, I had no proper musical training. At Wadham College I had a very good master in Dr. Roberts, who is perhaps the leading choir trainer in the United Kingdom."

.   .   .   .   .

"How have you got your orchestral experience?"

"Well, I had a little to do with an orchestra at Oxford, and I used to write things for college concerts and so on. Then, I have travelled a good deal on the Continent, heard all the best orchestras, mixed with the members and the conductors personally and picked up hints from them. In that way you hear good things. Mixing with conductors and experienced and eminent artists is of great value to one."

"People have commented, Mr. Beecham, that you seemed thoroughly at home on the conductor's pedestal. You seemed to like it."

"Yes, I have drifted into conducting because I am fond of it. It is by far the most enjoyable branch of music to me. I detest solo playing.* I am more or less nervous when solo playing but not in the slightest when I am conducting. That is a little strange. . . , because there is far more responsibility about conducting an orchestra."

"You seemed to know the symphony very well on Wednesday night. Is Beethoven your favourite composer?"

"Hardly. . . . Personally, if I were giving a concert to a musically trained audience, I should not give [Beethoven's Fifth]. It is so well

---

* At this time, nevertheless, he was still training as a concert pianist and entertained the idea of making the piano his basic or, at any rate, initial career.

known that it is a very favourite symphony for conductors to start with. It is popular with an audience because the expression is so immensely facile and easily understood. One of my favourite symphonic writers is Brahms, and Schubert is another; but all Beethoven's symphonies are interesting. . . ."

"May I ask how it is you have not yet taken any musical honours?"

"I was going to take a musical degree last year, but I was not so well at the time. I *may* take one, but I am not in a hurry. I can try any time I choose to go up for an examination. A degree is useful but, of course, nothing very wonderful. . . ."

"And now you have found how well you like conducting, do you intend to stick to it?"

"I think I may. I hardly know yet."

"Is there any field for clever amateur conductors?"

"Not much—unless a good man has a lot of money and can afford to get a tip-top orchestra of his own. There is very little field for conducting otherwise. Besides, orchestras like Hallé's are very rare indeed. . . . Mr. Wood's orchestra in London is one I like very much and is one of the best in the world. Wood's and Hallé's are the two best, and when you say they are the best in England you say they are the best in the world. They can compare with any Continental orchestras. I have heard all the best [Continental ones]."

The note of patronage on Beethoven—"hardly my favourite composer"—was often to recur. Sometimes it has developed into raillery or open disdain. "Hello, Beecham", said Cyril Scott, the composer, at a birthday dinner to Charles Kennedy Scott, the choral conductor, decades later, "I thought you were still in the country."

"To tell you the truth", drawled Beecham, "I had to conduct the *Pastoral* Symphony the other day. After that I couldn't stand the country any longer."

CHAPTER TWO

EWANVILLE

(1)

DURING THOMAS'S FIRST six years the Beechams lived at St. Helens in a sober looking house alongside the pill factory in Westfield Street. Here Thomas was born on April 29th, 1879, elder son and second child of Joseph Beecham, chemist, and his wife, *née* Josephine Burnett. His sister Emily, who was four years his senior remembers how sensitive he was to sound as an infant. He was especially allergic to brass bands. While yet in the nurse's arms he would "scream the house down" if a brass band played outside in the street. Here was another congenital loathing. Beecham's fumings against brass bands half a century later made every cornet fancier in the North of England shrink with guilt.

It was at the St. Helens house that Master Tom, in his sixth year, gave more positive signs of his interest in music. Taken to a piano recital at which new pieces by Grieg were heard, he went to bed in an ineffable condition. Unable to sleep, he got up in the middle of the night and went downstairs to the drawing room. "I want to learn the piano", he informed his startled parents. Next day a local organist was called in and began to give Tom lessons on an upright piano in the drawing room.

This first tutor was Mr. Unsworth, a mildly dignified man in his late fifties, who played the organ at a Roman Catholic church. At one time he gave lessons jointly to Tom and Emily. At some of these sessions Mr. Unsworth, a man of peace and patience, spent much time keeping brother and sister apart; they were more concerned to fight each other than get on with their scales and arpeggios. When order had been restored, Mr. Unsworth, for whom Mozart was all in all, would play the big numbers from *Figaro*, *Don Giovanni* and *The Magic Flute*, telling the stories of these operas as he went along. When not listening to Mr. Unsworth, Tom practised "the gentler flights of Dussek and Clementi" under his direction. The boy soon became a facile player; his fingers seemed born for the keyboard.

(2)

One day in the summer of 1885, mother and father and the four little Beechams packed themselves into the family landau and clopclopped sedately to Huyton, six miles south of St. Helens, a village

then surrounded by open country. At Huyton Joseph Beecham had
bought ten acres and a house more concordant than the old one with
his partnership in the pill-making enterprise founded by his father,
Thomas Beecham senior. Pills were booming. In that same year the
firm opened a new factory at St. Helens (the old house in Westfield
Street was pulled down to make way for it); and another factory—the
first of several overseas—was soon to be started by Joseph in New York.

Ewanville, the mansion he had bought at Huyton, was an outward
sign of Joseph's rising prosperity. Square and stolid in cream-painted
stucco, it stood on a turfed knoll at the top of a slope facing into the sun.
It had ugly chimney stacks and wide bay windows with looped lace
curtains flanking the front door. To the west Joseph had built on a
nursery wing and, running southward from the end of this, a lordly
glitter of conservatories. Under ornate glass grew palm trees, tropical
ferns, orchids and long white Muscat grapes which won prizes for
Joseph (in justice they should have gone rather to Oldham, his head
gardener) at all the big horticultural shows of the region. The lawns
were a rich man's lawns; they had a woven look. Oldham worked over
them with a patent mower which was hauled by a donkey.

The babies of the family were wheeled for daily airings in a two-
seater pram with a long wickerwork body. Their nurses (two) were
severely corseted and bodiced. Nurses and governesses brought up the
Beecham brood in almost royal isolation. "We were not a united
family", remembered one of the sisters. "We were kept in the nursery
and saw little of our parents." Owing to their mother's chronic illness
that little became less as the years went by.

Ewanville boasted two rooms of uncommon splendour. The drawing room had garlands and tendrils embossed on its plaster ceiling; the
walls were brocaded in shimmering greens and golds; the carpet was as
rich to the foot as Oldham's turf. In the window bay stood the grandest
of grand pianos. This wore a cover of burgundy velvet with scal-
loped and gold-embroidered edges. For Joseph greatly loved music.
His favourite composer was Wagner, his favourite Wagner *Die
Meistersinger*. But the billiard room was the place which truly revealed
his passion. In the middle of the floor, under six conical lamp shades,
reigned an eleven foot table by Burroughes and Watts. Visitors could
follow the play from a half-timbered inglenook alongside. The
grand function of the billiard room was not billiards, however, but
organ music. One wall was occupied first by a two-manual hand
blown organ, later by an electrically blown instrument of richer
specification. Against another wall, towering to the ceiling, stood an

orchestrion with gilded pipes and brazen trumpets encased in glass. Brought by Joseph from Geneva, the orchestrion fed on perforated rolls, emitted tuttis powerful enough to knock down a welter-weight, and had a repertory which took in all the Beethoven symphonies and many by Mozart, as well as copious operatic selections from Rossini, Verdi and Wagner.

Young Tom battened on this repertory. He had every piece played over and over again until he knew it by heart and could "strum" it (his own word) on the piano. The Wagner and Verdi selection were what he liked most. When he was eight somebody suggested that he should play the piano at a miscellaneous concert that was being got up in St. Helens. Father agreed. Thomas walked on to the platform and was quelled by the fog of faces in front of him. Hardly aware what he was doing, he managed to get through his piece, then walked off in a state of coma. The audience clapped enthusiastically and wouldn't stop clapping.

Thomas was told he must go on again and take his bow and, if fitting, play the "encore" piece he had prepared. At first he declined to do anything of the sort. Finally, after wheedlings and shovings, he yielded. This time he no longer saw the audience through a fog. He realised that, far from being dragons, as he had supposed, they were "just the ordinary people you see in shops and streets". He played his encore with aplomb—and from that day, he told Ethel Smyth, never knew what nervousness meant.

Is this claim to be taken literally?

Speaking of the early days of the London Philharmonic Orchestra when Beecham, in his early fifties, was at the peak of his powers, Paul Beard, first leader of the L.P.O., says: "He was a nervous man, whatever people think. Before Queen's Hall concerts he would disappear from the artists' room. Nobody had the faintest idea where he went. Probably for a stroll round to calm down. It wasn't until the interval that he could relax completely."

(3)

Down the slope from Ewanville, a little below the vinery, stood a private school run by one Norris. Tom was sent to Mr. Norris soon after the family settled at Huyton. According to his own account he was an idle and indifferent pupil; his head too full of the orchestrion and its marvels to cope with sums and pothooks. His piano lessons continued to prosper, however. Mr. Unsworth told Joseph Beecham very early on that Tom would go far. The boy himself would have preferred to go more quickly and in more directions. For Mr. Unsworth music stopped at the pre-Beethoven classics. Tom had to rely on other hands—and presently on his own—for Chopin, Schumann and Grieg. These romantics impassioned him.

Already his memory was prodigious. Asked by his father when in his eighth year to recite the witches' scene from *Macbeth* at a party, he obliged with the whole act and, greedy for further praise, had within a few days memorised the entire play. In the library of his Uncle William, the younger brother of Joseph, who for some years had a house at Huyton, he read ravenously, later claiming that there was hardly a novelist big or little, British or foreign, that he did not digest at this time.

For summer holidays the family went to Southport, where sailing dinghies on wheels cruised vast expanses of dry, hard sand. Winter brought concert-going and opera-going in Liverpool. These diversions entailed a fourteen-mile journey there and back by horse carriage. The Liverpool opera seasons, which ran from Christmas until spring, were by the celebrated Carl Rosa opera company. Full of Beechams big and small, the family landau drove to Liverpool as many as three times a week for a repertory which included—to name those works which particularly impressed Tom—*Aïda* and the *Romeo and Juliet* and *Faust* of Gounod. *Faust* was Tom's first operatic experience in the theatre. But he preferred *Romeo and Juliet* to *Faust* and *Aïda* to either. For a long time he considered *Aïda* "all that an opera should be". Straight plays were a bore. He regarded the theatre as a place where music and drama were meant to go hand in hand. Music on its own was, or could be, immensely exciting. Drama on its own was dull. By this time he was a boarder at Rossall School on the Lancashire coast. Coming home after his first term for the Christmas holidays of 1892, he was allowed to go to Carl Rosa performances at Liverpool either on his own or with a friend. Most of his pocket money was spent on gallery seats. Europe was being swept by an opera which had come out in Rome some two years earlier: the *Cavalleria Rusticana* of Pietro Mascagni. As sung by the Carl Rosa company, this went to Tom's head, as it had gone to the heads of millions more. He obtained a vocal score and played the opera endlessly on the upright piano which had survived from the St. Helens house.

(4)

The upright now stood in the little-used morning room which was regarded by the family generally not as a room in its own right but rather as a passageway to the conservatories. The piano was topped by a runner and a pot of ferns. On the wall nearby hung a potboiling print of Regency bucks taking their liquor outside an inn. The fireplace alongside housed a wheel of pleated paper and pampas grass dyed yellow and pink. Emily used to listen to Tom's *Cavalleria* sessions from behind the door. She found his playing impressive. So did all other members of the family, musical and non-musical alike. Old Thomas Beecham his grandfather, then in his seventies, who seems not to have had a spark of music in his soul, would clap his grandson on the back and shout, "Well, Tom, my boy, go to the piano and make some noise!" As Tom made "noises", his grandfather would listen from the depths of an armchair, hands folded complacently over his stomach.

As first source of the fortune which was to fund Beecham's orchestras and operatic enterprises, Thomas Beecham senior merits more than a casual reference. Born in 1820 at Witney, Oxfordshire, he settled in Lancashire in his early twenties, opened a chemist's shop in Wigan and, at twenty-six, married a girl whose father came from Bangor, Jane Evans. A year later he had invented the formula for his famous pill, which long remained a family secret. His first patent medicine licence is dated Liverpool 1847.

Twelve years later he shifted his business, still a small one, to the new town of St. Helens. He bought a house in Westfield Street, made up his pills in a backyard shed and sold them from a stall in the market place, aided by an extrovert nature, a commanding presence and powerful lungs. While he was haranguing the crowd one day about the merits of his pills, a woman interjected that they were "worth a guinea a box". He promptly replied that he would print this slogan on every box he sold in future. He ultimately spent, or watched his successor Joseph spend, £80,000 to £100,000 a year on advertising, a prodigious allocation for Edwardian times.

The house and shed in Westfield Street were pulled down; successive factories sprang up on the same site, others being built abroad, to cope with a demand which, by Joseph's maturity, involved a turnover of £360,000 a year. From the age of sixty-seven onwards he divided his time between St. Helens and Mursley Hall, his Buckinghamshire estate, where he indulged in "gentleman" farming. There is much of the farmer in the description his grandson gives of him: bluff, loud and addicted to thick, tweedy clothes (including "front-fall" trousers) which were more suited to cattle fairs than the opulence of his son's drawing room. He had taken Joseph into partnership in 1866. Nearly thirty years later he handed the business over to him and retired to a house at Southport which he had built for his declining years.

On his elder grandson, Tom, he doted in the manner proper to grandfathers. Even in sub-adolescence, Tom had an inborn dominance that matched certain traits in his grandfather. There is a photograph of the boy dating from about this time. It is a sunny afternoon. Tom stands alone on the tennis court at Ewanville, holding a racquet. Up the hill his small sisters, Edith and Jessie, are watching out of a window in the nursery wing. The boy is wearing a dark suit with long stockings, an absurdly small cap and what looks like a starched butterfly collar. Less suitable wear for tennis on a hot afternoon it would be hard to imagine. The face is chubby and unchildlike. The chin which later carried the famous beard is not noticeably strong, but the set of the mouth denotes an assertive will, and the imperious eyes sit in judgment on what they conceive already to be the phlegms and follies of mankind.

(5)

At Rossall Tom spent—and for the most part enjoyed—five years, 1892 to 1897. At first he was cut off from music. After months of deprivation, his first hearing of the "Prize Song" from Wagner's *Meistersinger* in an arrangement for solo violin and piano at a miscellaneous school concert gave him "a shock of joy". When a section of the Hallé Orchestra visited Rossall to play in celebration of the school's jubilee (1894), he was enrolled as a temporary member of the percussion department. In the cadet corps he played the bass drum with discomfort and distaste. In the same year (his fifteenth) he began to play the piano—rather badly, he confessed—at routine school concerts, thereby winning a prize volume of Beethoven sonatas. This gave him qualified satisfaction. After all, as he conceded shortly after his eightieth birthday, he had always liked *some* Beethoven. When he became captain of his house at seventeen he was allowed to have a piano in his study. On this he played much Mozart.

At the same time he met the "hearties" on their own terms, playing tempestuous football as well as cricket. In the course of later football playing at Oxford, "I dislocated two arms, put out two knees and injured a thumb." After these misfortunes, which he gaily enumerated sixty years later, he confined himself to cricket and tennis. At cricket he played on occasion both for his school and his college.

It had been no wish of Tom's to go to Oxford. The general assumption—against which he does not seem to have rebelled—was that he should in due time enter the family business. Oxford struck him as an incongruous probation for pill selling. In any case, his tastes beckoned him farther afield.

In his fifteenth year he had accompanied his father on one of his many business trips to America. Outward-bound on the *Campania* he played piano at the ship's concert, accompanying among other singers the fabulous Ben Davies who had a twenty-five year contract with the Royal Choral Society to sing for them twice a year and wore dress studs and cuff links from an admirer of his tenor voice, Kaiser Wilhelm II. Davies and others were on their way to the Chicago Exhibition. The Beechams went there, too. Tom saw Niagara, sailed the Hudson River and made a trip to Boston. On the return voyage he accompanied again at the ship's concert. The programme's main ornament this time was an elephantine Swede who, owing to his malady of overgrowth, could hardly walk and supported himself on two sticks. Frederick Lindquist was his name. He sang "O Star of Eve" divinely.

America opened one door in Tom's mind. The European Continent opened others. He spent his summer and other holidays in Southport no longer but, either with friends or alone, in France, Belgium, Switzerland, Scandinavia. Joseph was surprisingly casual in these matters. About Tom's companions—or whether he had any or not—he showed culpable incuriosity. Soon after Tom came home on holiday he would pull a handful of sovereigns out of his pocket and say to his son, "Here you are. Go to the Continent and enjoy yourself."

With its hundred opera houses and orchestras, Germany had an especial fascination for the boy. If he was to study anywhere, why not in the land of Richard Wagner? He put the matter to Joseph. As usual, Joseph put the matter in turn to the Reverend Alfred Carter, without whose advice—or that of his lawyer—he never took any decision in major family matters. Carter's counsel was adverse. He professed to be aghast at the idea of musical training in Germany. Tom, he decided, must go to an English university. He was sufficiently large-minded to leave the choice open as between Oxford and Cambridge. Tom chose Oxford because some of his closest friends were going up the same term.

Of Joseph's reverend adviser we get a supplementary glimpse from Emily Beecham's memories. One day she encountered Carter in the Ewanville lobby:

"My dear Miss Emily, it grieves me greatly to note that when you come to church you do not partake of the bread and the wine."

To which Emily, clenching her fists and frowning up at him from her tinyness, replied, "Mr. Carter, I would like you to know that I have no intention whatever of taking the bread and the wine in *your* church. If ever I do take the bread and the wine it will be in a church of a very different kind."

Even in the Ewanville days, Miss Emily had notions of her own. Later she was received into the Roman Catholic Church.

Another occasion:

"Pa, I like music so. *And* singing. Please may I go to Berlin and have lessons there?"

Pa snaps his fingers impatiently. "Don't bother me", he mutters. "I've enough to think about."

A day or two later Emily chances to pass the library door, which is ajar. Joseph and his spiritual adviser are in conference. Miss Emily eavesdrops. She hears Carter say, "Oh, no, no, no. It would be most unwise to send Miss Emily to Berlin. She can get all the training she needs at home."

A week's silence. Then Miss Emily pipes up again. She knows what the outcome will be. "Pa, what about Berlin? May I go?"

"Certainly not. I wouldn't dream of it."

At Wadham Tom spent an academically fruitless eighteen months. So that he should be able to play the piano as much as he liked, he took lodgings in Walton Street rather than live in College. At first his academic life was balanced. He played football devotedly, began to compose songs and what he called "little pieces", conscientiously attended classroom and chapel. An intoxicating Christmas vacation with friends in Dresden for "opera, parties and dances on the ice" sapped his academic zeal. He attended fewer and fewer lectures. His piano in Walton Street became the focal point of life. His early attempts at composition he handed for criticism to John Varley Roberts, organist of Magdalen, the choir-trainer whom he was to extol in his newspaper interview after the Mayor's concert. Roberts's advice to choristers, delivered in an aggressive Yorkshire accent, was one of Beecham's favourite quotations in later life. "Now lads", Roberts used to say, "you've heard a great deal about voice training methods, but I've just got this to say to you, and don't forget it. All you've got to do is stand up, throw your heads back and *sing*. All the rest is humbug."

In mid-term he broke away from Oxford for more opera in Dresden. His unauthorised absence would have led to instant expulsion had it been noticed by the College authorities. A trip to Italy in the spring of 1898 strengthened his dislike of university life. At the end of the summer he prevailed upon his father to let him go down. (Decades later he was asked by Ethel Smythe whether he was, in fact, sent down from

Wadham. He replied that, on the contrary, the Warden was sorry to lose him but said on parting, "Your timely departure has perhaps spared us the necessity of asking you to go.")

Back at Ewanville he told Joseph that what he wished to do was settle for a year or two in some Continental capital or capitals and prepare himself for the pill business by studying foreign languages while revelling in "that fuller musical life which was wanting at home."

As usual, Joseph put the case to the Reverend Alfred Carter; and again Carter said "No". Tom was told to come back to Huyton. He did so with dragging feet. He had no career plans. Joseph gave him a nominal job at the factory. The expectation was that he would stay on at St. Helens indefinitely. Actually he stayed for little more than a year.

(6)

To fellow townsmen in St. Helens he talked vaguely about having played clarinet and timpani in unidentified orchestras and of having "a little to do" with one orchestra in particular at Oxford. Already the need to conduct was strong upon him. His first act on settling at Ewanville was to found the St. Helens Orchestral Society. This was, in fact, the first orchestra to be mobilised and trained by Beecham. Comprising prominent members of the Richter and Hallé orchestras "from Liverpool and Manchester", as well as a large proportion of local players, Beecham's St. Helens band had eight first violins, eight seconds, four violas, five 'cellos, four double-basses, three flutes, two oboes, two clarinets, two bassoons, two horns, three trumpets, three trombones, harp and timpani.

Their inaugural concert—the first concert Beecham is known to have conducted publicly—had been given at the Town Hall about a month earlier than the Mayor's concert: on Wednesday November 11th, to be exact. Beecham took his forces on that occasion without mishap through Mendelssohn's *Ruy Blas* Overture, a *Peer Gynt* suite and the *William Tell* Overture. There were two soloists. A fellow townsman, Haigh Jackson ("principal baritone in the National Grand Opera Company; has sung at the Crystal Palace, Queen's Hall and St. James's Hall") sang the *Pagliacci* Prologue and *Even bravest heart* from *Faust*. Mr. Osborne Edmundson played solo in Mendelssohn's D minor piano concerto and was permitted to follow this up with his own adaptation of *The Lost Chord*, to which young Mr. Beecham listened with irony, no doubt.

The day after the concert Tom chanced to encounter his ten-year-old sister Elsie Olive at the gated entry to the Ewanville nursery wing. Beyond this point the younger Beecham children were never allowed to stray. Tom and Elsie had met so rarely that they were virtual strangers.

"Hello, little girl", condescended Tom, "how would you like to conduct a concert? It's easy. All you have to do is waggle a stick."

Although only ten, Elsie was quick to detect—and resent—the patronising raillery of this. She grew up, nevertheless, to worship her brother.

The Orchestral Society does not seem to have had a long life. We hear of it next—and finally—on December 14th, 1899, when it shared a programme with the Choral Society. Thomas conducted Beethoven's Symphony No. 1 in C major and a march by Mendelssohn. The choral part of the programme—Stanford's *Revenge* and Brahms's *Song of Destiny*—was directed by Mr. Elliott. At this second concert, we read, the reserved seats were well filled. The Mayor was there to admire his son's prowess, and with him sat an august M.P., Colonel Pilkington. The rest of the hall, said a newspaper account, was sparsely occupied, "and it was obvious that financially the effort .... must be written down as a failure." The reporter did not know just how prescient he was being. Financial insuccess was to be a blight on Beecham's career for a third or more of the coming century.

For the moment bills and balance sheets meant nothing. Music was his absorption and glory.

But he also saw and thought a good deal of Utie.

CHAPTER THREE

UTICA: AND THE BREAK WITH JOSEPH

(1)

WHILE ON ONE of his visits to the firm's factory in Brooklyn, U.S., in the late nineties, Joseph, accompanied by Emily who, as she puts it, was "looking after" him in Mama's absence, paid a social call on Dr. Charles Stuart Welles and Mrs. Welles at their home in 58th Street off Central Park.

Benign and trim-bearded, Dr. Welles began his career in the diplomatic service, later turning to medicine. On occasions of pomp he wore sword, pumps and knee breeches becomingly. He was of distinguished descent. One of his ancestors, Thomas Welles, of Warwickshire (Eng.) stock, settled at Hartford, Conn., in 1636 on land which he had bought from the Indians. He rose to be governor of Connecticut. Another notable of the family was Gideon Welles who wore a wig and white whiskers and had been secretary of the Navy in Lincoln's cabinet during the Civil War. Dr. Welles's daughter worked it out that she was Gideon's great-niece.

At the time of the Beechams' visit, Utica, known to familiars as Utie, was fifteen. She had dark hair, blue eyes and an oval face of uncommon mould. Her prettiness was incontestable. The portraits of that time or a little later suggest strong character as well. Joseph had already made friends in an avuncular way with Utie, who was something of a collector, by mailing her all the foreign postage stamps he could lay hands on at the counting house in Westfield Street. Emily took to her at once. Six years later she was to be Utie's bridesmaid. It was arranged that when the Welleses settled in London, which was to happen fairly soon, Utie should visit Ewanville as Emily's friend. Her visit lasted six weeks and coincided with one of Tom's vacations from Oxford.

In the drawing room Tom played on the caparisoned grand piano. What he played Utie never remembered. It was Tom who was the marvel. What did the music matter by comparison? Suddenly he stopped playing. Pushing aside the piano stool, he turned round, folded his arms and sat down facing her on the keyboard, producing a dissonance that was broad and complex. Utie listened to his bright, lordly words as much with her eyes as her ears. It was not so much Tom's ideas that weighed with her as the ebullient mastery he showed of everything and everybody about him. He was soaked in music and exuded it—without being committed to music as a career. There were other talents and ambitions in him. He said he might drop music altogether and go in for diplomacy. "I mean to be Prime Minister one day," he affirmed.

Utie was at Ewanville again in the autumn of 1899 and stayed there until the eve of the Mayor's concert. She charmed everybody, starting with Thomas senior, whose first present to Utie showed uncommon grace, comprising a golden sovereign, two yellow roses and one pink one. She and Tom went for a walk across the fields. Tom's head was full of Beethoven's C minor Symphony. He sang and shouted the music and waved his arms a lot, giving the beat and cues to imaginary players.

"That," explained Utie later, "was why I fell in love with him—because of his genius."

Between her visits to Ewanville, Utie was presented at Queen Victoria's last Drawing Room by right of her father's diplomatic status. On an easel in the dining room at Clopton House, Stratford-upon-Avon, sixty years later stood a painting of Utie wearing ostrich plumes and a lilies-of-the-valley shoulder spray as on the day of her presentation. Half or more of those sixty years had been years of separation and estrangement. As she showed me the painting Lady (Utica) Beecham, who bore her years with unquenched briskness, said, "I am the unhappiest woman in England. And the happiest. That is what it means to have been married to Thomas Beecham."

During the summer that followed the Mayor's concert, the Welleses holidayed in Devonshire. Tom went with them and expounded the history and the beauties of the county. "Tom", commented one of the party affectionately, "is a great fellow for showing off." From Minehead they drove in two carriages to Lynmouth. During the afternoon Tom and Utie fell behind and sat on a seat overlooking the tumble of rivers at Watersmeet. The proposal followed a well-known and light-hearted formula.

"I don't like your name," said Tom.

"Why don't you change it, then?" responded Utie, without quite realising what she was saying. When the realisation came she was radiant about it.

Tom kissed her. Then they walked back to the hotel. The first person they saw was Emily, who was also of the party. "We've become engaged", Tom whispered. "I'm going to tell the old people tonight." After dinner Tom informed Dr. Welles that he had proposed to Utie and hoped he would consent to their engagement. Dr. Welles said "Yes" straight away and was very benevolent. Tom fascinated both him and his wife; they had never come across anybody like him. The following day Tom took Utie round the Minehead shops and bought her presents. He knew she was fond of riding; the first present he bought her was a little china horse.

One shadow lay across their happiness. There could be no rejoicing at Ewanville. Tom and his father had become enemies. The Beecham family was bitterly divided.

(2)

The split had its origin in Joseph Beecham's treatment of his wife, which seems to have been unfeeling, to say the least. Josephine Beecham was approaching fifty when, on the testimony of his doctors and others, Joseph had her incarcerated in an asylum at Northampton. According to her champions there was little wrong with her except that she took brandy after her nerve attacks, behaved a little oddly in consequence and was subject to mental depression. Small and neat of figure, she had the mouth and intent eyes of a person easy to hurt. According to a tradition in the Beecham family she was partly of French extraction: it is said that one of her near forebears had been a silk merchant in Lille. Joseph married her in 1873 when already his father's manager and a man of growing means. Before the marriage Josephine and her family lived humbly, carrying on a small dressmaking business. In the subsequent alimony suit Joseph made a point of this. Josephine's family, he stressed, had no "position". The inference was that, having been lifted by Joseph from obscurity to the affluence and luxury of Ewanville she should have been grateful to him in perpetuity, however callous he might be.

Thomas did not share this view. To mark his disapproval of it he walked out of his father's house early in 1900, went to London and lived with the Welleses *en famille* at Roland Gardens, Kensington. He had deliberately cut himself off from his father's support and bounty. His early concert promotions—as well as his continued musical training, presumably—were to be funded mainly by his mother. Meantime his sister Emily returned from America. She had been perturbed during the latter part of her stay there by letters from home which first hinted, then disclosed, that for the good of her mental health her mother had been "put away".

Emily was as tiny as her mother and combative in inverse ratio to her size. She reminded, among other people, the governess at Ewanville

—a person for whom Joseph was in all things wise and impeccable
—that she had had medical training and intended to look into the case
of her mother personally. On hearing this the governess recoiled with
a startled look. It seems that she had had much to do with the testimony
which led to Josephine Beecham's incarceration. Following Tom's
footsteps, Emily settled as a guest at Roland Gardens and joined her
brother in a campaign for their mother's release. Brother and sister
brought in a mental specialist of their own and conferred with lawyers.
There was much coming and going between London and Northampton. It presently emerged that Joseph had been an inconsiderate husband in more ways than one. He had a woman friend in London
whom he visited regularly under an assumed name. He made a point
of taking her grapes, among other presents; whether these were from
the Ewanville vines is not recorded.

(3)

In June 1901 Josephine successfully petitioned in the Divorce
Division for judicial separation from Joseph on the grounds of his
adultery. The incarceration order was cancelled; release from the
asylum followed. Alimony was fixed at £2,500. Thomas and Emily
deemed this paltry. Just how much could Joseph afford? On Josephine's
behalf agents were sent down to St. Helens to find out—"not a right
thing to do", suggested Joseph's counsel later, with an air of pained
rectitude. Josephine's agents came back with the story that his income
was £85,000 a year.

This estimate is certainly concordant with later disclosures as to the
size of the family pill fortune. It is hard to see how Joseph could, in
years to come, have supported his son's musical ventures so lavishly
on less. Wrangling continued, in and out of court, until the spring of
1903. Joseph pleaded through counsel that it was almost impossible
to estimate the exact amount of his annual income but mentioned
£20,000 as a possibility. Unmoved by taunts from the other side that
he "revelled in every luxury and had only to put his hand in his
pocket for banknotes and spend them as freely as he liked", Joseph
admitted no more than that his income was "large enough to enable
him to pay any reasonable sum which the Court might think proper".

Josephine's application for increased alimony was finally granted
by the Court of Appeal. In announcing the settlement—which had
been reached at a private consultation between counsel on both sides
and Lord Justice Vaughan Williams—the learned judge thought it un-
desirable to state the amount by which the alimony had been increased.

The following day a country newspaper, *The Yorkshire Post*, reported—without being gainsaid—that the sum agreed upon was £4,500, an increase of £2,000 a year.

During the protracted hearings, counsel for Joseph had reproachful things to say about the motives which he imagined to have inspired Thomas and Emily. After her mother's victory in the Appeal Court, Emily published the following rebuttal:

"... Miss Emily Beecham writes to correct a misstatement contained in counsel's observations concerning herself and her brother, the two eldest children, who have remained with Mrs. Beecham. The statement in question is to the effect that her brother and herself had instigated their mother to bring the action for judicial separation in the hope of getting money from their father, as they feared they would not be left money in his will. The facts are, Miss Beecham states, directly opposed to that statement, because three days before the action in which Mr. Beecham's suit was served their father had threatened them irrevocably with disinheritance if they proceeded with the suit in behalf of their mother. It would therefore, adds Miss Beecham, be plainly seen that by aiding their mother in taking the action for separation (which they were informed by their solicitors was the only way in which her release from the asylum could be obtained), they knew they were being disinherited by protecting their mother."

This declaration was printed by *The St. Helens Newspaper* on May 1st, 1903. Joseph appears to have made no public riposte. No doubt the episode hardened his heart still more against the rebellious three.

His letter threatening Thomas and Emily with disinheritance had said, in these or equivalent words: "You will cease to be my children. You will be left to starve." In the case of Emily he appears to have persisted in his threat. There is no mention of her in his will, as published in January 1917, although four other daughters were remembered. In her brisk way, Emily set out to earn her living and did so to good effect in Italy as a ballet dancer and teacher and as an operatic singer.

Confirmed in her freedom and a considerable margin of comfort, including a carriage and servants of her own, Josephine (later the Dowager Lady Beecham) lived on for thirty-one years, surviving Joseph by fifteen. Most of these years she spent with her daughter-in-law Utica at Hamilton Terrace, Grosvenor Square or Mursley Hall, gentle, frail and sound in mind. There is a three-quarter length portrait of her at Clopton painted when she was in her sixties, the image of sweet benignity. She never lived under Joseph's roof after leaving the asylum.

Later there was some measure of reconciliation. For eight years or so before his death he used to visit her at Hamilton Terrace for amicable small talk. In 1903 Josephine's counsel had said Joseph was not likely to leave her anything in his will. Counsel proved to have been over-pessimistic. In the will that he signed less than a month before his death, in 1916, Joseph directed that the original allowance of £2,500 should continue to be paid to Josephine after his death. On Emily, however, the will was silent.

CHAPTER FOUR

ROLAND GARDENS

(1)

THE WELLESES' HOUSE in Roland Gardens, Kensington, where Beecham settled in 1900 after quarrelling with his father, was large, prim and gloomy of aspect.

The prevailing personality was his future father-in-law, Charles Stuart Welles, who wore broad-brimmed hats and old-fashioned cutaway coats. Although not from the South, he had the general air and manner of a Kentucky colonel. Engrossed in psychic matters, he would take people—ladies for preference—by the hand and look deeply into their eyes. This, he explained, was to diagnose their auras. Beecham was allotted a study on the first floor. Here, during the next two or three years, he tried to make his mark as an operatic composer. Like Wagner and Berlioz, he decided to be his own librettist. The first (and last) libretto from his own pen was based on Walter Scott's *Marmion*. On the words and music he spent long days, completely lost to practicalities. He was reluctant to leave his desk for meals, recalls Emily Beecham, and sometimes would not have eaten at all if the Welleses had not cajoled him into doing so. They sent him in nourishing trays "to keep his strength up".

Beecham is known to have written or sketched three pieces for the lyric stage. *Marmion* was followed by a work in "lighter vein" and by a second grand opera on the life of Christopher Marlowe, the (Italian) libretto of which was furnished by Puccini's collaborator, Luigi Illica, joint-author of the *Bohème*, *Tosca* and *Butterfly* "books". None of Beecham's operas ever saw, or neared, the footlights; and the manuscripts of two have disappeared. In 1910 Beecham told an interviewer that although gone they were not forgotten; at a pinch he could have rewritten every bar of *Marmion* from memory.

By that time, however, he had lost faith in his creative powers; he knew he was destined to perform music, not to compose it. Nevertheless, a professional friend to whom he played some of the *Marmion* music testifies that it was tuneful, well-shaped, and professional in quality.

The professional touch in Beecham's output was in part intuitive, in part acquired from one of the pundits of the Royal College of

Music, Charles Wood (1866-1926). Like his chief Sir Charles Villiers Stanford, Wood was an Irishman and an assiduous composer of pieces that are now as dead as a doornail. An authority on Tudor music, he was hostile to the new harmonic and aesthetic trends of Debussy, Richard Strauss and others. For two years Beecham went to him privately for composition lessons. He submitted to Wood as well as the *Marmion* score countless exercises in fugue, choral writing and orchestration. Not all his exercises were fruitful. He once spent three weeks trying to write a sonata first-movement, then gave up in despair.

Apart from Charles Wood, Beecham had four other teachers during the early years of the century.

One of them was Moritz Moszkowski (1854-1925), a Silesian composer resident in Paris who, after enjoying a certain international celebrity, died in wretched poverty. Beecham went to Moszkowski for orchestration lessons in Paris in 1904. He would compose a short piece of music or select one from the classics, then orchestrate it in the differing styles of, say Haydn, Tchaikovsky, Bizet or Moszkowski himself, handing the results to his master for excoriation or otherwise. Another composition teacher was Frederic Austin (1872-1952), who later sang baritone leads in Beecham's English opera seasons during the first World War and became eminent through his "realisation" of the *Beggar's Opera* tunes for the historic Playfair production at the Lyric, Hammersmith, in 1920.

While at Ewanville, Beecham had taken piano lessons from a Viennese master of wide prestige who had settled in Liverpool, one Steudner-Welsing (d. 1913), and continued to prepare for the recital platform after going south. His fingers were at the service of a seemingly inexhaustible memory. His friends boasted that Tom Beecham could sit down and play "anything" from memory. From Victor Maurel, the French baritone who created the Iago and Falstaff of Verdi at Milan in 1887 and 1893 respectively, he had lessons in "interpretation". At this time Maurel was regularly giving recitals in Bechstein Hall, where he sang arias to piano accompaniment. In his London studio he would make his appearance at morning sessions in pyjamas, dressing gown and silk hat, and oblige his pupils to repeat *en chœur* the same little song fifty times over in the hope—a vain one, it seems,—that they would master all its technical and emotional possibilities. Beecham played the piano for some of these one-piece marathons, which were apt to continue inflexibly for a week on end. That he and other pupils did not go mad is singular. They appear to have been sustained by the spark and majesty of Maurel's presence, which are still to be divined from the gramophone records, imperfect though they be, which he made about this time.

Among orchestral instruments Beecham had picked up "a working knowledge" of the oboe and the trumpet. While at Roland Gardens he took up the trombone also and, when holidaying at Lucerne, practised on it in a rowing boat in the middle of the lake so as not to disturb other residents of the *pension* where he was staying.

In one way or another, then, Beecham's musical training, although extra-mural and uncertificated, was varied and intensive. His assiduity makes nonsense of the whisper that he was an amateur. To call Beecham an amateur was as unfair as to call him a professional. No impresario or conductor can truly be styled a professional who so nearly equates his musical duty with his personal inclinations as Beecham did.

(2)

Round the corner from Roland Gardens and along the Old Brompton Road at a point then called Sussex Place stood a shop pleasantly crammed (as has been the case ever since) with harps. To Beecham in his comings and goings the sight was irresistible. He went into the shop one day and met its owner, Joseph George Morley, then in his middle fifties, a man with a flowing bow tie, a truculent moustache, reassuring eyes and hat brims almost as broad as Mr. Welles's.

In addition to being a considerable craftsman and musician, Morley had a talent for friendship, believed in Fabian Socialism (with which Beecham himself flirted for a while) and always kept good wine in his cellar and a barrel of Munich lager in his kitchen. He was a ravenous and proselytising reader. If a newly printed book caught his fancy, he would order a dozen copies and have them mailed to his friends. Morley's shop and the dwelling above it became Beecham's second home. Here he met musical people (not all of them harpists) from many parts of the Continent who had made Morley's acquaintance either through his thriving export business (the big Morley orchestral harp was in demand all over the world) or simply because Morley was a man one simply had to know.

On summer week-ends Beecham would go down to the Morleys' cottage at Chipperfield and join them at cricket on the green with the village postman, the village constable and other worthies. The day is still talked of when he requisitioned a loaf newly bought for the Morley's table and, for a wager, shied it over a high fir tree bough. Already he had a curious nervous trick, familiar to most who talked with him for any length of time, of screwing up—indeed rotating, almost—one side of his face while sniffing. This mannerism so fascinated the Morleys' small boy, John Sebastian, that he, too, found himself involuntarily sniffing and face-screwing while seated at the same table as Beecham. The guest did not notice. The Morley parents did. Afterwards John Sebastian came in for rebuke.

At Sussex Place Beecham often played chess and billiards with Morley and others of the circle. Two of his habits at billiards are particularly remembered. After making a stroke he would put the cue behind his back, bracing it horizontally with his elbows, and strut about the room oblivious to oddments he was knocking off tables and shelves with the cue ends. Another trick of his was to bounce the butt end of his cue on the linoleumed floor. Late at night the resulting tattoo used to keep Mrs. Morley awake. Morley therefore had every cue in the house shod with rubber buffers of the sort used for invalids' sticks. After that Mrs. Morley slept in peace.

(3)

For Beecham life was full; he lived it intensely from morning till bedtime. Yet behind the gaddings and the desk work lay a feeling of hollowness. His conducting of the Hallé Orchestra in 1899 had been as the taste of blood to a tiger. He would never rest until he was on the rostrum again, commanding torrents of tone.

Early in 1902 the news went round that, starting on Easter Monday (March 31), a newly-formed troupe called the Imperial Grand Opera Company would tour five London suburbs—Clapham, Brixton, Fulham, Stratford and New Cross—under the direction of its founder, one Kelson Trueman.

Here, Beecham told himself, was a prime opportunity. Perhaps Mr. Trueman, of whom he had never heard, would give him a conducting job; he might even produce *Marmion*. He put the *Marmion* score under his arm, called a hansom and drove to Trueman's audition room. As well as running the short-lived Imperial Grand Opera Company, a ramshackle concern that mocked its title, Trueman had a concert agency in or near Chancery Lane (an incongruous musical address) and occasionally sang tenor in miscellaneous concerts of his own promoting. His voice was of no account.

Beecham's call upon him coincided with a minor crisis in Trueman's affairs. Singers were awaiting audition—and the accompanist had not turned up. On learning that Beecham could play the piano, he pressed him into service. On discovering that the young man knew by heart a draft repertory that included *Carmen*, *Il Trovatore*, *Cavalleria Rusticana*, *Pagliacci*, *The Bohemian Girl*, *Maritana* and *The Lily of Killarney*, he invited him to become joint conductor of the tour. Beecham accepted, but wistfully mentioned that his original purpose in calling had been to suggest that Trueman might produce *Marmion*. "Good God, what an idea!" exclaimed the impresario; and the fantasy was dismissed.

Trueman's other conductor was an Italian, Emilio Pizzi, himself a composer of operas. (It was Pizzi who later put Beecham in touch with Luigi Illica over the *Marlowe* libretto.) Rehearsals were at the Old Vic. Beecham had little trouble with the chorus; most of the chorus men and women were old hands, wrinkled and toneless, but they knew their scores and sang accurately. The orchestra, thirty or forty strong, were a different matter. They were devoted drinkers to a man—Beecham later remarked that on tour they always had "a bar's rest" before a performance—and sulked when disciplined.

From the Old Vic the company moved during the Easter week-end to the first theatre of the tour, at Clapham. There Beecham had his first sight of the scenery and the wardrobe. They were makeshift and squalid. Certain of the principal singers—among them Blanche Marchesi, the prominently publicised star of the tour, who was making her first operatic appearance in England as Santuzza in *Cavalleria* —had brought their own costumes; the handsomeness of these made the drabness of the rest more excruciating still.

As was to be expected of a purely suburban event, the Imperial Grand Opera Company's tour went unreported in the national papers. It got short shrift even in the suburban ones. All the five theatres visited had sixpenny galleries and stalls at five shillings. Nowhere, either in advertisements or news paragraphs, do I find any mention of Beecham. Pizzi, who was his senior, crops up once. Trueman, who played Don José in *Carmen*, is said by one local reporter to have sung and acted very powerfully; but the same writer found everything splendid, even the staging. Business was patchy. While gratified that the cheaper parts of the house were full for *Faust*, the *West Ham, East Ham and Stratford Express* regretted that a community which prided itself on its love of music should leave so many of the dearer seats unoccupied.

Beecham's next musical adventure was of a staider and more satisfying sort.

Over the chess board in Morley's drawing room one night he met an earnest, courtly young man, Charles Kennedy Scott. Three years

Beecham's senior, Scott was impassioned about Tudor vocal music which, as it happened, had been one of Beecham's specialist subjects under Charles Wood. At Beecham's suggestion, Scott brought to Roland Gardens a load of Musical Antiquarian Society publications. The two of them, with half a score other singing friends, used to sit round the drawing room table, each with an immense Antiquarian tome in front of him, and sing madrigals. Beecham sang bass. His voice didn't amount to much. It was of the kind sardonically known as "a conductor's voice"; he could never have succeeded as a soloist.

Often he brought professional singers to these meetings, among them on one occasion, a soprano and a contralto from Covent Garden, who hid behind their propped-up copies and, so far as the rest could hear, did not emit a single note all evening. His associates at the Madrigal table were Kensingtonians whose musical keenness formed part of a broad general culture. Among them were two portrait painters, a sculptor, a doctor, a parson and a future Commissioner of Crown Lands. Where are such groups of amateur singers to be found nowadays?

Increasing in size and proficiency, Scott's madrigal group finally blossomed as the Oriana Madrigal Society. Beecham was among the basses at their first concert, in the Portman Rooms, Baker Street, in July 1905 and at their second and third concerts. What is more, he wrote analytical notes for their early programmes. The remarkable thing about these early Beecham writings is the calm omniscience of his judgments and the lulling smoothness of the language in which they are couched. The oracular tone suggests a mature lifetime's meditation rather than the relative rawness of twenty-six. Beecham's love of the Tudor madrigalists and his early expertise in this field must astonish later generations. From 1910 or thereabouts Beecham stood for music of such different sorts that one might have supposed the Wilbyes and the Byrds alien to his taste. Most other composers whom he took up during his formative years he went on propagating and conducting into old age. He remained actively faithful to Grieg, even to Grétry. The madrigalists, on the other hand, fell out of his life.

(4)

The madrigal table at Roland Gardens and the outcome of it have taken us a little ahead of our chronology.

Two years earlier, on July 27, 1903, to be exact, Thomas Beecham and Utica Celestia Welles were married, after banns, at St. Mary's Church, Cranley Gardens, a short stroll from the Welleses' house.

The feud with Ewanville was at its height. Joseph Beecham did not attend. He had not been invited. Probably he was not even informed. Emily Beecham was the bridesmaid. In the vestry the parson, Mr. Sopwith, told her that Utica was the most beautiful bride he had ever set eyes on. Among the witnesses were Utica's father and Beecham's mother. The honeymoon was spent in English cathedral cities and the Lake District. Somewhere on the tour, while out walking in the fields, they found a horseshoe. Beecham was a great believer in horseshoes. He took it back to the hotel and packed it in his travelling bag. With this extra weight the bag was heavy. Lifting it into the train next day, according to Lady (Utica) Beecham's recollection, he sprained and permanently injured his wrist.

After this he was never able to play the piano for more than fifteen or twenty minutes at a time without an incapacitating cramp or partial paralysis of the lower arm. There is no mention of the travelling bag incident in *A Mingled Chime*, which wraps the affair in mystery but speculates that the injury may possibly have been caused by overstrain in piano practice or by a blow from a cricket ball.

Whatever the cause, the effect was drastic. Beecham's ambition to become a concert pianist was killed overnight. The horseshoe was luckier than he knew. Fate was simplifying his professional choice. It only remained for him to become disillusioned with himself as a composer. Nothing would thereafter be left for him—in music, at any rate—but the rostrum.

(5)

Much of 1904 was spent by the Beechams on the Continent. They stayed in Paris, Lucerne, Milan, Parma, Modena, Bologna, Florence. After more than half a century the sequence of the year's events is blurred; but it seems that while in Italy he conferred with Luigi Illica on the now completed *Marlowe* script; and that through Illica he met one of the geniuses of the century, Giacomo Puccini.

Decades later Beecham told me that he stayed under the same roof as Puccini and Illica while they were revising *Madama Butterfly*. On its first performance in February, *Butterfly* had flopped calamitously. Their reshaping of it was "a marvel, a miracle".

He did not succumb entirely to Puccini's charm. Behind the charm—and the reticence—he diagnosed a mind that knew exactly what it wanted and was hard to please. He said later: "I never liked Puccini too well, but we 'managed'." It was not until 1920 that the two men really got to know each other. Visiting London that year for the first Covent Garden performances of his *Trittico*, Puccini went through the *Bohème* score with Beecham at the latter's request and corrected dynamic and other directions which, as printed, were contradictory or incomplete. It has been claimed for Beecham's performances of *La Bohème* that in consequence they were uniquely authoritative. It may well be that his 1904 contact with Puccini sowed in Beecham's mind the first doubt as to his own capacity as an operatic composer.

His stay in Paris was more productive. At the Opéra Comique he attended a performance of *Richard Cœur de Lion* by the French composer André Ernest Grétry (1741-1813). The music enchanted him. Instantly he set out to assimilate all the Grétry he could lay hands on. He combed the second-hand bookshops for full scores and, when these were wanting, turned them up in the Bibliothéque Nationale and either copied them himself or had others copy them for him.

From Grétry he passed to Grétry's contemporaries—Etienne Méhul (1763-1817), Nicholas Dalayrac (1753-1809), Pierre Alexandre Monsigny (1729-1817), Nicolo Isouard (1775-1818) and many others. He came back to England at the end of 1904 with a trunkload of likeable music which, even in France, had rarely been played in living memory. Much in this trunkload was to serve him for a lifetime. To mention two instances only, Méhul's piece *La Chasse du jeune Henri* was recurrent in Beecham programmes and recordings throughout his career; and as late as 1956 he produced Grétry's comic opera, *Zémire et Amor* in its entirety at the Bath Festival. The extent of Beecham's researches in Paris and elsewhere during the early years of the century is indicated by the range of works upon which he drew for his first concert series with the New Symphony Orchestra at Bechstein (now the Wigmore) Hall. In his prospectus to this series (November-December 1906), Beecham wrote:

"Though these concerts are devoted mainly to the work of 18th-century masters—rarely and in many cases never performed—they are not in any sense meant to be historical or 'antiquarian'. If it be remembered that it was no uncommon thing for a composer of the period to turn out in the course of his career some fifty or sixty operas (without taking into consideration other branches of composition), and that the number of these composers is almost bewilderingly numerous, it may be safely affirmed that there is a considerable quantity of fine and interesting music which, for no fault of its own, has dropped out of the ordinary orchestral repertory.

One of the chief causes for this has been the disappearance of the original publishing house, with the resultant difficulty and sometimes impossibility, of procuring scores and parts. Consequently, with plenty of good modern works near at hand and easy of access, the attention of both performer and public has been diverted from these productions of an earlier age. This is a matter for genuine regret, and it is the aim of these concerts to show that they possess all the elements of freshness, charm and originality that characterize this spring-time period of modern orchestral writing, and that they amply justify their revival."

Their revival by Beecham was, as yet, two years ahead. Most of those two years were devoted to preparation, contriving and career-planning. From this period dates a curious word portrait by the composer Cyril Scott. Scott met Beecham for the first time at the home of a fellow composer, Norman O'Neill. He recalls the Beecham of 1905 as a small figure in a frock coat, brown boots, pork-pie hat and dark woollen gloves (with pattern), who sat and talked with clasped hands, staring at the carpet and unable, apparently, to look anybody in the eye. Scott sensed in him a shyness amounting to inferiority. In his memoirs Scott reckons that it took Beecham five years, aided by one factor and another, to come out of his shell. He dramatically contrasts the diffident midget he met at Pembroke Villas with the mature Beecham who, around 1912, at one of Mrs. Charles Hunter's week-ends, sniffed at a proffered allowance from his father of £50,000 a year, exclaiming, "Such a sum is no good to me at all!"

It must be said that the Scott portrait is sharply at variance with the ebullient self-confidence which most contemporaries noted in Beecham. I have little doubt as to its truth, however. At this period there was an almost morbid element of self-questioning in Beecham. Most of the time his inner hesitations were concealed by the seigneurial front he put on.

Yet his mission was becoming clearer. One day he went on a train journey with Charles Kennedy Scott. The compartment was crowded. Beecham had a corner seat. He brought out a sort of chess board upon which were pegged symbols representing the "choirs" of the orchestra —all the strings, from first violins to double-basses, woodwind, horns, trombones, kettledrums, percussion and the rest. During the journey he "rehearsed" his chess board, flinging his arms about uninhibitedly, cueing in various sections or soloists with his left hand and humming, or rather snarling, the parts they were supposed to be playing.

Other people in the compartment, solid pipe-smoking Britons, wondered whether he might not be mad. Had they known he was preparing to give over fifty years of his life and spend one of the country's most considerable fortunes on giving people music they hadn't asked for and, for the most part, didn't enjoy, the pipe-smokers would have stopped wondering and said there was no doubt about his madness at all.

CHAPTER FIVE

"INSUBORDINATION"

(1)

In December 1905 Beecham hired forty players of the Queen's Hall Orchestra for his first public orchestral concert in London, which took place at Bechstein Hall. The programme was drawn mainly from the stock of 18th-century French and Italian pieces which he had been collecting on the Continent but included also *Fair Helen of Kirkconnel*, a ballad for baritone (on this occasion Frederic Austin) and orchestra by Cyril Scott. Six months younger than Beecham, Scott was one of several English composers who, in a country bemused by foreign music and musicians, benefited by Beecham's defiant and patriotic patronage. Thirty years later we find Beecham promoting, if not actually conducting, a new Scott piece, *La Belle Dame sans Merci*, at the Leeds Triennial Festival. But neither *Fair Helen* nor Beecham's 18th-century spoils served to galvanise this first Bechstein Hall concert. It appears, indeed, to have been a failure.

What went wrong? Our only evidence is a note by the critic of *The Times*:

> "Deference to the wishes of the conductor . . . was conspicuously absent from the performance of some well-known players. . . . The conductor suffered, as many a newcomer has suffered before, from what was practically insubordination on the part of the players."

Although it is significant that Beecham had no further dealings with the Queen's Hall Orchestra, he makes no reference to any recalcitrance on their part in his autobiography but rather blames himself, "My sensation . . . was one of definite disappointment with myself". he wrote. Throughout the concert he realised that he was failing to get from his players the tone, style and general effect he wanted. "Somehow or other the sound of much of the music was strangely different from the conception of it in my brain. . . . I felt I knew better and I knew I could do better."

Perhaps he had been trying to run before he could walk. He decided to spend most of a year in the study of orchestral techniques. He would bury his head in scores. He would attend every concert at the Queen's

Hall, watching and listening with ruthless eyes and ears. The gifts and errors of others should be the springboard of his own career. And the Queen's Hall should be his classroom.

(2)

Reduced to a shell by Hitler's bombers in May 1941, the Queen's Hall now belongs to memory and will soon be merely a page in history. Even the shell has disappeared. Let us visualise the hall as it looked at the time of Beecham's "visitations".

There was a backing of mirrors all round the stalls. Medallions of great composers dominated the platform from either side. The paint-work was in two colours, terracotta and light grey. Knightley, the architect, had specified that the grey should be that of the belly of a London mouse. While the job was in progress he had a row of dead mice hung in the paint shop as a colour guide. The ceiling had been painted by a decorator from the Paris Opera with "attenunated Cupids ... clad in sallow pantaloons". (The phrase is E. M. Forster's.) At a point near the platform on the right-hand side a hole was constantly wearing in the carpet where male "prommers" concentrated in force to watch the girl harpist, who was accounted pretty.

Such was the Queen's Hall in its early years: not much to look at according to contemporary *art nouveau* canons but clear and mellow for listening, with a reverberation of 3·7 seconds when empty, fining down to 1·5 seconds ("too short for good choral tone", finicked the acousticians) when packed. The 1906 season brought to the rostrum a procession of conductors, mostly foreign: Raabe, Steinbach, Stanford, Colonne, Safonoff, Grieg, Cowen, Nikisch, Richter and Wood. Of these ten only the last three were destined to leave an ambience and legend in this country on the strength of their rostrum techniques and personalities.

At this time Nikisch was fifty, ornate as to neckties, whiskers, cuffs and hat brims. He controlled his baton with the fluid wrist proper to a former violinist. People credited him with mesmeric gifts. At rehear-sals of Tchaikovsky's Fifth Symphony, he would fix his eyes during the horn solo which opens the slow movement upon Adolf Borsdorf, principal hornist successively in the Queen's Hall and London Sym-phony orchestras. At the same time he would sing the melody. At the finish Nikisch would murmur, "Beautiful. But let us do it again, Mr. Borsdorf." Invariably the second version was more beautiful than the first—and had something of Nikisch, swore connoisseurs, in every note. In players' pubs it was contended that, away from Nikisch,

Borsdorf could not have phrased the solo with the same nuances to save his life.

Something has already been said about Richter. In 1906 he was at his apogee. In the Queen's Hall bandroom his lightest word became law. There was a leader of second violins, one Eayres, who exasperated lesser conductors by buttonholing them after rehearsal and saying he didn't agree with their *tempi* in such and such a movement, because The Old Man took it more quickly or, as the case might be (and probably was) more slowly.

Severe on wrong-doers, Richter combined a long and unremitting memory with parades of humility. If Mr. X, woodwind player, committed a wrong note in, say Richard Strauss's *Zarathustra*, he was sharply reminded of the fact when *Zarathustra* next came into rehearsal a year or more later. Richter would say, "And remember, Mr. X, three bars after figure 32—E *flat*, not E natural!" In Manchester a cymbal player disastrously mistimed an entry in the finale of Dvořák's *New World* Symphony. Richter glared at him until the end of the movement and went on glaring for a full second after the music stopped. Seasons afterwards he rehearsed the *New World* again. Meantime the offending cymbalist had been dismissed. On reaching the fateful page, Richter pulled up the orchestra two bars before the cymbal stroke and inquired in a stage whisper, "Iss he still alife?"

Humility came into the picture when he publicly committed a mistake himself. If he fumbled a beat and dislocated the playing, he would turn round to the audience, utter a *mea culpa* that cleared his minions and start the piece again. Occasional self-abasements of this kind put a finishing touch to the imported Father Figure of English music.

Certain of his traits and limitations were not as well known. In Vienna, after running through the *Penthesilea* tone poem with the Vienna Philharmonic Orchestra, he had shabbily derided its composer, a starveling young genius named Hugo Wolf. As viewed from Wahnfried he was not altogether the authority on *The Ring* and its *tempi* that London supposed him to be. Although he entrusted the first *Ring* performances to Richter, Wagner found his rhythm excessively four-square. He won high praise for his notable Elgar premières; but *Gerontius* caught him out badly. We know now that after the first rehearsal of Elgar's oratorio at Birmingham he spent half the night with the score propped up on his bedroom mantelpiece, agitatedly trying to master Elgar's idiom and memorise its terms. Handicapped by too short a rehearsal schedule, the choir were even more baffled.

Richter appears to have erred markedly in not ordering a postpone-
ment of the performance. The few who knew *Gerontius* then and
several present who came to know it well later agree that the première
of October 1900 was woefully bad.

Richter's beard, crinkled and untidy, suggested brimming beer
steins and salted horse-radish. Henry Wood's beard, on the other
hand, was in the same torpedo class as those of Nikisch, Beecham and
Tsar Nicholas. At the time of Beecham's Queen's Hall studies,
Wood was thirty-seven. For over fifty years he worked for music
and his Queen's Hall public as tirelessly as a gin horse, if not as un-
complainingly. At the height of the summer musical season he
rejoiced in a schedule of up to eight concerts and four rehearsals a week
and contrived, nobody will ever know how, to give five hundred
singing lessons a year as well. With August Manns (of the Crystal
Palace concerts) he gave London music lovers their first regular access
to what became the standard orchestral repertory, Bach to Brahms.

His famous Promenade Concerts began as a startling *olla podrida* of
cornet solos (Schubert's *Serenade* was the most highly prized among
these), "selections" from *Carmen*, *Trovatore* and the like, bassoon
fantasias of the *Lucy Long* genre and single movements by Beethoven
as well as whole symphonies. But, both at the Proms and in Wood's
other series, aesthetic growth was quick. Within a few years his
programmes were sane in taste and balance. He gave a first hearing
to masses of new or unfamiliar music, some of which (though not
much, to be sure) has survived. In 1896 he gave his public Tchaikovsky's *Casse Noisette* suite. They bellowed with delight. Three
of the movements had to be repeated. In 1901 he introduced Elgar's
Pomp and Circumstance March in D major, the one to which A. C.
Benson later fitted his *Land of Hope and Glory* text. Britain was
at war with the Boers. Beholding in the music an image of their
patriotism, the crowd exploded with enthusiasm and would not let
the concert continue until Wood had repeated the march *twice*.

Wood was either first or early in the field with rarer stuff than this
however. Before Beecham appeared on the scene he had already
conducted a good deal of Rimsky-Korsakov, Dukas's *Apprenti Sorcier*,
Sibelius's Symphony No. 1, three of the Sibelius tone poems, Gustav
Mahler's Symphony No. 1 and, among Richard Strauss pieces, the
then formidable *Ein Heldenleben*. His production in 1912 at the Queen's
Hall of Schönberg's *Five Orchestral Pieces*, for which he was barbar-
ously hissed, is to be coupled historically with Monteux's conducting
of Stravinsky's *Sacre du Printemps* at Drury Lane two years later. In

the annals of the mind, not merely of music, both were peak occasions of a sort that London experiences rarely in any half-century.

During the Edwardian decade Wood was, in his field, supreme. A young aspirant called Landon Ronald (later Sir Landon) concluded there was no room on our rostrums for any other English conductor and accordingly sought engagements in Germany, Austria and Italy. "You drove me out of London", he told Wood in a burst of forgiveness many years later. Wood's energy, patience and adaptability amounted to something like greatness. But along with the greatness went touches of pettiness. In the years to come Beecham's immense vogue irked him. It was not that he denied Beecham's musicianship. It was merely that, as he saw it, Beecham often reaped prestige as a musical pioneer which should more properly have been enjoyed by him.

"What d'you think of that?" he chuckled to Benjamin Dale, the composer, shortly after the appearance of his autobiography *My Life of Music* (1938)—"four hundred and ninety-five pages; and not a single reference to Beecham!"

Nikisch, Richter, Wood: these were the monoliths who confronted Beecham at the outset of his conducting career. Ronald might run away. Not he. All three monoliths must be met and outrivalled on their own ground.

(3)

What of the human raw material on which he would have to rely? What manner of men were the mass of orchestral players in mid-Edwardian times?

The answer is brief. They were a harried proletariat. There were no permanent orchestras then. Hence there were no regular jobs. Every man was a freelance, who worked from a personal diary which was in perpetual revision as he jockeyed daily for betterment, dropping poorly paid assignments in favour of more rewarding ones, when these came his way. Such chopping and changing sometimes involved a rejigging of teaching dates, for most players eked out by giving lessons on flute, fiddle or what-not in their front parlours.

In a gruelling vocation, the musician enjoyed one prescriptive liberty: that of picking and choosing. Let us take a case. A 'cellist is booked to rehearse at the Queen's Hall on Friday morning and play there on Friday night. The day before he is offered a more tempting Friday night engagement; he is invited to play at some duchess's soirée in Mayfair at five shillings more, hock and sandwiches thrown in. He accepts the second job, attends the Friday morning rehearsal (for which he gets a fee) and finds some brother 'cellist to deputise for him at the Queen's Hall concert.

The anomalies of the deputy system were excellently hit off by an honorary treasurer of the (now Royal) Philharmonic Society. "A, whom you want", wrote Mr. John Mewburn Levien, "signs to play at your concert. He sends B (whom you don't mind) to the first rehearsal. B, without your knowledge or consent, sends C to the second rehearsal. Not being able to play at the concert, C sends D, whom you would have paid five shillings to stay away." When, as periodically happened, the freelance pool was creamed off for lucrative musical festivals in the country, Wood found himself faced at the Queen's Hall on more than one Monday morning with an orchestra of a hundred including seventy or eighty new faces. To induct the newcomers into his technical methods and needs on the spur of the moment was hopeless. In any case, the turnover of deputies being what it was, he had no guarantee that all or any of them would turn up "on the night".

Clearly, the abuse was not to be borne. Early in 1904 he struck at the roots of it. At Wood's instigation, Robert Newman, his manager, went on to the platform before rehearsal one morning, moustaches bristling, a militant glint in his blue eyes. Reading from a bit of paper, he delivered his and Wood's ultimatum: "Gentlemen, in future there will be no deputies. Good morning!"

Half the players handed in their resignations forthwith and changed the musical scene almost overnight by founding the London Symphony Orchestra. The L.S.O.'s first concert, conducted by Richter, was on June 9th, 1904. Within a year the L.S.O. directors had themselves begun to reprimand and fine players for practising that very deputy system in defence of which they had seceded from Wood.

The older hands of the epoch were tough, nimble and laconically humorous. Seen from the opposite end of the concert room they looked well groomed. At closer range you noticed the lapel stains, the grubbiness of the white tie. Drinking was a right, almost a ritual. Their resort during concert intervals at the Queen's Hall was a public house in Great Portland Street known then and now as The Glue Pot, whence they were summoned by a man with a handbell. Their fathers and grandfathers had played at the Opera and at the Philharmonic under Mendelssohn and Richard Wagner. At best their playing seems to have had exactness and a purely physical gusto. The more velvety nuances were excluded. In rehearsal they smouldered resentfully under martinets and were benign towards good natured oldsters of limited musical vision. A snatch of conversation which Henry Wood overheard in the nineties is illuminating.

Lamenting departed days, one old hand says to the other:

"Remember how we used to stroll in at half-past ten for a 10 a.m. rehearsal? No stop watch on the desk then."

"True", sighs his friend. "And there wasn't all this fuss. In the old days the conductor would say, Fifth Symphony, Beethoven, gentlemen. No need to rehearse *that*. We all know it!"

As we have seen, much music was played unrehearsed. By *force majeure* London players became supremely good sight readers. As such they were esteemed from New York to St. Petersburg. Rehearsals, when there were any, commanded a separate fee but, especially in the theatre, were alarmingly elastic. An easygoing musical director might dismiss the band after fifty minutes instead of drilling them for the statutory three hours. On the other hand the three hours sometimes multiplied unconscionably. I heard a Beecham veteran of 60 remark that a Wagner rehearsal, called for 10 a.m. at Covent Garden in the 'thirties, lasted until 4 p.m. "And we were back in the pit again for *Mastersingers* at six."

"That's nothing", commented a bassoonist of 80. "The longest rehearsal I ever did was when Beerbohm Tree put on Stephen Phillips's *Herod* with incidental music at His Majesty's. We went in one Sunday afternoon at four o'clock. We came out at six-thirty next morning. We didn't get an extra penny for that. And we thought Tree was a fine chap because he sent sandwiches and bottled beer down to the pit at four in the morning!"

Probably through the influx of a new generation of student players, as well as growing musical awareness on the part of concertgoers and conductors alike, playing standards were already on the upgrade before Beecham first raised his baton in London. In 1899, at a rehearsal in the Queen's Hall of Bach's E major Violin Concerto, Ysaÿe, before whom Europe touched its forehead in the dust, plaintively said, "Gentlemen, I am not a trombone—only a solo violin." This suggests a certain heavy-handedness in the accompaniments. Fifteen years later, apropos a performance by the same orchestra in the same hall, Arnold Schönberg in an open letter to the players, wrote of

"the unexcelled qualities of your ensemble, the precision, beauty of sound, noble taste and careful thoroughness of detail which are the merit of every single one of you and of all of you together . . .

On the Continent there are only two orchestras which could be compared to you—the Amsterdam Orchestra and the Vienna Philharmonic."

That was written in January 1913. It may be doubted if Schönberg could have written as warmly in 1906. Beecham's electrifying advent in the meantime had sharpened public expectation and, in consequence, playing standards all round.

Beecham ended his studies at the Queen's Hall in a mood of disdain. He felt that other conductors were being as futile with the Queen's Hall Orchestra as he had himself been at his "pilot" concert of 1905. Uniformly, he found, the playing lacked "true balance or adjustment of component parts." Fifty-three years later, on the eve of his 80th birthday, he was asked whether the standard of orchestral playing had improved since the beginning of his career. "Oh, incontestably", he replied. "At the beginning of the century there was no standard to speak of."

The thing to do, he told himself in 1906, was to enrol some group of skilled players who would respond to the conceptions and ideals that were so imperiously fermenting inside him. He had already found what he wanted in a little theatre called The Coronet at Notting Hill Gate.

CHAPTER SIX

ENTER DELIUS

(1)

THE SECOND LONDON orchestra to be used by Beecham was originally a nameless body of sixty players, mostly first-rate men. Their principals included John Saunders (leader), Eli Hudson (flute), Waldo Warner (viola), Charles Draper (clarinet) and Aubrey Brain (horn). These were among the aristocrats of their profession.

The sixty had come together late in 1905 for a series of Sunday night concerts at The Coronet conducted by Howard Jones under the banner of a transient Sunday Concerts Society. Like the Imperial Grand Opera Company, they played to a sixpenny gallery. The dearest seats were four shillings. Even on this basis the concerts failed to prosper. After two or three ill-patronised essays, the committee announced that the remaining concerts of the series would have to be "postponed" through lack of support.

That was the end of symphonic music at The Coronet—but not of the sixty. The organising spirits were Saunders (who became their chairman) and Draper. We gather something of Saunders' standing and enterprise from the part he played in promoting a new toy which wrongheads were beginning to take seriously as a musical instrument. The thing called itself the gramophone and was made by a firm that made typewriters, too. In a well-filled Royal Albert Hall—i.e., before 5,000 or 6,000 listeners—Hudson played the piccolo in duet with W. H. Squire's 'cello to organ accompaniment. At the end of their piece the trio retired and were heard, as pre-recorded, through apparatus which incorporated a primitive form of amplifier. Patti, Melba, Plançon, Journet, Caruso and Scotti were heard as well but did not grace the occasion in person. "To musical people", sniffed *The Times* next day, "such sounds are but a travesty of the real thing."

It came to Saunders' ears that a newcomer called Thomas Beecham (soon to be simplified throughout the profession to "Tommy") was on the look out for a chamber orchestra and proposed to give four concerts between November 1906 and January 1907 at Bechstein Hall. It was Saunders' lieutenant, Draper, who negotiated with Beecham. Their meeting was at the conductor's home in the country. Beecham had already heard the sixty in rehearsal and found them to his liking. With Draper he went for a walk across the fields and talked of the music he proposed to play. Draper was dizzied by a string of unfamiliar names and titles—*Le Petit Chaperon Rouge* and *La Fête du Village Voisin* by Boieldieu, Méhul's *Les Deux Aveugles* and *Horatius Cocles*, Cherubini's *Les Abencerrages*, Cimarosa's *Giannina e Bernardone*, Paisello's *Proserpine* and equally unheard of things by Louard, Dalayrac, Paer and Grétry.

Beecham's business manager, Leslie Hibberd, had warned him, with reason, that nobody would buy seats to hear unknown composers. During their walk Beecham and Draper came upon three horsehoes. These they regarded as a sign. Beecham wrote his prospectus and sent it to the printer. The series was announced as The Thomas Beecham Orchestral Concerts. A seventeen-year-old Westminster boy named Adrian Boult, who toyed with the idea of becoming a conductor himself, remembered in later life the poster displays in Wigmore Street. There were glossy half-tone portraits on view of the new maestro. He had a piercing eye. His handsome beard, which it was Utica's prerogative to trim, was fuller than the one he wore later. The prospectus was topped by a line from *The Times* notice of his "pilot" concert—"He is a conductor of remarkable ability."

In these preliminaries the orchestra remained anonymous. Beecham described it reticently as drawn from the best London permanent orchestras and as comprising thirty-five to forty instrumentalists, all chamber players of skill and experience. By the first concert (November 2nd), however, he or Saunders and Draper had thought up a title: The New Symphony Orchestra. Beecham's association with the N.S.O. lasted for two years. Technically it was the making of him.

As usual he wrote his own programme notes. In view of the revival of *Medea* by Callas in our own time, his cool appraisal of its composer, Cherubini, makes piquant reading. In the programme for the third concert, which included the *Medea* Overture, Beecham wrote:

"The music of Cherubini is a somewhat strange thing and dallies alternatively with two widely differing moods—an impressive serenity, which occasionally declines into dullness, and a sparkling gaiety which, however, seldom develops into real humour. Of these the former is inclined to predominate, with the unfortunate result of having obtained for the composer an exaggerated reputation for stiffness and pedantry. It is true that on listening to much of his music, one is tempted to paraphrase a criticism on Arturo Graf's verse and say, 'If this be poetry, it is poetry cast in steel!' "

With a Mozart Symphony, the No. 38 in D major, as its centre-piece, the first programme ran to ten items and finished so late, complained the *Morning Post* critic, that he could not dwell on many of the performances, pleasant as it would have been to do so. Save for minor pinpricks the critics were cordial. At the first concert Beecham conducted without a baton. In this, noted the *Morning Post*, he followed the example of M. Safonoff. At the third he stopped beating time for the finale of Haydn's E flat Symphony, letting the orchestra conduct itself. The critic of *The Daily Telegraph* gave a deprecatory cough; the last word in such tricks, he suggested, had been uttered by "the admirable Sousa" The most popular piece in a programme dedicated mainly to antique music appears to have been a modern one, Järnefelt's *Praeludium*, which had newly caught the public fancy. Beecham had to repeat it.

Obscure arias were sung at the first three concerts by foreign artists or, at any rate, by artists with foreign names—Luis Alvarez, Lydia Obrée, Julien Henry and Hilda de Angelis. A rising young English tenor, John Coates, was to have sung Boieldieu and Paisello numbers at the concluding concert (January 23rd, 1907).

This concert, however, did not take place. There was no public explanation of its cancellation. Perhaps Hibberd's forebodings about lack of support had come embarrassingly true. It was certainly the fact that, until his personality finally bewitched the public—a gradual and lengthy process—Beecham's esoteric programmes kept thousands away from his concerts and piled up deficits that would have intimidated any other man.

Again Beecham retired to his tent and meditated. The lesson of the Bechstein Hall venture was clear. If the New Symphony Orchestra was to compete successfully for public favour with the Queen's Hall and London Symphony orchestras, it must drop its "chamber" status and approximate in size to its rivals. During the summer of 1907, Beecham accordingly reorganised the orchestra and brought it up to full symphonic strength.

(2)

His first concert with the expanded New Symphony Orchestra, on the night of October 19th, 1907, was in the "ampler accommodation" of the Queen's Hall. Uncowed and confident, he put on a programme which was even more certain to deter the public then than it would be in our own day. The principal pieces were Vincent d'Indy's symphonic ballad *La fôret enchantée*, Smetana's symphonic poem *La Sarka* and Edouard Lalo's "practically unknown Symphony in G minor".

Beecham could not have failed to realise that such a programme would be a box office handicap. Throughout 1907 and for a considerable time after, reconciliation with his father not having been effected, he was intermittently hard-up and dependent for his enterprises largely upon his mother's help plus domestic cheeseparing. One can only conclude that his playing of highly individual and non-commercial programmes was part of an astute, long-term policy. Only by being innovatory and, up to a point, perplexing, could he hope to rise above the conventional ruck of London musicmaking and command attention. At twenty-eight he considered that the first essential, if one wanted to be better than anybody else, was to be *different*.

While he was turning these thoughts over in his mind at the end of his Queen's Hall concert, a stranger was shown into the artists' room. Monkish, keen-eyed and reserved, he was introduced as Frederick Delius, composer. With him was Fritz Cassirer, conductor of the Eberfeld opera house, Germany, who, seven months earlier at the Komische Oper, Berlin, had produced an opera by Delius, *A Village Romeo and Juliet*, which Beecham himself was to champion fervently in years to come. Delius and Cassirer said they thought the New Symphony Orchestra very good indeed and asked if they could hire it for a concert at the Queen's Hall on December 1st, at which Cassirer proposed to conduct Delius's *Appalachia* Variations and Strauss's *Ein Heldenleben*. Arrangements were concluded on the spot.

Beecham took to Delius at once. For the first time in his life he found himself in the presence of a personality unmistakable in stamp, full, mellow and unchanging. In the whole of Beecham's egocentric career, Delius was the only contemporary who could, from time to time, pull him out of orbit. If Delius in middle life was really concerned to find an ideal interpreter—a thing by no means certain, for he seemed sardonically indifferent to his own interests—he could have found nobody to match Thomas Beecham, whose care in Delius's case for the integrity of the notes as set down was uniquely counterpoised by a sense of that reality beyond the notes which is said to be the ultimate truth of any music.

Beecham attended the *Appalachia* rehearsals at the Queen's Hall and was there on the night of December 1st. The score's loveliness of tone and variety of atmosphere astonished him then and for the rest of his life. He was not the only one to be carried away. In the galleries people stood up to applaud. At an English symphony concert this was the nearest thing known to hysteria. When Delius came on to the platform the applause became thunderous. Characteristically, his smile was of surprise and amusement rather than of appreciation. Delius had no great regard for his fellow men, even when they were worshipping his music.

In 1907 he was in his middle forties. He had written five operas, of which *A Village Romeo* is the only one of note nowadays, and, among outstanding miscellaneous works, *Paris: the Song of a Great City* (1899), *Sea Drift*, after Walt Whitman (1903), *A Mass of Life*, after Nietzsche (1904-5), *Songs of Sunset*, after Ernest Dowson (1906-7) and *Brigg Fair: an English Rhapsody* (1907). History offers no ready example of a composer whose music, in essence and feeling, was more at variance with his temper and tongue. Delius's music is compounded of dawn pipings, sultry noons, orange afterglows, the incense of burning leaves and the gripings of nostalgia. Delius himself, as is clear from the memoirs of Fenby, Philip Heseltine and Clare Delius, as well as from such letters of his as have so far been published, was cranky to a malignant degree, incapable of seeing the point of anybody else's music (except, perhaps, that of Grieg, who was in some measure his precursor) and as fanatically hostile to received opinions—simply because they were received—as warped egocentrics usually are. Son of a well-to-do West Riding wool merchant, he had roamed in early manhood as far as Florida and was now settled on independent though modest means in the village of Grez-sur-Loing, near Fontainebleau. As a rising composer he found Germany his best market and cultivated it in a casual way.

During his London visit of 1907 he ran into or heard about several young English composers—Cyril Scott, Arnold Bax, Balfour Gardiner, W. H. Bell, Ralph Vaughan Williams, Joseph Holbrooke and others —who, notwithstanding that Beecham was doing what he could to give their works a hearing, were apt to rail against the indifference of the English public and English institutions.

The most voluble of the railers was Joseph Holbrooke, then twenty-nine years old, who had a lean, saturnine look and intense eyes behind silver framed lenses. Holbrooke, whose *Apollo and the Seaman* was to be produced by Beecham in fantastic circumstances at the Queen's Hall, went on railing for fifty years. Delius had a realistic, even brutal reply to him and the rest.

"You complain (he told them) that you rarely get a second hearing of your works. You ought to be thankful you get a first! Consider the position in Germany. There's a society with headquarters in Berlin, the Tonkünstlerversammlung, for the encouragement of new music. Well now, last year the Tonkünstlerversammlung had 280 new symphonies sent to it. It was able to arrange performances for six of them. Think of the years spent in composing the other 274! Don't ever dream of becoming a "professional" composer unless you have private means. If you're sure of your three meals a day, good. In that case write individualistic music to your heart's content. You can afford to wait for recognition. . . . Of course, there are always shop ballads. In England you can earn your living by writing stuff that wouldn't be listened to in Germany."

In a musical society which had more than its share of smooth humbug, the sardonic and combative flavour in Delius's talk had a tonic effect on Beecham. More often than not he disagreed with Delius's sentiments and views: but the man's personality was vivi-fying, his music a greater marvel, as Beecham heard it, than any written since the height of the Wagner-Tchaikowsky epoch. At his first Queen's Hall concert with the N.S.O. in 1908 (February 26th) he produced the *Paris* tone poem. On March 31st he produced *Brigg Fair*, on May 16th the tone poem *Over the Hills and Far Away*. During the next two years he conducted two important choral pieces—*Sea Drift* (of which Henry Wood had conducted the first English performance) and the *Mass of Life*—in London, Manchester and Hanley.

Beecham quickly discovered that the worst enemy of Delius's music was Delius himself. The man had little notion of writing music beyond setting down the mere notes on paper. His indications of speed, dynamics and phrasing were vague or misleading. Such works of his as had found their way into print were, in Beecham's phrase, vilely edited. Nor did he seem to care what happened to his creations once they had left his desk. At rehearsal Beecham would turn round to him and query some technical point. "Is that right?" he would ask. Delius always replied, "Take it just as you think, my dear fellow."

(3)

For his early *Sea Drift* performances, Beecham invariably used the North Staffordshire Choral Society. This entailed many visits to Hanley, at least two of them in Delius's company. The more memor-able of these occasions occurred in April 1908, when Delius, who was no more a conductor than a tightrope walker, took it into his head to conduct the Choral Society in his own *Appalachia* Variations. During the rehearsals it was difficult to keep him to the matter in hand. He was for ever wandering off to Liverpool to stare at shipping in the Mersey. At the last rehearsal in Victoria Hall, Hanley, the orchestra turned up with seven important instruments missing. White with fury, Delius turned on Jennings, the luckless Hallé secretary, and shouted, "Call yourself an orchestra? You're no better than a bloody village band." Then, his voice rising to a scream, as we are told by an eye-witness: "My God, if this country goes to war with Germany, what a hiding you'll get! You don't know anything about organisation."

Beecham sat through this unhappy scene and the floundering rehearsal that followed with marmoreal calm. Having a pretty gift for tantrums himself, he was never moved by the tantrums of others. Not only were seven instruments missing; it further appeared that they had not been cued into the other band parts. (A cue in a band part warns the individual player exactly what is being played by what other instrument during the few bars that precede his own entry.) At the end of the rehearsal Beecham sauntered along to the artists' room. His notion was to borrow the score and cue in the missing parts himself. He found Delius gone and the score locked up. Unperturbed, he went round the players' desks and cued in the missing parts on their copies from memory. Technically *Appalachia* seems small beer today. In 1908 Beecham's feat rightly gave rise to startled admiration. It showed a detailed grasp of unfamiliar musical textures which was without parallel.

The man's uncanny memory was further shown when, again accompanied by Delius, he came to Hanley to conduct *Sea Drift*. Between the last rehearsal and the time fixed for the performance the score disappeared and has never been traced since. Philip Heseltine (who wrote music under the pen-name of Peter Warlock) hints that the score was stolen by some enemy of the conductor or the composer. He adds that Beecham, not in the least disconcerted, gave as fine a rendering of the work as he ever gave with the score in front of him.

The Hanley choir greatly pleased Beecham. He booked them for his historical performance of the *Mass of Life* at the Queen's Hall in June 1909. Their performance on this occasion was described in *The Musical Times* as a triumph. "Tone, expression and efficiency", added the writer, "were always admirable and often verged on the miraculous."

"Why did you go to the Potteries for your choir?" Beecham was asked later.

"Because", he answered, "I couldn't get a good enough choir in London."

Although preposterously busy at the time with other projects and enterprises, including preparations for his first independent opera production, he used to shuttle between London and Hanley for choral rehearsals, always using the night train for his return journeys. In Hanley he saw much of the choir's trainer and regular conductor, a brooding and clairvoyant genius called James Whewall. Inducted to music as a boy singer in a parish church out on the bleak Staffordshire moorlands, Whewall was at one and the same time kindly and aloof. In singers' pubs after concerts he would stand aside, lost in uncanny meditation. One morning he caught an early train from Hanley to Birmingham. With him was the composer Havergal Brian.

"I was wakened by my wife this morning in good time to catch the train," volunteered Whewall.

"But", objected Brian, "your wife is dead."

"Yes", said Whewall, "but it often happens."

And he started talking about something else.

Any genius of Beecham's compulsive power is served by smaller geniuses, oddities, keen talents, even freakish ones. There were many oddities within Beecham's orbit. Whewall was the most singular of all—and not the least gifted.

The ovation that attended Cassirer's performance of *Appalachia* in 1907 seems to have been a flash in the pan. After it Delius slumped badly. There was a woeful night at the old Free Trade Hall, Manchester, when Beecham took combined choral and orchestral forces of 400 through *Sea Drift* before 300 ticketholders in an auditorium built for 2,600. It took the critics and pundits a long time to get the point and savour of any Delius score. Their imperviousness was a matter of ironic indifference to Beecham. The essential thing was that he saw the point himself. He saw it with an intoxicating assurance and clarity that were proof against all the box office deficits in the world.

He lived to see Delius become, largely through his own persistence, a dominating English cult. There was a time when gramophone records of *On Hearing the First Cuckoo in Spring*, *In a Summer Garden* and the like were as much a part of the cultivated or aspiring Englishman's life and home as the latest Hemingway or colour prints of Van Gogh's *Sunflowers* and Cézanne's *Card Players*. Beecham lived also to see the Delius cult wane. One has seen an all-Delius programme of his ruthlessly cut at the last moment for want of public support, the *Appalachia* Variations and the first Dance Rhapsody being jettisoned to make way for a box office lifesaver in the shape of Sibelius's Symphony No. 1. This happened at the Festival Hall, London, in 1958.

Beecham's immense prestige failed to fill the hall on this occasion. Beechamites stayed away in their hundreds, repelled, it would seem, by such Delius works as were retained.

The moral seems clear. Music which is inevitable and ripe for one generation often has little savour for the next.*

The Beecham-Delius friendship was close-knit from the start. In the summer of 1908 it withstood the strain of a mountain-walking holiday in Norway. From a letter by Delius to his wife dated August 18th we gather that the rigours of glacier-climbing told more severely upon Beecham than is to be gathered from the racy account in *A Mingled Chime*. They trudged and climbed for fourteen hours at a stretch with no food but scraps of bread and butter and a cup of coffee and no rest before or after, except what could be snatched on twig beds in mountain huts that were either waterlogged or flea ridden. After crossing Jostedal Glacier they started on the descent to Mysahytten.

"Beecham", wrote Delius, "seemed quite done up and faint, and I thought we should have to turn back. He pulled together, however, very pluckily. I carried his rucksack and the guide carried mine. . . . Ultimately Beecham could scarcely walk any more. We had to wade a stream which took me almost up to the waist. The man carried Beecham across. . . ."

* Against this conclusion stands Beecham's extraordinary claim, unsupported by figures or analyses, in the last chapter of his *Frederick Delius*, that between 1949 and 1959 the performances of Delius's works, including broadcasts, had doubled in number.

CHAPTER SEVEN

THE PINCHED YEARS

(1)

RUNNING A SYMPHONY orchestra in halls a third full or less was an expensive business even in Edwardian times. What, in modern jargon, was Beecham using for money?

There had been a slight easing in his circumstances. To mark his marriage with Utica, old Thomas Beecham had made him a present of Mursley Hall, a Buckinghamshire shooting box which had cost him £10,000 to build. Dying four years later, Thomas senior left his grandson the equivalent of £300 a year. For a man of Beecham's upbringing and ambitions, these resources hardly amounted to a bread and butter voucher.

They were supplemented from Josephine Beecham's purse; had it not been for his mother's £4,500 a year, the concerts with the New Symphony Orchestra would have been out of the question. In those days it cost £500 (the equivalent of £2,000 today) to promote a massive choral-orchestral concert, with eminent solo singers. At this stage, it is true, Beecham was not conducting many such concerts, but there is evidence that sometimes the shoe pinched. Every pound that could be scraped in was swallowed up by the gap between concert costs and concert takings.

Of Beecham's 1909 series, the composer Ethel Smyth noted in her diary that she and her friend Violet Gordon Woodhouse, later a harpsichordist of renown, were agreed that they had never heard orchestral music played so superbly. But "the money someone must have dropped over these concerts, each one emptier than the last, owing to the programmes being devoted to the music of totally unknown composers, was an inspiring thought."

Often professional people had to wait for their money. Mewburn Levien, who was an organ builder, supplied Beecham with a single organ pipe for some experimental effect at one of his concerts. The bill was ignored for a long period. "What *is* young Beecham up to?" asked Levien testily of another instrument maker who was in like case.

The Beechams now lived in the country, at Boreham Wood on the rim of Greater London. Already there was a nursery. Adrian had been born in 1904. Thomas III arrived in 1909. Utica ran Highfields, as the house was called, on six pounds a week "to help pay for the orchestra". Years afterwards she commented, "I didn't mind much. If you love anything enough, everything comes right in the end." One day they had a considerable surprise. A pony and trap turned up at Mursley Hall: a present from Joseph Beecham. The seed of reconciliation was thus sown. It did not sprout for some years.

Meantime Beecham went ahead valiantly with his New Symphony Orchestra projects. Veteran instrumentalists remember how sometimes they had to wait for their money; how they even, on occasion, went round to Beecham's flat, when he was staying in London, to dun him in person. However long they had to wait they were confident, generally speaking, that they would get their money in the end. Beecham's like had never happened to them before. He had flame, tranquillity, wit, an incredible memory and the most splendid angers. The young players had naïve and boundless faith in him; they would follow him anywhere, through anything; even through the scores of these new young English composers in whom they were often puzzled to know what Beecham saw. Merely to read a list of the homegrown—and mainly stillborn—pieces he produced with the New Symphony Orchestra and in the early days of its successor, the Beecham Symphony Orchestra, is enough to turn one liverish with ennui. But Beecham had made up his mind. Not only was he going to produce new English music; he was going to produce it with a splash.

(2)

Preceded by reams of patriotic leaflets, a send-off meeting was held in a fashionable Hampstead drawing-room. Everybody was in evening dress. Among other persons one W. H. Bell aired his views. Bell had composed a tone-poem, *Love Among the Ruins*, which Beecham had undertaken to produce.

While Bell was giving utterance to some unexceptionable thesis, a parade ground voice unceremoniously broke in, "There I join issue with you, Mr. Bell!" The voice was that of Ethel Smyth, composer of *The Wreckers*. In tweeds, boots, deerstalker hat and divided skirt, she cut a singular figure among the white ties and gleaming shoulders. She had parked her bicycle in the porch. At Miss Smyth's voice Mr. Bell winced. Luckily she caught sight of a musical banker in the audience and called out, "Hallo, Sir Hamo, I haven't seen you for years." Mercifully Mr. Bell was forgotten. Not long afterwards he went to South Africa and became principal of a musical academy there.

Around this time Miss Smyth's relations with Beecham were cordial in a truculent way. She was given to large pronouncements and proof against scepticism.

"In England," she told a *Daily Mail* reporter, "we have a new school of composers both scientific and subtle, richer [than whom was not stated] in what I will call the freshness of youth."

"Who are they?" inquired the reporter wickedly.

"Who", inquired Miss Smyth crushingly, "is anybody until he has had time to make himself felt?"

Miss Smyth was not the only oddity among Beecham's early protégés. There was, for example, young Percy Grainger, from Australia, more admired for his *Molly on the Shore*, *Mock Morris* and *Handel in the Strand* than for, say the *Marching Song of Democracy* or *Morning Song of the Jungle*. Grainger looked out on life with darting eyes from beneath a tousle of curly hair. On hot days in Chelsea he was seen abroad in a blue and red shirt open across the chest, shorts made of Turkish towelling and white linen puttees. An assiduous collector of percussion instruments, he would set off for concerts of his own devising with a load of tubular bells and tuned gongs on his back. Long before his lighter pieces had taken the popular ear, he allocated his hours with the nicety of a dentist. Acquaintances who wished to see him gave advance notice and were invited to call, "punctually please", at, say 4.20 p.m. on a given day and not to stay after 4.40.

Balfour Gardiner (1877-1950), whose *Fantasy for Orchestra* and *Shepherd Fennel's Dance* were in Beecham's early repertory, had a more casual nature. A former master at Winchester College, he held decided opinions on most things under the sun, from Woman's nugatory influence (as he saw it) on civilisation to the Zeppelin as a future instrument of war. He had large and trusting blue eyes behind myope's glasses; and he hated mountains ("those regrettable shapes"). He listened to his own music with a detached ear and in the end became embittered about its shortcomings. Dropping music altogether, he took up pig-farming in Devonshire. Devoted in this as in all things, he broke off a holiday in Central Europe because a favourite sow was in farrow and hastened home to be in at the births.

Among scores by Granville Bantock (1868-1946), Beecham produced two cycles for voice and orchestra, one a setting of Sapphic poems, the other of *Ferishtah's Fancies* by Browning. *Ferishtah* caused puzzlement among the more philistine critics, one of whom asked why so clever a musician should select such "queer verses" for musical illustration. The writer thought it unfair (as, indeed, I do) that John Coates should be required to sing such lines as:

What lay on the floor to trip your foot?
    Each object, late awry,
Looked fitly placed, nor proved offence
    To footing free—for why?
The lamp showed all, discordant late
    Grown simple symmetry.

Critical bewilderment left Bantock unmoved. Outwardly he was of massive calm, with a sage's beard and pondering blue eyes in a sallow face. At Birmingham, where he had a musical professorship, he and his wife lived in a décor of prayer mats, oriental rugs and Japanese prints. He sought relief from composing and lecturing in "magic". His pockets were full of multi-coloured ribbon and crumpled playing cards. After the production of one of his more mountainous choral pieces in Manchester, the critic Gerald Cumberland found him at his hotel practising a new trick with a penny that folded on itself.

The new English works were strategically distributed by Beecham over programmes otherwise compounded of Mozart, Berlioz, Dvořák and his French and Italian antiques. Young Arnold Bax's tone poem *Into the Twilight*, which its composer later defined as "a mild and rather hesitant Celtic essay" had a Mozart violin concerto and Rimsky-Korsakov's *Antar* as its bedfellows. Bax (1883-1953) was at this time in his middle twenties. He lived to be Master of the King's Music and the composer of seven symphonies which have been neglected from birth, scandalously so in the opinion of partisans.

Bax had sent the score of *Into the Twilight* to professional copyists. The band parts were delivered on the day of the concert. Being unschooled in these matters, Bax did not realise that they would inevitably swarm with errors. The rehearsal that morning was a shambles. Listening to the welter of wrong notes, Bax shrank into himself with humiliation. Beecham made no comment; he did not even cock an eyebrow but maintained a steady beat and ploughed through chaos to the end. Most other conductors would have stopped at the fifth page and caustically washed their hands of the business. Without any word with or from Beecham, Bax, aided by Bell, worked solidly for eight hours correcting the band parts. That night the performance went reasonably well. When it was over Bax asked himself (he felt much too sheepish to ask Beecham) what "impish perversity" had prompted Beecham to leave the piece in the programme.

An even more memorable English première was that of Joseph Holbrooke's *Apollo and the Seaman* at the Queen's Hall in January 1908.

Holbrooke, who died in 1957, was then thirty years old. He bustled, bickered, made troops of friends and enemies and went about on a motor bicycle. Little has been heard, since they first came out, of his vast operas, choral works and symphonic poems. In 1908 and for some time later their impact—upon a limited circle, to be sure—was startling. "A genius bizarre and tantalising . . . a real and unmistakable genius", pronounced Gerald Cumberland. He and Cumberland journeyed across London by cab to a Fauré piano quartet rehearsal one wet Sunday afternoon. He talked impulsively about himself most of the way:

> You belong to the agnostic set, Cumberland, don't you? I've heard so. Well, I'm a believer. I'm a very humble member of the Church of England. . . . In many ways I'm a Puritan. . . . Faith is a huge driving force. . . . Without religion I should do little or nothing. Religion is a daily necessity.

(3)

Such was the man who set Herbert Trench's narrative poem *Apollo and the Seaman* to music and magic lantern slides. Holbrooke described his score as "an illuminated dramatic symphony with choral epilogue." Trench's words, stanza by stanza, interspersed with apt pictures, were projected on to a screen in front of the Queen's Hall platform. Behind the screen Beecham and his players worked in their shirtsleeves amid cowled desk lamps. The orchestra was vast and of unusual specification. An old man of bibulous habit had been brought over especially from Paris to play the sarrusophone. He missed his first cue, fumbled several others, then lapsed into prudent silence: a good thing, perhaps, for his phrases were interspersed with groaning intakes of breath which, at rehearsal, had made neighbouring players writhe with laughter.

From time to time Holbrooke could be seen on the outskirts of the orchestra with his head in a huge beer tankard. This made Beecham envious. During a few bars' rest he exclaimed "My God! I've the most colossal thirst! Let me see—ah, yes! Third trumpet, you have nothing to do for pages. Just run out and get me a brandy and soda, there's a good fellow."

Afterwards there was a celebration. The poet Trench sat at one end of the table, Beecham at the other. Someone got up and lauded Trench's verses and said how excellent it was that they had been disseminated by magic lantern that night. As the speaker resumed his seat and the applause was dying down, Beecham called up the table in an indolent way, "Do you know, Trench, I really think I must read your poem!"

Apollo had two performances. There was no public clamour for a third. Far from pin-pointing the pictorial and emotional intentions of the music, the magic lantern texts were projected in so fragmentary and confused a fashion that it was found impossible to read the poetry and hear the appropriate music at the same time. *Apollo* by no means liquidated Holbrooke in Beecham's estimation, however. More than a year later his *Ulalume* tone poem shared a Beecham programme with music by two other Britons—J. B. McEwen's *Gray Galloway* and W. H. Bell's *Arcadia* Suite. The attendance at the Queen's Hall on this occasion (May 17th, 1909) was characteristic—"sparse enough", said one observer, "to make the patriotic musician's blood boil."

A diary-keeping concertgoer of noble family, young William Maitland Stritt, found *Ulalume*, with its extensive use of string mutes, rather thin and monotonous. But he was obliged to simulate enthusiasm as, "before the work was played, an old gentleman in the next seat who, throughout Mozart's C major Symphony K. 425, had been casting sidelong glances at me, confided that he was 'Holbrooke senior'. There followed a brief discussion of his son's music and chance of recognition from the public. I opined that popularity would hardly come just yet, and the old man sadly agreed. He went on to deplore . . . that Joseph would not write in a more popular and therefore more lucrative style."

After the concert Joseph set down on paper his elated wonder at Beecham's bounty. At this time most people of the official and academic sort still responded with a blank stare when Beecham's name was mentioned. To the relatively limited circle who knew him, however, he was already a demigod. This attitude is aptly reflected in Holbrooke's 1909 diary entry. After dwelling on the "dreadful loss to the purse" entailed by promoting new music, he says:

"A truly formidable young man! A giant and an egotist of the first degree! One who *makes* difficulties rather than avoids them! Such are the men who make history after all. . . . I am astounded when I think of the power and virility of Mr. Beecham's conducting in many of our young men's works, such as Vaughan Williams, Norman O'Neill, Havergal Brian, W. H. Bell, John McEwen, Frederick Delius and Granville Bantock. . . . All our finest work has hitherto been repudiated by our judges; by musicians most of all. Hence the power and praise . . . which Beecham deserves from all of us, for . . . he does not go in for such modern and intense art except for the love of it . . .; and his curious genius, his Parisian refinement in reproducing the works he chooses, is quite too much for the heavy perception of our islanders. It is not likely that he will ever have the slightest reward for his extraordinary endeavours. His recent efforts in conducting an English orchestra on tour (the most extensive, I think, ever given in England, covering some 25 towns, where *also* he lost a great deal of money in the cause of art) were another feather in his cap."

That same spring Frederick Delius was writing in much the same vein, though more concisely, to Ethel Smyth: "Beecham . . . is wonderfully gifted and destined to play perhaps the most important part in the development of modern music in England. My prophecy! Don't forget it!"

One last word about British concert music.

Fortuitously aided by patriotism during the first World War, Beecham's early crusade in this cause reached its climax at a Queen's Hall festival in May 1915. He and others conducted "the best and most characteristic music" written during the preceding decade by sixteen composers including, apart from those I have already named, C. V. Stanford, William Wallace, Elgar, Hamilton Harty, Frederick Austin and Percy Pitt. Again my sympathies go out to the critics who were obliged to sit through these refined chauvinistic revels.

To what extent did Beecham have his tongue in his cheek? After conducting one of the festival's more ill-balanced and unwieldy programmes he is said to have remarked, while putting on his overcoat in the artists' room, "Well, I think we have successfully paved the way this afternoon for another quarter of a century of German music!"

CHAPTER EIGHT

THE FIREWORKS ORCHESTRA

(1)

PEOPLE IN MUSICAL high places preened themselves on having neatly parcelled out music-making to their mutual convenience for a generation at least. Beecham threatened to upset their snug arrangements. "Who", they asked each other in their clubs, "is this extraordinary young man?" On one thing they quickly agreed. Whoever he might be, he must not be allowed to poach.

For the *Apollo* concert, Beecham's "fixer", Verdi Fawcett, booked Haydn Waud to lead the double basses. Waud happened to be principal double bass of the Queen's Hall Orchestra. It was, or seemed to be, a free enough world. There was no reason on the face of things why Waud should not do an odd stint for Beecham in and among his obligations to Wood. Waud attended the first two rehearsals. At the final rehearsal, on the morning of the concert, he did not appear. News went round that he had withdrawn under duress. The managers of the Queen's Hall Orchestra made it known that any of their members who played for Beecham would lose their Queen's Hall jobs. Young Eugene Cruft, newly recruited from the variety pit, took Waud's place.

The London Symphony Orchestra became equally frigid. A promising young L.S.O. bassoonist was offered a contract by Beecham for a given number of concerts annually at a guinea and a half per concert. The bassoonist mentioned Beecham's offer to the directors of the L.S.O. "Fair enough", said these gentlemen. "We don't want to stand in your way. But if you join Beecham you'll have to resign from the L.S.O." The bassoonist resigned at once and went down to His Majesty's Theatre, where Beecham had an office, and signed the contract over whisky and soda. Beecham loved to sign contracts. He brought to such ceremonies a grand and swelling geniality.

Not only did other big London orchestras strive to hobble their players. The freelances of the New Symphony Orchestra, too, became uppish. Their first indiscretion had been to form themselves into a limited liability company. Beecham and limited liability companies were concepts that did not mix. A second shortcoming was that they persisted in that deputy system against which Wood and Newman had revolted in 1904. As Beecham experienced it, the deputy system led to weighting the orchestra's average age. If a man could not play at a given concert, he tended to nominate a deputy a bit older than himself rather than a bit younger. Even when riddled with deputies, the New Symphony Orchestra were a seasoned band. They read unfamiliar music to admiration. But they lacked two qualities on which Beecham was intent: resilience and fire. These qualities, both the marks of youth, were to be Beecham's twin gifts to English orchestral playing. He delivered an ultimatum to the N.S.O. in December 1908. He made it clear that, if the N.S.O. did not conform to his wishes in the matter of deputies and kindred matters, he would wash his hands of them.

"In that case", retorted orchestral spokesmen, "you'll find yourself without an orchestra."

"Nothing of the kind. I shall form an orchestra of my own."

"You can't do it. Where are the players?"

"Wait and see."

Whereupon he strutted out. The New Symphony Orchestra sat disconsolate for some weeks in their Shaftesbury Avenue rehearsal room, offering practice sessions to this conductor and that. At length they were taken over by young Landon Ronald, who was back from his successful Continental tour. They survived hardily enough. In 1920 they became the Royal Albert Hall Orchestra.

Meantime, Verdi Fawcett worked arduously. Fawcett, who had played in the N.S.O. second violins under Beecham, was one of a big musical family from the North whose males, as occasionally happened in Victorian times, were named after great composers. His kinsmen included a Handel, a Mendelssohn and a Weber, who played respectively the trombone, clarinet and oboe. Verdi Fawcett was well-thatched, beaming and rubicund. Comradely by nature, he knew everybody in the orchestral world and, what is more, knew precisely where any player of note could be laid hands on at any hour of any given day. For new young talents he had a sure ear. This gift was as much the making of the fabulous Beecham Symphony Orchestra as Beecham's own arts. Like Napoleon and certain other eminences, he had a way of snatching sleep in odd quarter-hours. In bandrooms between rehearsal and concert or on railway stations between trains, he would lie on benches and sleep like an infant through all commotions.

In recruiting the new orchestra Fawcett fished adroitly in theatre bandrooms, local symphony societies, the palm courts of hotels and the commonrooms of music colleges. The Beecham Symphony Orchestra —the first fully professional orchestra that was truly Beecham's own in the sense, almost, that a painter's finished canvas is his—was enrolled from all over the country. The players were young men. Their typical age was twenty-five. And, a point of which Beecham was proud, they were all Britons.

(2)

The Beecham Symphony Orchestra made its first public appearance at the Queen's Hall on February 22nd, 1909, with a markedly Beecham-esque programme: Berlioz's *Carnaval Romain* Overture,* *In the Fen Country* (R. Vaughan Williams), *Sea Drift* (conducted from memory, of course) and Berlioz's *Te Deum*. One often heard Beecham conduct the *Te Deum* in later decades. What did he make of the immense *Judex crederis* at the age of thirty? From *The Musical Times* we gather that the brass instruments were too much in evidence. Beecham has never at any time been accused of flaccidity, but later generations, it seems, have little notion of the rhythmic and tonal excesses he was wont to commit in his early sessions. If a concert's opening item was of a lively nature he would lift his stick and exclaim in a high pitched voice that could be heard in the front seats as well as throughout the orchestra, "Now then, gentlemen, do your *worst!*" This, noted Eric Coates, sitting among the violas, always brought out the "devil" in the players. The performances that followed were uniformly tempestuous. Audiences, even small ones, positively exploded. Saturday nights at the Proms were tea parties by comparison. The things that counted on such occasions were the blowtorch of Beecham's ego and the enormous smartness of his players. Essentially, music had little to do with the case.

The Beecham Symphony Orchestra did not reach the height of its form at one leap. There were rejectings and reshufflings. In the midst of these Beecham and his father, as will be narrated, became friends again. With comforting funds at his disposal, he became the ruthless perfectionist. The shining and the elect of other orchestras were sure

---

* With this same Overture Beecham opened the sensational inaugural concert of his London Philharmonic Orchestra on October 7th, 1932.

The principals and sub-principals at the opening concert in February 1909 were: violins, Philip Cathie and A. E. Sammons; Second Violins, Horace Fellowes and F. Shelley Pearce; Violas, Lionel Tertis and Eric Coates; 'Cellos, Arthur Trew and Walter O'Donnell; Double-basses, Noël Morel and Eugene Cruft; Flutes, G. Ackroyd; Piccolo, M. Donnawell; Oboes, Walter Hinchcliff; Clarinets, Emile Gilmer; Bassoons, Edward Dubrucq; Horns, B. J. Muskett; Trumpets, D. Flynn; Trombones, A. E. Matt; Tuba, J. Collins; Timpani, H. Lockett; Harps, Jeanne Chevreau.

of a welcome—to his back desks. Of the eleven violas behind Lionel
Tertis, leader of this section, eight were former or future principal
players. Choice of the first violin (who is also the orchestral "leader")
hung fire for some months.

Accounts were circulating of a new lounge band at the Waldorf
Hotel whose first violin was a remarkable young talent. He made his
own fiddles, always had a fiddle in his hands and constantly "fingered"
it with his left hand when conversing or consulting railway time-tables.
He was credited with a marvellously noble yet seductive tone. Beecham
looked in at the Waldorf one night. There he was, the young fiddler
who was being so much talked about: mane of fair hair brushed back
from a pale profile with cavernous eyes. The young man played the
finale of the Mendelssohn violin concerto at breakneck speed. Beecham
scribbled on a card, "Splendid, but the tempo is so and so." Back came
the answer, "Many thanks. I'll play it for you again a little later on."
The two were afterwards introduced. The fiddler's name was Albert
Sammons. After a spell as sub-principal, he became leader of the
B.S.O. and stayed with the orchestra for five years. "The best
all-round concert-master I have met anywhere", Beecham wrote of
him.

Sammons was the first leader to enjoy Beecham's characteristic
asides and confidences from the rostrum in mid-performance. Some of
these were revealing. During a Diaghilev ballet season, Beecham was
called to the rostrum unexpectedly because all other available conductors
were sick. The programme included among other pieces the Polovtsian
Dances from *Prince Igor*. Did he wish for a rehearsal with the dancers?
inquired the management. Not at all, drawled Beecham benevolently.
On the night, at a point usually taken two-in-a-bar, he suddenly let
fly to the general consternation with a one-in-the-bar beat which had
the dancers winded after a couple of pages. "Too fest, too fest!"
they gasped every time they came within earshot of the rostrum.
Beecham's face remained ironic and inflexible. At the end he leaned
down to Sammons and said, "We made the b——s hop, what?"*

At its first concert the new orchestra had ninety-nine players. Of
these ninety-five were "regulars". On the opening night triangle and
tambourine were entrusted to a personality met in the preceding
chapter, H. Balfour Gardiner, composer. One has met men of sound
judgment who worked day by day, season after season, first with
the Beecham Symphony Orchestra, then, after a generation, with its

* I have heard the same incident ascribed to another occasion by another orchestral
leader. It seems to have happened more than once.

successor, the London Philharmonic. On certain points they are in substantial agreement. The L.P.O. brass and woodwind had greater power and mellowness; but when it came to string tone and attack, say these witnesses, the B.S.O.'s fire was unmatched. And unmatched it remained.

(3)

Mischief and irresponsibility were important spices in young Beecham's career. After half a century it is hard to decide whether his escapades were considered or impulsive. My own leaning is to the former hypothesis. Never was he more gaily preposterous than in 1909.

As soon as the Beecham Symphony Orchestra was firmly on its feet he took it out on tour. Within a matter of weeks it had become known to amused porters and frowning railway officials as the Fireworks Orchestra. Every time the B.S.O. train pulled into or out of a station showers of lighted crackers were thrown on to platform and permanent way by Beecham's high spirited protégés. The station which suffered most from these salvos was Crewe Junction, where the orchestra regularly changed on its way to various northern concert halls. There were grave complaints by other passengers. Officials were reproving in a fatherly way. A joke was a joke, they conceded, but this one had gone far enough. The joke went on just the same. At Birmingham a giant cracker of the sort known as a cannon was hidden by the first 'cello with time fuse lighted under a luggage trolley immediately before the train steamed out. The explosion was so alarming that the stationmaster had the train stopped and backed into the station. Going aboard, he threatened to have every member of the orchestra, Beecham included, arrested.

When firecrackers were wanting, electric bulbs served. At the old Adelphi Hotel, Liverpool, late one night, Beecham and two or three of his principals climbed the spiral stair from the lounge and collected high power bulbs from each landing.

They bundled their spoils into a bedsheet and, arrived at the top floor, shot them over the balustrade. The detonation on the ground floor was judged first-rate. Instantly the Adelphi was turned upside down. Hall porters chased after culprits up stairs and down corridors. When taxed with the prank Beecham said in tired tones, "Put it on the bill!" and went to bed. Next morning he rose impenitent at an early hour and caused hysterical commotion by changing shoes outside

bedroom doors a few hours before the departure of the American boat.*
Juvenile high spirits needed, and found, a butt.

Signor Tamini cuts a grotesque and pathetic figure in the Beecham
story. He professed to be an Italian tenor. Actually he was a forced-up
German baritone. He had made a first appearance at the second of the
B.S.O.'s Queen's Hall concerts in March 1909 and turned popular
tenor arias into a sequence of heavy and tuneless shouts. He offended
further by adding unsolicited encores to an already overlong programme. Yet Beecham not only tolerated this in London; he also
took Tamini on tour. "It is difficult", noted William Stritt in his diary,
"to imagine how a musician of Beecham's calibre came to engage such
a singer; and I always supposed that Tamini contributed his share to
the programme gratis." There is no limit, of course, to the illusions of a
baritone who thinks he is a tenor. Tamini regarded himself as a hit.
And his bosom swelled with gratitude.

One night after a concert, seeing Beecham in a crowded hotel lobby,
he rushed over and embraced him. Beecham turned scarlet and sput-
tered. For what seems to have been the only time in his life words
failed him. As the tour progressed so did the length of Tamini's top
notes. His favourite top note was the last note but one in *Lohengrin's
Farewell*. To this he clung increasingly. The noise was execrable. It
made the orchestral players hold their breath. One night Beecham took
out his watch a beat before Tamini's top G and, turning deliberately
towards the singer, affected to time him. After this practical jokes began.
Like most practical jokes, they were oafish. On one occasion Tamini
turned up at a railway station with a notice pinned to his back, I AM
A TENOR. On another occasion he was fetched down from his hotel
room in his dressing gown to take a long distance call from his wife.
The call was a hoax. While the poor man was trying to cope with the
situation in broken English, a conspiring group raced up to his room
and threw his dress suit out of the window. The night was rainy. The
suit was found on the pavement next morning in a sorry state. Before
the B.S.O. train steamed out that day there were detectives on the
station platform. They questioned many suspects. Nobody knew a
thing. By this time the culprits must have been harried by guilt.

A triviality, perhaps. But trivialities can leave a lasting mark. Two
generations later the incident was narrated to me by an old B.S.O.
player who took no part in it. There was shame in his face.

* According to another account the incident occurred at the Grand Hotel, Sheffield;
but the Adelphi, Liverpool, is mentioned by two eyewitnesses, Eric Coates (memoirs)
and Lionel Tertis (private information) and therefore carries the day.

(4)

Aesthetic sentimentalists will argue that so long as Beecham and his orchestra behaved like angels in the concert hall it mattered little how they comported themselves elsewhere. But they were not always angels in the concert hall. Their treatment of Elgar's Symphony in A flat is one of the scandals of musical history.

This noble symphony had had its first performance the previous December in Manchester under Richter: not the most auspicious of launchings from Beecham's point of view. It had a take-up without precedent in English symphonic music. Within a year there were nearly a hundred performances in this country alone. Foreign audiences, too, were responsive.

Obviously the A flat was not a symphony to be ignored. In the autumn of 1909 Beecham put it into his tour programme and conducted it nightly. From the start he boggled at the symphony's length: fifty minutes normally. At first he made carefully considered cuts,

> but, as time went on, these became more and more drastic (wrote Eric Coates) until, one night just before the performance, he announced that there were to be cuts of the most ruthless nature, from here-to-there in each movement, and he ended up defiantly with the words, "I don't know how it sounds, and I don't care!"

Far from caring, he plumed himself on his brutal surgery. On reaching Bournemouth he met Dan Godfrey (afterwards Sir Dan), the local conductor, ex-bandmaster and scion of bandmasters. To Godfrey he detailed the Elgar cuts "with great glee". Whether Godfrey demurred at the time is not clear. In his memoirs fifteen years later he exclaimed over the "enormity" of Beecham's offence but blew so cold and patronisingly on Beecham's conducting ability that it seemed to matter little in his eyes whether Beecham offended or not. Young Havergal Brian's fury was more purposeful. Brian was then twenty-three. He lived in the Potteries, composed vast symphonies and wrote criticism for *The Musical Times*. He was friendly with Elgar and fervent about his music. In the Victoria Hall, Hanley, he assisted at one of Beecham's routine maulings of the A flat. He expressed his disgust in a note to his Editor. The Editor of *The Musical Times* wrote back saying that he had had similar reports from other parts of the country, and would Brian state his opinion in the form of a letter to the Editor? Brian complied. He wrote:

"To the dismay of those who knew [the Symphony], Mr. Beecham ... chose to give his version of it in preference to the composer's. The first movement was cut down one half: part of the "exposition" and the whole of the "development" were cut out, and some minutes were sacrificed in the succeeding movements. Those who know the Symphony will be astonished to hear that the actual time occupied in its performance was only thirty-eight minutes!* It was an insult to the composer and also to those responsible for the concert. This is surely not the use to which so exceedingly fine an orchestra should be put, to say nothing of the genius with which nature has endowed Mr. Thomas Beecham."

In another column the Editor, too, was deprecatory. "The mutilation of Elgar's Symphony", he wrote, "calls for severe censure. . . . We understand that the sanction of the composer was not obtained for such a drastic treatment of the work as that accorded by Mr. Thomas Beecham. How is English music to be held in respect if it is to be so badly treated by a native conductor?"

Connoisseurs in the human comedy will be amused by the sequel to Brian's letter. Beecham did not turn a hair. He was as cordial to Brian after it as before. Elgar, on the other hand, became noticeably distant to his champion. Brian's biographer hints that maimed performances of his works pleased him better than no performances at all, and that the crusade on behalf of the A flat by his young worshipper irked instead of pleasing him.

For Beecham Elgar had a high regard which does not seem to have been altogether reciprocated. Nor was it wholly shared by Alice Elgar, the composer's wife, who, meeting Beecham at one of Lady Cunard's parties, was ruffled because he insisted on being called "Thomas". She found him, according to her diary, "very Phantasmagoria", whatever that meant, and said he didn't appeal to them *at all*.

In later years Beecham sharply reacted to any suggestion that he underestimated Elgar's music. Running through the London correspondence of the *Manchester Guardian* one morning in 1936, his eye came upon a light-hearted suggestion, apropos a concert the previous night, that the Elgar Violin Concerto "is plainly not one of Sir Thomas's major enthusiasms." He composed a crushing eight-point manifesto in self-defence. This appeared in print the following day. The effect of it is as follows. He had known and admired the Concerto

---

* According to Coates, the cuts at their most extensive reduced playing time to thirty-five minutes from an average of fifty. Thus fifteen minutes were sacrificed. As Coates observed, fifteen minutes is a lot of music.

for nearly thirty years, had discussed its interpretation several times with the composer, the last occasion being eighteen months before his death, when they went exhaustively together over his minutest wishes and indications; had given special study to the records of the Concerto which Elgar made with Mr. Menuhin; had laboriously rehearsed the piece with the London Philharmonic Orchestra, preparing and polishing every detail to the last degree in accordance with Elgar's ideas; and could say without fear of contradiction that "never in the history of this piece has it received a more accurate, a more faithful and a more pointed performance."

This reads most convincingly; but Beecham's evident anxiety to put himself in the right is out of proportion to the occasion and almost suggests a guilty conscience. Not long before he died, Elgar, old and ill, wrote commending Beecham's attention to his Symphonic Study *Falstaff*. The score might, he submitted, have been expressly written for Beecham, whom he would love to hear conduct and record it. The letter left Beecham unmoved. "My dear boy", he said to a young assistant who demurred, "Elgar's music is like the façade of Euston Station."

One is driven to conclude that he underrated Elgar as compensation for overrating Delius. Such trimmings of critical balance often occur in music. An earlier generation had found it impossible to like Brahms without automatically hating Wagner, or the other way round.

In their provincial wanderings the B.S.O. entered the Elgar country (Worcester-Gloucester-Hereford). Here it was found prudent to do repair work. The A flat, it was announced, was to be played without cuts. These had, unhappily, become second nature to the players. Their first efforts to play the Symphony *intacta* suggested a parcel of incompetent sight readers.

(5)

On this and other early tours of the B.S.O. odd things were always happening. At Exeter, where the orchestra played in a variety hall, Debussy's *L'après-midi d'un faune* was ruined in its first diaphanous bars by the barking of a sea lion which had been left backstage in a tank from the previous night's show. After the sea lion had been pacified, they started the Debussy again. The sea lion then disported itself so exuberantly that water slopped over from the tank and trickled down the stage under the players' feet into the stalls.*

* Extraordinarily enough, the same mammal seems to have inhabited the same tank when Henry Wood visited Exeter. At rehearsal Wood noticed an appalling smell of fish. "Oh", said the manager, "that's the sea lion." "What sea lion? Where?" "The one in the tank under the stage." "I never knew sea lions smelt like that." "Oh, *he* doesn't smell. It's the fish we feed him on."

But the mishaps which raised the biggest laughs were caused by fatigue. After a chain of one-night stands and sleepless nights in trains the players hardly knew what they were about until Beecham regalvanised them. At Southampton two percussion players, one nicknamed Mr. Jolly, the other Mr. Merry, fell off their perch at the back of the platform and took the bass drum with them. When they and the drum reappeared a great cheer went up. At Hanley the first clarinet went to sleep and dropped his intrument during a silent bar; it rolled down a ramp with its keys clicking all the way. At the end of the tour a young conductor arrived brightly at the Royal Opera House at 10 a.m. one day to rehearse Beecham's orchestra for a police orphanage charity concert. After half an hour a few stragglers turned up in the orchestra pit. Somnolent and unshaven, they were understood to say they had just got off the train from a concert in the remote provinces the night before. The young conductor, one Percy Pitt, withdrew on tiptoe and left them to their slumbers.

CHAPTER NINE

MAUD CHRISTIAN FOSTER

(1)

IN THE EARLY years Beecham had a devoted court of women helpers who either came to his aid outright or buttonholed, telephoned and mildly intrigued in his behalf among the fashionable, the titled, the well meaning and the moneyed. Four of these women, as well as his wife, were from America: Mary Dodge, a spinster millionairess; Katherine Ruth Heyman, a striving concert pianist known to her friends as Brangaene; Lady Cunard, whose name was to be coupled with Beecham's on many a resounding musical prospectus well into the 'thirties; and a charmingly snub nosed blonde, Maud Christian Foster, who was marked out for a brief and uncomfortable celebrity.

Maud Foster wore the boas, umbrageous hats and shapely tailoring of the day with distinction. She was married, not happily, to George Sherwood Foster, who had upturned moustaches and a ploughshare chin. Foster organised arts balls, turned biggish houses into flats, lived on the rents and painted portraits. Maud Foster, too, painted. Her talents were multiple, indeed. She was credited by her friends with an excellent singing voice. Coming to Europe with her widowed mother who, like herself, was of independent though limited means, she saw much of musical life in Paris, Dresden, Bayreuth and Berlin. She gushed about England in her letters. It was "a dear old place" and "ever ripping". Beecham later swore that she was not merely enthusiastic about music but also an authority on it. She gave it to be understood that she had been booked to sing at Covent Garden and His Majesty's Theatre as well as for the Philharmonic Society, three institutions which Beecham's presence was soon to enliven. Unhappily she had been obliged, owing to maltreatment by her husband and consequent ill health, to renounce these projects. So, at any rate, she alleged.

Beecham met Mrs. Foster at his father-in-law's house in March 1909. Having painted—or at least begun—a portrait of Princess Marie Dolgorowki, Mrs. Foster was now at work on one of Charles Stuart Welles. Most of Welles's sittings were at her studio in Redcliffe Square, Kensington. Beecham and Utica accompanied him there at least once and stayed on for a musical party. The circle in which

Maud Christian Foster moved was of the kind then known as Bohemian. Painters, theatre people, musicians and dilettantes, none of them raffish, most of them fashionably tailored, chattered, smiled a lot and darlinged each other in an aura of cigar smoke, flowers and champagne cup. Much was seen in this milieu of a whiskered Russian playwright, Prince Vladimir Bariatinsky, whom Mrs. Foster familiarly called "Vladdy". The Prince's wife acted in her husband's plays as Lydia Yavorskaya. Saluted by her publicity agent as the Russian Duse or the Sarah Bernhardt of the Snows, she was described by the same source as of an ancient and noble French family. In September the Princess Bariatinsky was to be among guests at a house party at the Beechams' home which had unhappy consequences. But as yet no shadows had fallen.

Beecham was full of the new orchestra which he and Verdi Fawcett were getting together. At Redcliffe Square he talked endlessly and brilliantly of his projects.

Maud Foster listened devotedly, then put pleading questions. Could she not help in some way? Surely her musical contacts on the Continent and back home might be of use to him? Already Beecham dreamed of touring America with his orchestra. She knew many people in the States who could further this project if only he would authorise her to approach them. Another person she knew was Vincent d'Indy. (As composers went d'Indy inclined to truculence. One winter morning a little more than a year earlier, he had fought a harmless duel with his librettist in the Parc au Princes.) Beecham planned to produce d'Indy's tone poem, *Jour d'été à la montagne* at his opening concert with the B.S.O. Would he like her to run over to Paris and arrange a meeting with d'Indy before the rehearsals? Finally, there was a matter which had been mentioned to her by Emily Beecham: the estrangement of Beecham and his father. If, as a humble intermediary, she could bring father and son together it would give her untold joy.

(2)

Such to begin with seems to have been the relationship between Beecham and Maud Foster. In the free and easy green room spirit which prevailed at Redcliffe Square, she took to calling him first Tommy, then Tom. To familiars she spoke of him as The Boy. Beecham gave her a signed authority to attend his rehearsals and apparently encouraged her collaborative efforts. She seems to have found Beecham's ways disconcerting. Soon after their first meeting he had occasion to write her a soothing letter:

"Dear Mrs. Foster,—It is evident that my fascinating, offhand manner, which is the despair of all my friends, has been perturbing your simple soul. Pray have no such fear. I am really only too delighted to find someone who is intelligent enough to be interested in my doings. I am most grateful for your energy and kindness in relation to d'Indy and meeting with him.

Anything you care to do will be immensely appreciated by me. There are really few people who care twopence for the sort of thing I do . . . I rest sincerely yours,—Thomas Beecham."

Other notes of the period to Mrs. Foster make it clear that they had discussed his early operatic projects. Beecham advised that these had better be kept in abeyance until his concert schemes had fully matured. He was averse, in the meantime, to allowing people's minds to "wander off on the vague subject of opera." His tone was exceedingly cordial. "I am delighted to hear of your activities on my behalf", he wrote. ". . . I am most tremendously delighted."

A glimpse of Mrs. Foster's crusading endeavours is afforded by a letter she wrote to Welles's solicitor, Sir Henry Paget-Cooke, in the early summer of 1909. Paget-Cooke had invited Mrs. Foster to an "at home". Replying to the invitation, she said:

"Instead of bringing some lady friend to your 'At Home' I mean, if I can, to bring Tom Beecham. Did you hear *The Wreckers* [see pp. 82–86.]? That is a stupendous triumph for the boy. . . . He was presented with enormous laurel wreaths, and is really a wonderful fellow and so fine, sweet and good with it all. I suppose you know he has been accepted to conduct the Philharmonic Concerts. No greater tribute could be paid one.

"He certainly is the greatest musical personage of today, and will place England musically ahead of other nations, given time and courage. He is so courageous a soul. I say courage, because the boy has lost all interest in life. He has not felt any for years and years, and I think that perhaps I am the only person who knows this and to whom he talks. He longs for his father, not the money, Sir Henry, for he says, quite broken-heartedly, 'What can that buy back? My father does not care for me. That is what I wanted all these years, and there was not an hour in the past eight or ten years that I would not have gone straight to him, had I not been tied hand and foot.' He admires his father tremendously, and is nearly crazed for fear of losing his father.

"I ask him why, in God's name, he does not tell all this to his

father, and he only answers: 'He does not believe.' It is too perfectly terrible. I think it is the greatest tragedy I know of. It grieves
me to death, who am an outsider and can do nothing to help. His
orchestra is doing splendid work in a national cause. . . . Both he
and his wife go without continually, and he has to borrow a coat
to conduct the concert in. It is Mr. Beecham's dream that His
Majesty will befriend the movement. That will save it."

This picture of Beecham as pathetically dependent on his father emo-
tionally and psychologically hardly squares with what we know
of him otherwise. Nor is it entirely in harmony with Beecham's own
estimate of his father. *A Mingled Chime*, after depicting Joseph Beecham
as bashful, pusillanimous and prosaic, says, "Our relationship [was] a
strange one; outwardly there was an apparent formality, but inwardly
an actual sympathy, almost an affinity between us. He was, I think, a
little inclined to be afraid of me; and I, for some reason I could never
explain to myself, generally felt rather sorry for him."

By the time of Mrs. Foster's letter to Paget-Cooke the great reconciliation was under way, though not, it seems, through her doing.
Before dealing with this, however, and with the sequel to Mrs. Foster's
friendship, I must deal for chronology's sake with his first opera
season.

(3)

For five years Ethel Smyth, wearing mannish tweeds and an assertively cocked felt hat, had been striding about Europe, cigar in mouth,
trying to sell her opera *The Wreckers* to timorous or stubborn impre-
sarios. There had been a production at Leipzig with a butchered third
act. When the management refused to "restore" the cuts, she raided
the orchestra pit early one morning, collected her material from the
players' desks and made off with it to Prague, where they treated her
score more circumspectly. At the Queen's Hall in June 1908, Nikisch
conducted two of the three acts in concert version. She hoped that
Nikisch's patronage would unlock doors at Covent Garden. In this
she was naïve. Written originally in French by her philosopher friend
and belated lover, Henry Bennet Brewster, the libretto of *The Wreckers*,
which was later done into painfully stilted English, dealt with adultery
unto death in an 18th-century Cornish fishing village where the
profession of wrecking was enjoined from the pulpit as a basic Christian duty to oneself and the community alike. Brethren who, in
moments of weakness, lighted warning beacons at danger points

along the coast usually repented in public when found out and were put to death by drowning in a sealed cave.

Miss Smyth's sturdy but (as it sounds to some of us today) slightly drab music, with its modish whole-tone touches, was admired by many; among others by Bruno Walter, then Gustav Mahler's assistant at Vienna. But the sound was one thing, the sense quite another. A libretto which no doubt delighted Delius's cynical soul—it might, indeed, have been devised with Delius specifically in mind—could not be expected to win over the Edwardian directors of the Royal Opera. "Frankly", they wrote to Miss Smyth, "there is no hope of our being able to produce *The Wreckers*. To announce a new work by a new composer is to secure an absolutely empty house. . . . I feel sure you will understand we are not justified in embarking on expeditions into *terra incognita* at the expense of our shareholders."

It was at this point that the American millionairess, Mary Dodge, put in a providential oar. Miss Dodge, who had recently settled in England and lived at Warwick House, St. James's, was described by Ethel Smyth as ". . . one of the noblest characters I have ever met and one of the very few people who . . . come relatively unscathed out of the ordeal of possessing great riches." If Covent Garden wouldn't back *The Wreckers*, said Miss Dodge, well then, she would. "You are always telling me", she remarked to Miss Smyth, "what a wonderful conductor Thomas Beecham is. Couldn't your wonderful Mr. Beecham be roped into the scheme? And do you think £1,000 would cover the production?"

Mr. Beecham, when the idea was put to him, was delighted. He forgot to be casual. Indeed, he beamed. Here, he said, was the chance he had been waiting for. At last he could introduce himself to the West End as an operatic conductor. Yes, he would gladly conduct *The Wreckers*, which he regarded as a piece of "real musical merit and vitality". He would, in fact, conduct it for nothing. His Majesty's Theatre was hired by Miss Dodge for six afternoon performances. Beecham's own orchestra—already talked of by some as the finest orchestra in Europe—was to occupy the pit. The scenery was makeshift, a vest pocket version of grand opera, and the chorus, though willing, betrayed its origins: church choirs and musical comedy, mainly. But the principals—headed by Miss De Vere Sapio as Thirza (soprano lead) and John Coates as Mark (tenor lead)—were singers of merit, even of distinction. They had been picked by Miss Smyth herself.

The preparations were a nomadic whirlwind. Although the chorus had a margin of special training as compared with the other forces, the essential rehearsals under Beecham were crammed into ten days and nights and were divided between His Majesty's, the Queen's Hall and a number of private houses. In the midst of the flurry Beecham kept darting away to Hanley for choral rehearsals of Delius's *Mass of Life*. To make an ideal job of *The Wreckers*, as of any new production, he should ideally have worked at it on and off for two months. Looking back, he admitted this. At the time, however, nomadic whirlwinds were to his taste.

(4)

Beneath a veneer of bland confidence he was very much the greenhorn in the opera house. With her own experience, a considerable one, of Continental theatres, Miss Smyth found his airy impracticality about rehearsals and such matters galling. He was rarely less than an hour late for rehearsals, a peculiarity for which he quickly became notorious among orchestral players. To the composer's metronome marks he paid little attention, imposing speeds of his own upon her music as the impulse or preference seized him. Rehearsals developed into a battle of wills. Miss Smyth made it clear that when it came to the handling of her music she had no intention of being complaisant, like Delius. Not for her the shrugging abdication, the attitude of "I leave it to you, my dear fellow." At the last rehearsal she sat crosslegged on the stage, beating one tempo while Beecham in the pit beat another. Naturally, it was Beecham who won. But Miss Smyth's opposition was splendidly overt.

What are the rights and wrongs of such a situation? There are rigorists who say that the composer's thought and intention must always be decisive and final, and that if these have not, by any chance, been made clear in his score the music cannot be worth performing anyhow. An alternative view places greater stress on the demands and rights of the paying public. A conductor of vast experience often sees potential effects in a new score to which the composer is oblivious. By judicious changes of tempo, "louds" and "softs" and even of instrumentation, he is able to bring out these effects and make a correspondingly greater impression on the listener. Whether Beecham was capable of working such wonders in 1909 is doubtful. His operatic experience, far from being vast, was a beginner's merely. Intuition and electrifying leadership were there. But no mellowness and little technical shrewdness.

Singers he tended to flail. At a *Wreckers* rehearsal, as he was approaching the final drowning catastrophe, John Coates, as Mark, the doomed hero, suddenly stopped singing. "What's the matter, Mr. Coates?" inquired Beecham, halting the orchestra. "I was just wondering", replied Coates—"is this the place where I'm supposed to be drowned by the waves or by the orchestra?" Of another rehearsal Miss Smyth has left accounts which are disquieting. The long Act II duet between Thirza and Mark was scheduled for its sole run-through with orchestra. On the appointed morning London was shrouded in impenetrable fog. No sign of either singer. Beecham cheerfully began rehearsing the orchestra. After half an hour a telegram was handed to him. He read it out with a joyful gleam—" 'Held up at Bedford by fog. Can't get any further—Coates.' Go on, gentlemen, please!" Five minutes later a second telegram came—" 'No trains from Willesden. Not a taxi to be had—De Vere Sapio.' Glorious! All right! Go on, gentlemen!"

To Miss Smyth it was obvious that from the start he had gloated over the chance of holding an orchestral rehearsal without the singers. "Any conductor I ever had dealings with", she added, "would have manifested signs of distress and at once have tried to fix another rehearsal of Act II. Not so Beecham!" In another autobiographical passage she commented, "I . . . noticed that not only was it an effort for him to allow for the limitations of the human voice, to give singers time to enunciate and drive home their words, but that quâ musical instrument he really disliked the genus singer, which seemed an unfortunate trait in an opera conductor. In short, my impression was that his real passion was concert rather than opera conducting."

Miss Smyth not only confided these opinions to her diary; she expressed them to Beecham in person. One can imagine the raised brows, the eyes dilating in offended surprise. How, inquired Beecham, could a person who had loved opera from the age of five be suspected of disliking the genus singer? The answer is that consistency has rarely been a virtue of the more highly energised personalities. Beecham himself in a note to Miss Smyth twenty years after The Wreckers production spoke witheringly of "bungling asses who have no apprehension of the inner forces (often conflicting and paradoxical) that sometimes, after much secret struggling, occasionally unite to offer an outward entity in harmony of result." In the case of The Wreckers in 1909 and also, as will be shown, in the case of Beecham's coming Elektra productions, inner conflict and paradox remained unresolved, with the result that the singers went to the wall and the orchestra enjoyed a deafening right of way.

With The Wreckers Beecham scored his first operatic deficit. The production cost Miss Dodge £558 8s. 6d., which was judged to be

"not discouraging". Despite her wrangles with Beecham—which did
not impair their lifelong friendship—Miss Smyth was faintly pleased
with it all; after a pint of champagne with dinner she went so far as to
assert that *The Wreckers* was quite a good opera, a judgment which
posterity has not so far underwritten. She retouched her score lovingly
and often. One afternoon Henry Wood arrived at His Majesty's with
Lady Speyer and Lady Maud Warrender fifteen minutes before a
performance was due to begin.

"Where's Ethel Smyth?" asked Wood. "I don't see her anywhere.
It's a wonder she hasn't been down in the orchestral pit by now to make
a few alterations in the band parts."

Lady Speyer objected that she would never do that as late as 2.20
p.m., ten minutes before the start.

"I don't care", persisted Wood. "Just you wait. She'll be down there
with her little revision slip to pin on before the first bar."

"No!"

"I'll bet you a pound she does."

"Right!"

At 2.25 p.m. the composer duly crept into the pit as Wood had
forecast and fixed alterations over certain brass parts.

"What did I tell you?" exulted Wood. "I don't suppose for a
moment she has warned Beecham, either. He'll wonder what on earth's
happening when he comes to the rewritten bit."

During the week receipts began to rise. Miss Smyth argued that
the management might see their way to extend the scheduled run
(July 5-10). Beerbohm Tree's man of affairs, a Mr. Dana, would not
hear of it. Stubbing her cigar in an ashtray, Miss Smyth voiced her
opinion of Mr. Dana, an uncomplimentary one, in vivid terms. Witnesses were present. The upshot was a slander action. This was settled
out of court. The angelic Miss Dodge paid a hundred pounds to Mr.
Dana, bringing her total bill to £658 8s. 6d.

(5)

A more important outcome of *The Wreckers* was that it cemented
Beecham's reconciliation with his father. That something of the kind
was imminent was clear from a letter which Beecham had written to
Maud Foster as early as May 25th. In this he said:

"You will be interested to know that I am to have an interview with
him [Joseph] tomorrow, the first for almost ten years, but whatever
happens, please understand that I have no intention of allowing you

to relax your efforts on my behalf. On the contrary, it is most necessary to prove to the 'old boy' that my musical ventures are sound finance as well as 'high falutin' ' art. This you can do better than anyone I know, so please don't slack off, there's a dear. Come to some of my rehearsals and let us lunch together afterwards and talk."

Apparently Joseph's anger at Thomas's siding with Josephine over the alimony suit had long subsided. His son's achievements with the New Symphony Orchestra and now with the Beecham Symphony Orchestra flattered the old man's fatherly pride and were congenial to both his tastes and his patronal itch. For some years he had been in the habit of sneaking into his son's concerts incognito. He would sit in a back row and slip out before the end in the hope that nobody would identify and report his presence. The way Tom lorded it on the concert platform impressed him deeply. But had Tom the necessary stability? Was he *serious* about music, truly committed to it as a career? Like certain more schooled observers, Joseph wondered whether his son might not be a little too brilliant. The boy's darting and omniscient versatility might, he reflected, turn out to be his undoing.

While yet in his twenties, Thomas combined fifteen talents at least. According to Ethel Smyth's enumeration, he was potentially, at any rate, a poet, a savant, a lawyer, a traveller, an actor, a politician, an Extension lecturer, an adventurer, a financier and six musicians rolled into one. A similar thought struck Philip Heseltine a year or two later. "Beecham", wrote Heseltine, "is a man of extraordinary versatility; . . . there are few subjects to which he has not devoted a great deal of thought and about which he does not hold an individual and finely reasoned opinion. . . . But"—and here Heseltine struck a bodeful note which Joseph, too, must have experienced—"music cannot satisfactorily be one interest among many. Music demands the whole man, with all his faculties focused upon it." In these matters everything depends upon the individual. In some cases—and Beecham is a conspicuous example —musical accomplishment is enriched rather than sapped by widely ranging intellectual appetites.

That was not how Joseph saw it, however. Beecham's friends decided that something irresistible must be done to win Joseph over. The initiative was taken not by Maud Foster but by the resourceful Ethel Smyth who, not only in her own cause but in that of friends, was wont to enlist a social network that took in Mayfair duchesses, the ex-Empress Eugénie and the Palace itself. The thing to do, decreed

Miss Smyth, was to get King Edward to a performance of *The Wreckers* and have Beecham presented to him. Anything that smacked of royal approval would bring Joseph hastening to His Majesty's with open arms and cheque book.

The plot worked. A highly placed friend of Miss Smyth had it brought to the King's notice that a young man of genius was conducting at His Majesty's Theatre who, if rightly encouraged, would work marvels for English music. In musical matters Edward was no fool. He listened with a connoisseur's ear to Melba's *fioriture* at the Opera, saw the point of Elgar as early as anybody, and was moved to tears by the incomparable Gilibert as the Father in *Louise*. On the Tuesday of *The Wreckers* run it was announced in the Court and Social columns that the King, accompanied by Queen Alexandra and the Princess Victoria, would attend a special performance on the following Thursday night. The news was murmured in advance to Joseph by some intermediary. He was drawn to the theatre as by a lodestone. At a rehearsal before the royal visit Beecham told Ethel Smyth not to look now, but the left-hand man of two men trying to hide behind pillars at the back of the stalls was *his father*!

The gala performance went off without mishap. There was much *élan*—too much, perhaps. The composer's brother, Bob Smyth, who later became a general, said that the chorus overacted terribly; they waved their arms about so long and so much that they reminded him of a class of soldiers learning semaphore signalling. The King sent for Beecham at the end and said civil things. Behind the expression of fatigued indifference which he subsequently assumed, Beecham was jubilant. And with reason. He and Joseph had another meeting, this time in a lawyer's office.

Joseph smiled wryly and, in extenuation of nearly a decade's aloofness, said, "You know, you annoyed me." Beecham retorted, "And *you* annoyed *me*!" Recrimination stopped at that. Thereafter they were firm friends, each knowing much of the other's mind.

Joseph promptly undertook to back a projected opera season at Covent Garden. When his son suggested that two Covent Garden seasons were better than one, he assented: two seasons it should be— one in the spring, the other in the late autumn of 1910. Joseph was under no illusion on financial counts. He knew as well as any Covent Garden actuary that when box office takings are set against costs, grand opera invariably makes a loss; and that unless rich men put their hands in their pockets accordingly impresarios have no choice but to put up their shutters. On the day of the gala performance at His

Majesty's he looked in at Christie's saleroom and there met his crony Thomas J. Barrett, the soap "king". In his diffident, almost furtive way, he told Barrett he was prepared to spend £200,000 on opera promotion. Turning his attention to the bidding, he bought a George Vincent landscape for 1060 guineas—320 guineas more, it was respectfully noted, than the price at which it had last changed hands, twenty years before.

It was Joseph Beecham's prerogative and glory for a pitifully few golden years to keep the shutters out of Thomas Beecham's operatic career. Between 1910 and 1920 about £300,000 of pill money was poured by Joseph and his son into the box office breach. It is not to be forgotten that, for all his prosaic ways, Joseph had a genuine liking for music. He used to say edifyingly, "My family and myself need a certain amount of money to live on. When that is deducted from my income there's a lot of money left. How could I spend the balance more profitably than by giving the same pleasure to thousands that I myself derive from this glorious music?"

(6)

For Thomas Beecham the way was now wide and clear. His mind danced exhilarating jigs. On the night of his meeting with Joseph he sat down at the Langham Hotel and wrote triumphantly to Maud Foster. Triumph was not, it will be noticed, the only characteristic of his letter:

"I have been with my father all day, from 10.30 a.m. till the present moment. We have lunched and dined together and played duets on organ and piano, and we are once again as brothers. I think you will admit your boy is developing diplomatic capacities. . . . All my heart is with you tonight and always. My love, my darling.—T."

This note had a curious history. Mrs. Nash, the housekeeper at Redcliffe Square found it in a white stocking which Mrs. Foster had put out to wash. Mrs. Nash judged rightly that it would be of interest to Mrs. Foster's husband. Accordingly she handed it over to him. Some days later Foster steamed open and, before resealing, photographed another note to his wife in Beecham's handwriting which said in part, "Please tell me where we meet tomorrow. . . . I have had a terrific day, but I will try to steal an hour to see YOU. No old Russian princess, I can assure you—only YOU, YOU, YOU!"

George Sherwood Foster went off in dudgeon to his lawyers. The two Beecham notes and certain others that came his way were made much of in the Divorce Division later. Divorce preliminaries are often leisurely affairs. The parties in the Foster-Beecham suit were not "called" until October 1911. During the intervening two years, thanks to his ebullient ways, his musical prowess and his father's money, Beecham became one of the three or four most fashionable celebrities of his generation. When the summons came for him to enter the witness box as co-respondent he was spared nothing of spotlight, stenography or newsprint.

Before attending to the proceedings before Mr. Justice Bargrave Deane, let us watch the prodigious blooming of a personality whose contemporary peers were Winston Churchill, David Lloyd George, F. E. Smith and George Bernard Shaw.

CHAPTER TEN

ENTHRONED

(1)

CREDITORS BREATHED freely at last. The ambience of bailiffs and hair's-breadth expedient of which Ethel Smyth writes was dispelled overnight. On one occasion during the lean years, according to a story that reached Dame Ethel's ears, he was laid up and dead lame through having hurriedly left a friend's house by a second storey window, presumably down the fall-pipe. He could now confidently leave by the ground floor. One morning a lawyer went the rounds with a fistful of banknotes. He settled among other neglected bills that of Mewburn Levien for the organ pipe. On chill mornings Beecham henceforth appeared at rehearsals in a fur coat. Often he did not turn up until noon. Prosperity made him increasingly casual.

"We would report for a three-hour rehearsal", a B.S.O. veteran remembers, "at ten in the morning. No sign of Beecham. We would hang around the stage door smoking and yarning. He would arrive at 11.30 or thereabouts, peel off his coat and plunge into the first 'tune'. Not a word of apology. Once he started Beecham never wanted to stop. He wanted to go on and on. In those days the Union had little power. We had to cope with the problem ourselves. Around one o'clock we'd become restive. 'What about a breather?' somebody would shout. Beecham always took the hint. He'd put down his stick and order a second rehearsal—paid for—at two o'clock. 'Standing money', as we called it, came to four or five pounds a week with Beecham, as compared with two pounds five in the average theatre pit. Extra time through afternoon rehearsals bumped up our weekly earnings to about eight pounds. Before the Kaiser's War a pound went a long way. I must say that Beecham paid well. In fact he overpaid. He could have saved a lot of money by turning up on time. Also by giving backword to players who wouldn't be needed. Many's the time an unwanted cor anglais or side drum has got his half-guinea for turning up and merely signing the rehearsal book." Dan Godfrey, who rarely spoke of Beecham save acidulously, agreed that Beecham had plenty of rehearsals and that these were well paid for. "But", he characteristically added, "the result did not always justify the means."

Fifty years after, white-haired players with service in a dozen leading

orchestras look back on the Beecham Symphony Orchestra with
something like awe. All are agreed that for verve and warmth there
has never been anything to touch the B.S.O. strings. Rehearsals were
held in odd places, among them the basement of a waiters' club in
Soho. On blazing summer days Beecham would appear, an hour late as
usual, in a splendid white suit. The proceedings were a sequence of
rages, cowed silence, quips and roaring laughter. The prevailing feeling
was one of elation. Everybody knew that music was being made with a
dash and a finesse never before known in London and rarely in any
part of the world.

This feeling communicated itself to audiences, even to unschooled
listeners. Done with a precision of detail and at a speed which none dared
essay but Beecham and his young bloods and blades, such opening
pieces as the *Bartered Bride* and *Carnaval Romain* overtures made people
bounce in their seats and stare at each other while applauding with
shining eyes; they remained Beecham's slaves not merely for the rest
of the concert but also for the rest of their lives.

He is known to have bored his players occasionally by over-rehears-
ing Delius. At the threat of yet another session devoted to *Paris*,
the leaders begged to be let off, arguing that, unless rested for a while,
the piece would go stale on them. There were no gramophone records
of *Paris* then. The probability is that Beecham rehearsed *Paris* mainly
for the pleasure of hearing it. The "chess board" orchestral model
which he once conducted on railway journeys was by this time discarded. On railway platforms and in hotel lounges he now conducted
orchestras of the mind, lunging, scowling and stamping alarmingly at
imaginary trombones, 'cellos and whatnot. Again in these exercises his
favourite composer was Delius. Hotel managers and station masters
were at a loss what to make of this spry, prosperous looking little
man with beard, fur coat and perpetually indignant eyes. At a glance
they concluded he was a foreigner. Then they heard his commanding
drawl, that of the English governing classes. Who would have suspected that his grandfather, recently dead, had hawked pills in a
Lancashire market place?

(2)

His tantrums had an awesomely spontaneous look and sound. I
suspect that actually they were unleashed in accordance with plan and
policy. In the autumn of 1910 a story (true, I believe) went round that
he had stopped a big scale choral-orchestral rehearsal with a stentorian
shout and threatened to pack everybody off home like ill-behaved

children. Musicians who panicked at his adroitly produced rages were
undone. It would be a mistake to mourn them. Musicians prone to
panic were of little professional use to Beecham. What he wanted—
and what he usually got—was natural aplomb plus the stamina of a
tiger. As well as furies there were kindnesses, some of them entirely
unforeseen. For one of his early Covent Garden seasons he took
on a sixteen-year-old harpist of Italian blood. The boy was of brilliant
promise. But in the immense orchestra pit, straining his eyes and ears
for cues and trying to cope with tricky parts whose context was unknown to him, he felt bewildered and acquitted himself badly. Most
other conductors would have dismissed the boy without compunction
after half an hour. Not so Beecham. Taking on a substitute player,
he invited the boy to continue at rehearsals merely as a listener, for
the good of his musical education—and paid him full salary for a
fortnight.

With correspondents he was less considerate. He rarely replied to
letters. He rarely read them, indeed. Havergal Brian sent him three
orchestral scores in the hope of getting performances. One of these, the
Second English Suite, was never returned. At the time of the receiving
order against Beecham some years later, search was made for the
missing MS. It could not be found. The executors mentioned to
Brian, however, that they had discovered an accumulation of two
thousand letters addressed to Beecham. All were unopened. It is
doubtful whether this news was any consolation to the symphonist.

The hours and the nervous energy which Beecham devoted at this
period to the study and memorising of new music would alone excuse
his lack of business method. Probably they explain also the unpredict-
ableness of his comings and goings, his failure to keep appointments,
the inability of his most trusted lieutenants to lay their hands on him
at any time and place except those to which he was committed by
advertised concert and opera schedules. As time went on even his
conducting commitments were no guarantee that he would turn up.
At the Drury Lane, Aldwych and Shaftesbury theatres during the first
World War and also on many concert platforms he often substituted
assistant conductors (he had quite a constellation of these), without a
word of regret or explanation, at the last moment. Conversely, when
the whim seized him he would occasionally displace some assistant and
himself appear unheralded on the rostrum, to the surprised delight of
the audience and the dismay of any singer who feared his preparation
of a given part wasn't up to Beecham standards.

His elusiveness was an especial trial to society hostesses. They invited in vain. "I can never get hold of him", they lamented one to another. "Where *does* he go to?" He had three addresses and was rarely to be found at any of them. "No one", said Ethel Smyth, "ever saw him go in or out of any of the three front doors. Even if you could have sat on all three front doorsteps all day long, never, never could you have speech with him."

The more houses Beecham owned or leased, the more he tended to use hotels. This was a foible of his for decades. Only his valet was capable of forecasting Beecham's whereabouts. But Beecham's valet was no more accessible than his master.

(3)

In the glow of the pill fortune Beecham's faculties flourished exceedingly. He had made himself an opulent kingdom. On its throne he sat like a lawgiver and from time to time indulged in sonorous generalities. After waiting for two hours an Edwardian writer on music, Reginald R. Buckley, conversed with him at one of his three homes, a place with a lot of rich brown paint, Turkey rugs on polished floors, old oak furniture, one or two "quaintly oriental" pieces, a flower stand of branching gold and glass and a conspicuous copy of Nietzsche's *Beyond Good and Evil*. From upstairs came pleasant nursery noises.

Clearing his throat, Beecham said to Buckley: "There is no such thing as nationality in music. Music is universal. We have northern and southern music if you like. Grieg was northern, not Norwegian. The melody of Strauss is not German at all. It is Italian."

Of two main propositions in these five sentences each is arguable. The trouble is that they contradict each other, a fact that seems to have eluded both Beecham and his interviewer. If music is of its nature universal, it cannot be confined in a regional strait-jacket any more than in a nationalist one.

In his new-found self-sufficiency, Beecham busily resented the excessive praise which foreign musicians, then as now, enjoyed in Britain automatically and almost as a matter of right. Britain a musical nation? Not a bit of it!

"Surely (he was quoted as saying soon after the *Wreckers* production), if we were a musical nation we should have fine English artists, opera houses, provincial orchestras and a hundred and one musical things which other countries can boast of. . . . The truth is, we have allowed ourselves to be flattered up into such a state of self-conceit that, apart from being the musical laughing stock of the world, we are looked upon as mugs who can continually be taken in by foreign artists, because we are content to listen to rotten foreign pianists, rotten foreign singers, rotten foreign orchestras, to be content with rotten foreign conductors and so on."

It was the first time in history that the British musical public had been dismissed as a parcel of mugs by one who sought their suffrages and guineas. They did not resent it in the least. On the contrary, they arched their backs with pleasure. It was a pleasure they were often to experience.

CHAPTER ELEVEN

AN ORGY OF OPERA

(I)

In 1910 LONDON heard—or had the opportunity of hearing—more opera than ever before in its history. Between mid-February and New Year's Eve, Thomas Beecham, financed by Joseph, either conducted or was responsible as impresario for 190 performances at Covent Garden and His Majesty's Theatre. While he was away at His Majesty's the Grand Opera Syndicate put on a concurrent season of their own at Covent Garden. This brought the year's grand total to 273 performances, far more than London could stomach.

For his two Covent Garden seasons, the first early, the second late in the year, Beecham had eight assistant or guest conductors. Among them were the expensive Richard Strauss, who for two *Elektras* advanced his conducting fee from 100 guineas to £200 a night, Bruno Walter, whose memoirs are singularly reticent about the musical aspects of his visit, and young Percy Pitt, whose association with Beecham culminated twenty years later in his appointment as "musical controller" of Beecham's ghostly and short-lived Imperial League of Opera.

The demands on Beecham's nervous and physical energies, notwithstanding his eight rostrum "reliefs", were prodigious. The "musical Maecenas", as the papers were beginning to call him, was equal to everything. Some of his 1910 endurance feats smack of bravado. One afternoon he rehearsed at Covent Garden from two till five; put in an hour's telephoning and letter-writing; motored to the Queen's Hall to conduct two pieces (the *Carnaval Romain* overture and the Prelude to Holbrooke's *Dylan*) in the London Symphony Orchestra's opening programme of the season; then left for the Royal Opera with five minutes in hand to conduct *Elektra*, regarded at that time as enough of itself to sap the strongest constitution for a week. The day of his first appearance at the Philharmonic Society's rostrum (December 7th) was even more prodigal. He spent the morning taking the Philharmonic Orchestra through new or unfamiliar music (Delius, d'Indy, W. H. Bell). After lunch he directed the dress rehearsal of another Straussian head-breaker, as it was then considered to be, *Salome*, before an open-mouthed gathering of musical pundits who, in the main couldn't make head or tail of it and wondered what the world was coming to. In the evening he returned to the Queen's Hall for the Philharmonic concert proper in roaring form. He lunged at the trombonists like a duellist. This was the period of Lloyd George's diatribes against the "idle rich". Beecham, observed a newspaper commentator, might be rich; nobody could call him idle.

By an alchemy of which Beecham alone had the secret, grand opera suddenly became "news" in the most breathless sense of the word. Looking back over yellowed newspaper files, one notes with astonishment that, both as to advance publicity and notices after the event, the big Beecham nights at Covent Garden were given more space by the popular halfpenny sheets than by their staider Fleet Street sisters. the *Daily Mirror* and the *Daily Mail* garnished their notices of *Elektra* with music-type illustrations which must have sent many an earnest reader to his cottage piano without enlightening him in the least. Both *Elektra*, and its equally sensational twin *Salome*, got a flatteringly high readership rating in a vintage Fleet Street year that produced two General Elections, King Edward's death, the Crippen case, the Houndsditch murders, the Sidney Street siege and incredible feats every other day, some of them fatal, by men in string-bag flying machines and floundering dirigibles. It is doubtful whether Beecham employed any elaborate publicity machine. He did not go to the reporters. The reporters came flocking to him. When the publicity pandemonium was at its height, George Sherwood Foster lodged his petition (dated March 18th, 1910) for divorce against Maud Christian Foster. Beecham was cited as co-respondent. It was evident that, as his counsel put it later, an adverse outcome of the case would be of serious import for a man of such eminence in the artistic world. Beecham must have been perturbed. But there was no outward sign. His calms were as magnificent as his furies.

His operatic doings that year were, as has been said, in three phases. From February 19th to March 19th he ruled at Covent Garden (27 performances); from May 12th to July 30th at his Majesty's (81 performances); and from October 3rd to December 31st at Covent Garden again (82 performances). During these three phases, which together lasted twenty-eight weeks, he mounted thirty-four operas, a high proportion of them either new to London or almost unknown there. He played sometimes to packed, tumultuous houses, sometimes to wretchedly small ones, grossly miscalculated public taste from time to time or blandly ignored it in favour of his own, lost an undisclosed amount of Joseph's money (in terms of 1910 it must have been a substantial fortune) and ended the year in a state of verbose frustration.

Of the 190 performances he conducted or promoted, 109 were at Covent Garden. In a curious autobiographical passage, Beecham suggests that his choice of this theatre as the venue of his crucial 1910 seasons was suggested to him by "advisers". I doubt whether anybody in Europe was capable of telling Beecham anything about Covent Garden of which he—and musical people generally—were not already aware. His own ideas and practice were in some ways sharply at variance with those of the Garden's principal tenants, the Grand Opera Syndicate.

As the Syndicate viewed matters, what made Covent Garden prosper was first-rate voices, backed in some cases by first-rate stage personalities. The gallery and the amphitheatre public, no less than the box-holders, wanted above all to enjoy the tone and technique of the Melbas, Destinnovas, Tetrazzinis, Carusos, McCormacks, Martinellis, Scottis, Journets and the rest. As well as hearing these people, they wanted to assess them as humans and respond to their acting—if any. Emmy Destinnova on her first night as Madama Butterfly had everybody, merchant bankers included, in tears. When McCormack, as Don Ottavio, sang *Il mio tesoro* a transforming ray seemed to play upon the squalid earth. Coming unheralded to London, Tetrazzini sang Violetta to a heavily "papered" and, at the outset, tepid house. After *Ah, fors' è lui*, news of her brilliance sped all over the town. From then on every Tetrazzini night was jammed. Late-comers were turned away from the box office in droves.

At Covent Garden, then, the voice was supreme. The singers were demigods. In the eyes of the paying public nobody else counted except, possibly, the composer. Conductors were an essential though subordinate part of the outfit. You applauded politely when they climbed on to the rostrum—and dismissed them from your mind for the rest of the night. As to the orchestra, its basic function was accompaniment, except in the case of Wagner, who attracted an odd, slightly vegetarian public of his own.

(2)

Such, roughly, was the scale of aesthetic values which prevailed at Covent Garden before Beecham's advent in 1910. It was a scale at which he snapped his fingers. This is clear from a vital sentence in the prospectus which signalled his first Covent Garden season. "In modern opera", he wrote "the Conductor and the Orchestra *play as important a part as the singers.*" (My italics.) His initial repertory of eight operas included five by living composers and therefore to be classed, in the sense of the prospectus, as "modern". These were *Elektra, A Village Romeo and Juliet, Hansel and Gretel* (Humperdinck), *The Wreckers* (Smyth) and *L'Enfant Prodigue* (Debussy). The remaining three works were *Tristan, Carmen* and Arthur Sullivan's *Ivanhoe.* Out of the five works named, Strauss's *Elektra* was the one to which Beecham applied most conspicuously—and exaggeratedly—his doctrine of equality between the conductor-orchestra plexus on the one hand and the singers on the other. It is a doctrine which makes nonsense as much of *Elektra*, or any other "modern" opera, as it would of *Aïda* or *Don Giovanni* or *Tosca* or *Fidelio.* Exactly as in the case of these earlier works, the structure, impact and purpose of *Elektra* are determined first and last by the moods and moves of the people on the stage and what comes out of their mouths. Because he denied this in principle and (most deafeningly) in practice, Beecham's performances of *Elektra*, although lavishly praised at the time, seem to have been unbridled and bad.

When Beecham first took it up, *Elektra* was little more than a year old. Its blood-boltered tale of palace murders, fortified by Strauss's often daring and subtle harmonic procedures, had put audiences as far apart as Dresden and New York into a state of bemused consternation. Most professional musicians were bewildered and inwardly frightened by a score which, for all its innovations, was a good deal more traditional and luscious than they suspected. When told by young Eugene Goossens (now Sir Eugene), a pupil of his, that he had been to one of Beecham's *Elektra* performances, Charles Villiers Stanford denounced it as "pornographic rubbish" and said that if Goossens persisted in such tastes he would give him up as a lost soul. *Elektra* was, in short, one of the world sensations of the epoch. Everybody expected to be horrified by it; everybody fought for seats, accordingly.

That January there were notable *Elektra* performances in Vienna. Beecham went out in the middle of the month to hear some of these and, as was officially explained, to "renew acquaintance" with the work. Already he had every note of it "photographed" on his brain. Thirty-seven years later he told this writer that *Elektra* took him one week to memorise at the rate of three hours a day. When he came back from Vienna he had the score on his desk during rehearsals. Often he staggered his players by rehearsing with the score closed. The score wasn't there at all on the first night.

The rehearsals were extraordinary affairs, nagged by empty stomachs and frayed nerves. The lunch-break system completely broke down. The players would be in the pit by ten. Beecham would appear at 11.30 a.m. and run on without pause until three or four in the afternoon. According to Eric Coates, this routine brought the orchestra near to breakdown. In his own department (violas) there were three successive leaders during that first short Covent Garden season, two men successively throwing in the towel because the pace had become more than their nerves could stand. It soon became evident that Beecham's point about equality as between the orchestra and the singers was, if anything, a humorous understatement of his actual intentions. Coates says:

"It was a gruelling business: Beecham coolly continuing to rehearse from hour to hour, with the orchestra becoming more exhausted: Richard Strauss standing in the front row of the stalls . . . directing, suggesting, interrupting; the artists in a state of bewilderment, not knowing which was more important, the voice parts or the orchestral part: Beecham, just before the curtain rose on the first night of *Elektra*, shouting at the orchestra, 'The singers think they're going to be heard, and I'm going to make jolly well certain that they are not!' "

For the new tribe of newspaper photographers there were "photo calls". The popular papers carried "spreads" showing flimsy Maecenean masonry and Greek maids with plastery make-up and hair like disordered bird-nests, carrying wine jars or playing syrinxes. Beecham stared from montages with mesmeric eyes. There were pictures even of the gentleman in his orchestra who played the heckelphone, or baritone oboe, an instrument recklessly asserted by one writer to have been invented expressly for the *Elektra* music. Confusing *Elektra* with Strauss's *Don Quixote* Variations, another paper promised orchestral noises like the bleating of sheep.

Before the curtain went up Beecham had spent £20,000 on preliminaries for the season as a whole, including £1,500 on each *Elektra*. So far as *Elektra* was concerned, he seemed likely to get his money back. For the opening night of this production he could have filled the theatre three times over according to some gossips, six times according to others. Tickets exchanged hands at fancy prices on the Floral Street kerb. On the morning of the dress rehearsal muscular scrutineers were posted at every door to keep out gate-crashers. When Beecham appeared at the conductor's desk he was cordially applauded by his players, who had evidently forgiven him their six-hour re-hearsal sessions, and by an invited audience including Granville Bantock and Pierre Monteux, who sat in the stalls and followed the the music from the score.

The Elektra was Edyth Walker, a former American school-marm who as a seventeen-year-old did her first singing in a hometown church choir. A million or two readers had been informed how Miss Walker trained her voice (contralto) on £200 put up by an unnamed American millionaire and changed to soprano register at the suggestion of no less a maestro than Kaiser Wilhelm, who heard her sing in Berlin. During one of Elektra's more impassioned pages, Miss Walker lost two combs from her hair and put them back without missing a beat or a note, a feat much admired by the rehearsal audience.

Two nights later came the first public performance, which was also the opening of the season. A doctor stood by in the wings "in case the strain upon Miss Walker proved too great." His services were not needed. Miss Walker sang and gyrated gamely to the end. An audience who in the main didn't know what to make of the music and couldn't understand what few words they heard, cheered and clapped their hands sore. Covent Garden had known few if any ovations like it within living memory. In the royal box, King Edward, who usually left the theatre at the first curtain, sat and applauded until the sixth. Queen Alexandra, with Prince Henry of Prussia and his Princess, were still there at the twelfth curtain, when Beecham came up from the pit and joined the singers before the footlights. Somebody gave him an enormous, beribboned wreath.

He ought in fairness to have brought up his orchestra as well, especially the percussion section. His rehearsal threat to the singers had been no jocular one. George Bernard Shaw, once a music critic, after hearing two *Elektras* at Covent Garden that season, wrote to Willy Levin, the dedicatee of Strauss's opera: "Mr. Beecham conducts *Elektra* extraordinarily well; but he certainly does occasionally make the score sound like a concerto for six drums, whereas when Dr. Strauss conducts it I totally forget that there is any such thing as a drum in the world; I hear nothing but just what the score means." There are other testimonies to the same or stronger effect. Beecham had not yet done his worst, however. When he revived *Elektra*, with *Salome*, three years later, Alfred Kalisch wrote that he allowed the orchestra to "run riot" even more flagrantly than in 1910. Kalisch was a good judge. As translator of their texts, he knew every cranny of each score.

In Beecham's time at Covent Garden, *Elektra* declined fairly quickly in box office favour. King George V, whose musical tastes were less adventurous than those of his late father, was among its adverse critics. Inspired by the Beecham performances, Bandmaster Williams of the Grenadier Guards ran together an *Elektra* potpourri, drilled his band for months and played it one morning in the Buckingham Palace forecourt following a Changing of the Guard. Soon after the final chord, a liveried page came out of the Palace, with a personal message for Williams. "His Majesty", said the note, "does not know what the Band has just played, but it is *never* to be played again."

(3)

Salome did not come into Beecham's repertory until ten months later, near the end of his second Covent Garden season. It may be conveniently dealt with on the heels of *Elektra* because it is by the same composer, had roughly the same object, that of titillating and shocking middle-class susceptibilities, and caused the same kind of talk and stir.

The first performance, conducted by Beecham, was scheduled for December 8th. As early as the preceding January it had become known that the Lord Chamberlain declined to license the opera as it stood. His objection, after reading Wilde's text and the accompanying stage directions, was to the proposed appearance on the stage of a biblical character, namely, John the Baptist, to the display of the Baptist's head after he had been decapitated at Salome's instance and to any word or hint in the libretto that the princess was animated by any such thing as lust. The perturbed composer was reported to be ready to "meet" the Lord Chamberlain in any way possible—a hint that expurgation might be accepted as the way out. In the controversy that followed the Lord Chamberlain was twitted for inconsistency. Had he not recently, or relatively so, licensed Saint-Saëns' *Samson et Dalila*, Massenet's *Hérodiade* and Goldmark's *Die Königin von Saba*? Were not these just as much biblical subjects as *Salome*? If there was to be discrimination against one, why not against all?

As the first night approached, rumours spread that Beecham, despairing of any accommodation with the official censor, had resolved to dodge the ban by conducting *Salome* at a series of "private" Sunday performances. These and other speculations stoked up public excitement and had a stimulating effect along the Floral Street kerb. Places in the queue for the half-crown unreserved gallery sold at a guinea; guinea stalls sold for five guineas; tickets in pairs earned even higher premiums, often changing hands five times, with a profit for each holder. Again the picture papers came out with their spreads. Due allowance made for the crudity of contemporary half-tone reproduction, it is clear that, as staged at Covent Garden for Beecham in 1910, *Salome* was an uninspired spectacle.

But another thing emerged from advance publicity: that Aino Ackté, from Finland, Beecham's Salome, was uncommonly good to look upon. She was, in fact, svelte, to use a word which had just been discovered. Of her voice Beecham tells us dispiritingly that it was "adequate". Vocally she must have been greatly inferior to Ljublja Welitsch in her prime and certain other post-1945 Salomes. But a thing that distinguished Ackté's Salome from all Salomes before her was that she actually *danced* the Dance of the Seven Veils instead of sneaking off behind a palm tree and letting a stand-in from the ballet dance it for her.

"Did you know", she surprised a reporter, "that the Seven Veils [which Salome peels successively while seductively prancing before Herod] represent different passions and moods—anger, hatred, jealousy and so forth? It is a fine idea, is it not?" When the news was released that Worth of Paris had designed her costume and that she would wear two jewelled snakes, one twined around her upper arm, the other rising to strike from her hair, the kerb quotation for stalls went up another half guinea.

(4)

Meantime, much had been going on behind the social scenes. Beecham manœuvred an invitation for himself to a house party in Gloucestershire where the Prime Minister, Asquith, was to be among the guests. On the second afternoon the two men found themselves alone together. Asquith stared at Beecham as at something new in the realm of fauna. After making it clear that he knew nothing about music, he put a surprising request. Would Beecham play him the *Tannhäuser* March? There was a piano to hand. Beecham played the March twice and, the night before he left, a third time. Asquith listened with an air of marvel. Beecham broke in upon his musings with an account of the *Salome* dilemma. Asquith listened like one newly converted. He promised to take the matter up with the Lord Chamberlain personally.

Soon afterwards Beecham was invited to attend at the Lord Chamberlain's office, St. James's Palace. It was made clear to him that, unless Wilde's text was ruthlessly cleansed the ban would remain. After a deal of bargaining, Beecham accepted a list of points which were to be altered or deleted from the libretto. He handed the list to Alfred

Kalisch and, since *Salome* was to be sung in German, instructed him to revise the German libretto accordingly. Kalisch, a multi-lingual barrel of a man, lighted another cigar, his fourth that day, and cheerfully set to work. His revision was a root and branch job. He shifted the scene of action from Judea to some vague terrain in Greece. John the Baptist (Jokanaan in operatic German) became "Mattaniah the Prophet". No biblical phrase was allowed to pass his lips or any other on the stage. He sang mostly on social and political topics, and was listened to not by Jews and Nazarenes but by "Cappadocians" and "Learned Men". Salome's role was disinfected unflinchingly. In the original text she yearns to kiss Jokanaan dead or alive. In the Kalisch version kisses were out; she yearned merely to "follow" him and be true until death to his teaching. Her last line, "If you had looked upon me you would have loved me" became "If you had looked upon me you would have blessed me."

On one point agreement was deferred. The wrangle over what should be substituted for the Prophet's head, which is supposed to be handed up on a charger from his place of execution, continued until the dress rehearsal. A compromise had been suggested by the Lord Chamber-lain's staff. Instead of the Prophet's head, the bloody sword which had chopped it off should be given to Salome. Under official pressure Beecham accepted even this absurdity. At the dress rehearsal the bedaubed sword was duly proffered. Miss Ackté took it gingerly, then put it down, bringing the rehearsal to a halt. The "blood", she com-plained, was dirtying her hands and would almost certainly ruin her beautiful dress. Could not the Lord Chamberlain think of something else?

Myrmidons behind the scenes telephoned in agitation to St. James's Palace. Presently the stage manager rushed on excitedly, his shirt-sleeved arms aloft. Kneeling down near the footlights he shouted through the music to Beecham: "We can use a tray instead of a sword —so long as there's no head on it."

Clearly, the show was saved. But what happened at actual per-formances? At this point the fog of history overtakes us. Either different things were handed up from the dungeon on different nights or the witnesses contradict each other. Beecham himself writes of a large platter covered with a cloth and nothing underneath it. Accord-ing to other accounts the article was (*a*) a simple empty tray (*b*) a silver charger filled with the Prophet's lifeblood (*c*) a dish of what looked like pink blanc-mange and (*d*) a loaf of bread covered by a towel.

(5)

The first night outpaced even the *Elektra* première. The crush at the back of the amphitheatre and in other "standing places" was stifling. A frock-coated music student who was then seventeen remembers being so wedged in the crowd that he could not insinuate his hand into his tail pocket for sandwiches which he had hoped to eat as the music went on. He and his companions stood shoulder to shoulder in pinioned ranks. Silhouetted against desk lamps in the pit, Beecham flung his arms about imperially and roared like a teamster. Again the little man was giving the singers hell. The orchestra was supreme and deafening. Kalisch must have wondered why he had been at such pains to bowdlerise a libretto which was bound in large part to be smothered anyhow.

The only person who realised what happened to Kalisch's handi-work was, apparently Beecham himself. Under the stress of first-night excitement, according to *A Mingled Chime*, Miss Ackté forgot two or three lines of Kalisch's version at an early stage and started singing the banned text, which was presently taken up automatically by everybody else on the stage. And so it continued until the end. In a box almost overhanging the stage a party from the Lord Chamber-lain's office were listening with cupped ears. At the end there were sixteen curtain calls. Beecham joined the singers at the twelfth. He looked at the crowd with head back, lids lowered, a touch of insolence in his regard. Then as later, his ironical detachment from the crowd increased in the same ratio as their incense and clamour.

But behind his crumpled shirt-front there was a stirring of un-easiness. What would happen when the Lord Chamberlain learned that his ban and most of the bowdlerising had been ignored? Beecham had visions of Traitor's Gate and a block on Tower Hill, or so he playfully asserted later. After the last curtain he learned that the Lord Chamberlain's party were asking for him backstage. He steeled himself for an icy reproof. What he got was an effusive compliment.

Smiling from ear to ear, the Lord Chamberlain's spokesman said, "It has been wonderful. We are all delighted. I felt I could not leave the theatre without thanking you and your colleagues for the complete way in which you have gratified our wishes." Beecham never dis-covered whether these unmerited thanks were due to the imperfect diction of the singers, ignorance of German on the part of the Lord Chamberlain's party, or a diplomatic resolve to pretend that nothing untoward had happened.

A fourth possibility, which he overlooked, is that owing to the excesses of his orchestra the visitors may not have heard any words at all. Of one thing at any rate they were sure. Salome made love not to a severed head but to a salver. That made everybody happy at St. James's Palace.

Of Beecham's other Covent Garden productions that year, Delius's *Village Romeo and Juliet* was the one he prized most. The sad, small tale of Sali and Vrenchen and their ill-starred love made as little impression on critics and public as Delius's music. Philip Heseltine, as good a judge of Delius performances as anybody in Europe apart from Beecham himself, found the singing "passable"—which usually means poor the orchestral playing marvellous and the stagework marred by old stock scenery and stock gestures of the "operatrical" sort which made the work's fundamental purpose unintelligible. For the second scene of the middle act, where Sali and Vrenchen wander into a fairground, Beecham had hired an enormous merry-go-round from a travelling circus. This delighted him greatly. At a rehearsal he climbed on to one of the wooden horses and gave himself a ride. With some difficulty, noted Ethel Smyth from the stalls, the stage manager directed his attention to more pressing matters.

"That would never do in Germany," said Miss Smyth's companion, who happened to be a German singer.

In contrast to Heseltine, Miss Smyth proclaimed that *A Village Romeo* came off brilliantly. Her paean had a resentful undertone. The truth is she felt piqued about the treatment given to her *Wreckers* which, although it had two performances, one conducted by Beecham, the other by Walter, "went to the wall" in her judgment. "And this", she added bitterly, "was to have been the great model performance . . ., the previous affair at His Majesty's being merely six preliminary canters."

The second (autumn) season at Covent Garden opened with Ambroise Thomas's *Hamlet*, sung to a tiny, tepid house. Orchestral veterans recall this and other insuccesses—among them Eugen d'Albert's *Tiefland*—with a shudder. The rows of empty seats and factitious optimism behind the scenes contrasted eerily with the great Strauss nights. In some ways Beecham's eleven-weeks summer season of *opéra comique* (as he advertised it) at His Majesty's Theatre was equally luckless. The note here was to be discreetly "popular". People were not to be scared by Covent Garden prices or crush room pomp. Stalls were down to twelve-and-six. On the second day of the season the management put out a comradely notice: evening dress was not compulsory in any part of the house.

Beecham and his players and singers moved into the theatre for rehearsals in mid-April, a month before the advertised start. His cast lists were revolutionary. Never before had there been so defiant a breakaway from the Italo-German stranglehold on London's operatic stages. Of seventy principal singers forty were English or had Anglo-Saxon names. Some of these forty played an illustrious part in establishing what, after two generations, is beginning to be recognised as a native operatic tradition. As subsidised State theatres, Covent Garden and Sadler's Wells would not be where they are today had it not been for pioneer native talents and the unique framework and opportunity which Beecham gave them from Edwardian times onward.

But the Edwardian decade was running out. On the night of Thursday May 5th, 1910, Utica Beecham dreamed the King was dead. He breathed his last the following day at ten to midnight. Saturday morning's newspapers were blackbordered and crammed with obituary articles. All theatres were closed at a stroke as a mark of mourning. Beecham's opening night, *The Tales of Hoffmann*, was put off from Monday until Thursday. For the commercial insuccess of the season, Beecham puts some blame upon the gloom which overhung London and the nation that summer. A more germane factor seems to have been the limited or non-existent drawing power of half the operas in his twelve-piece repertory.* Of the other half only two could be relied on at any time to fill the theatre. These were *Hoffmann*, which Beecham transferred to Covent Garden in October and played fifty times before the end of the year; and *Fledermaus*, which depended for its popularity in part upon Walter Passmore, the celebrated D'Oyly Carte droll, inheritor of Grossmith's parts in the Savoy operas, as the Prison Governor. These two works and the two Strauss "sensations", *Elektra* and *Salome*, were the only unqualified successes of the year. Of the thirty-four operas which Beecham had produced in twenty-eight weeks thirty were outright failures or partial failures.

The average production standard was abysmal. Most of the operas were shovelled on to the stage. A disturbing survey of the 1910 season was printed three years later by Richard Capell, one of the most highly considered critics of his generation.

"We have said (wrote Capell) that there were blunders. . . . One

* *Tales of Hoffmann, Hansel and Gretel, Shamus O'Brien* (Stanford), *Mugette* (by Edmond de Missa, after Ouida's *Two Little Wooden Shoes*), *Werther* (Massenet), *Feuersnot* (R. Strauss), *Die Fledermaus* (Johann Strauss) four Mozart works, *Figaro, The Seraglio, Così fan Tutte* and *The Impresario*; and an English novelty, George Clutsam's *A Summer Night*.

season was actually inaugurated by a perfectly abominable French travesty of *Hamlet*, served up anyhow and Heaven knows why. The haste of omnivorousness was generally felt through those 1910 days. So many exciting things (the feeling seemed to be) remained to be done that time was not to be wasted on vain refinements of representation. The inequalities in execution were fantastic. Much was splendid, much was simply sketchy; one recalls a night of *Tristan* that seemed only to be kept going in pure desperation, and a *Fidelio* that was as bad as could be. . . . Most people seemed . . . disconcerted and vexed that Mr. Beecham should be out on a grandiose musical 'lark'; they wanted to know solidly just what they were going to be given, refused any supplement out of their own imaginations, and mostly stayed away, discouraged."

There could never be another operatic year like 1910. Even Joseph's patience and resources had limits. To attempt other seasons in the same circumstances and on the same scale would, as Beecham saw, bring disaster. On whom lay the blame? To this question Beecham returned different answers at different times. In his memoirs he took much of the blame upon himself. "In those early days", he confessed, "I lacked the experience to gauge the capacities or incapacities of my artists *and frequently mounted operas more for the purpose of hearing the music myself than for giving pleasure to the public*." The italicised sentence goes to the root of Beecham's aesthetic motivation. His duty to music, as he conceived it both then and later, coincided approximately with his personal tastes. On the morrow of the débâcle, however, his tendency was to round on the public because their tastes differed from his own.

"Are you satisfied", a reporter asked him, "with the results of your operatic labours?"

"I am profoundly *dis*satisfied." he replied.

"Why?"

"Because nobody ever came to see my productions. You cannot run a grand opera house for the benefit of a hundred persons."

"But has no progress at all been made?"

"I think the position is just the same as it was a year ago; or rather, it is worse, because now we have had the opportunity of a year's opera, and we can see what the position really is. A year ago the public cherished the fond delusion that it was only necessary for opera to be given on a large scale for everybody to take it up, especially opera in English. For years everyone has been grumbling and crying out at the lack of opportunity. Now they have had it for a year, and they have never come anywhere near the place."*

"But surely there have been some fairly good audiences?"

"There is no question of fairly good audiences or even small ones. There is no audience at all for opera. As for an audience for a new work, to put on a new opera is like raising the most deadly danger signal. People at once avoid the district for weeks as though it were infected by the plague. A new work absolutely sends a shudder through people."

"But what of the furore caused by your productions of *Elektra* and *Salome*?"

"Get an elephant to stand on one foot on top of the Nelson Column, and you will draw a much larger crowd than twenty-five *Salomes*. It is no credit for people merely to patronise these productions and stay away from everything else."

"Perhaps, however, you see some greater hope for the future?"

"I don't know anything about the future. The past year has shown indubitably that so far as 1910 is concerned no one in England has wanted to see grand opera. . . . There was then no public demand of any kind. On certain occasions I brought celebrated artists to this country to sing in celebrated operas, and frequently the house has not been one-seventh part filled. To give opera for the next five years in the same circumstances and with the same public results I should require to be a Rockefeller and a Carnegie rolled into one."

"But there are at least a few people who would like to know your plans for the future. Will there be another season under your guidance?

"Oh, very likely. But I cannot say anything about my plans. The future requires a great deal of consideration."

Consideration, among other factors, of a new operatic rival.

(7)

In the autumn of 1910 workmen began digging a vast hole in Kingsway, not more than a trumpet call from the Royal Opera. A boastful billboard fronted the excavation. It read:

ON THIS SITE
THE LONDON OPERA HOUSE IS TO BE ERECTED
BY OSCAR HAMMERSTEIN, BUILDER OF OPERA HOUSES

* The delusion that a massive public demand existed for opera was peculiar to Beecham. There is no evidence that in 1909-10 "everybody" or even any respectable mass of opinion was crying out for seasons of the kind Beecham put on at Covent Garden and His Majesty's Theatre.

Mr. Hammerstein figured eminently among the marvels of his age. Hamburg-born, he descended penniless upon New York in his early 'teens and gratified a passion for grand opera, composing bad music and building excellent theatres, on money earned by making cigars and making machines to make yet more cigars. In 1910 he was a tubby sixty-two-year-old with a pug profile and a hard, appraising eye. He wore a custom-built silk hat at all times and, smoking a cigar against theatre bye-laws, used to sit in his own wings listening to performances of his own ordering and funding. His new Manhattan Opera House proved so acutely competitive a menace to the immensely powerful New York Metropolitan Opera House that the directors of the latter had smoked him out of New York altogether with, so it was said, a cheque for a million and a quarter dollars. In consideration of this bribe, Hammerstein undertook to promote no more opera in New York and its precincts. Since it was not in the man's nature to abstain from opera promotion altogether, he brought his million and a quarter dollars, or the first sizeable instalment of it, to London.

The billboard on Kingsway was the sequel. Having bought a 99-year lease of the site at £4,000 a year, Hammerstein purposed to build and open in little over one year (the provisional opening date was November 1st, 1911) a model opera house with seats at two shillings to a guinea, every seat having a perfect viewline, and three opera companies embodying the cream of international talent, who would sustain glittering repertories in Italian, French and German.

When Hammerstein's prospectus came out, Beecham had commented: "I am delighted that Mr. Hammerstein is coming to London. I am pleased if only for the cause of British music. But what Mr. Hammerstein does is no concern of mine. A dozen impresarios may come to London to give opera. It is generally known, I think, that I do not produce opera for the love of money but rather to increase the love of opera among the British people."

Privately he was not delighted at all. Both he and the Grand Opera Syndicate were feeling wary, perhaps apprehensive. Clearly the town could not nourish three rival operatic enterprises. The time had come for a closing of the ranks at Covent Garden against Hammerstein's intrusion. Half-way through Beecham's second Covent Garden season the newspapers announced that he had accepted an invitation to become a member of the Syndicate's board of directors. Having burnt his father's fingers financially, Beecham deemed it prudent to withdraw from the field entirely until Hammerstein showed what he could, or could not, do.

Nineteen-hundred-and-eleven was to be a relatively fallow year for him. But only in a professional sense. Outside the professional domain trouble lay ahead. The case of Foster v. Foster and Beecham was called for hearing in the Probate, Divorce and Admiralty Division, Court 1, before Mr. Justice Bargrave Deane and a special jury at 10.30 on October 18th.

CHAPTER TWELVE

"WHO IS MR. ROCHE?"

(1)

THE HEARINGS OCCUPIED eight days but, with long week-end adjournments, sprawled over a fortnight. Newspaper readers thus had convenient intervals in which to digest what had gone before and speculate about what was to come.

The proceedings were copiously reported in the newspapers. One national daily averaged 5,000 words a day. There was no legal restriction upon divorce court reporting in 1911. The new picture papers were even more attentive than they had been to the *Salome* and *Elektra* premières. They showed Utica Beecham at home with her babies; Thomas Beecham sitting magisterially in a carved armchair with baton and handlebar moustaches; Thomas Beecham darting a worried sideglance at the photographer while on his way to court, a dapper figure in high starched collar and curly brimmed hat; Maud Christian Foster in a pencil drawing by some anonymous artist, looking cultured and pretty in a fragile way; Maud Christian Foster taking veal and red wine with her friends Katherine Ruth Heyman and Prince and Princess Bariatinsky in the Law Courts restaurant; the gaping crowds that gathered in the Strand to watch these and other celebrities come and go; and so on.

The case of the husband, George Sherwood Foster, was presented by Mr. Montague Shearman, K.C., and spoken to by the petitioner and four servants—two from the Foster household at Redcliffe Square, Kensington, and two from Highfields, the Beechams' cottage at Boreham Wood. The essence of it was as follows.

The Fosters married in 1906. Owing to money difficulties and a malign mother-in-law, the marriage began to break up two years later. In 1908 the husband took preliminary steps towards a judicial separation. All sorts of stories, he complained, were in circulation about his wife, "some scandalous, some absurd". Matters came to a head in the summer of 1909, when Mrs. Nash, the Fosters' housekeeper, discovered and handed to the petitioner the letter signed "T" and admittedly in Beecham's hand (see p. 89) which exulted over his reconciliation with his father and ended, "All my heart is with you tonight and always. My love, my darling." Foster engaged a private detective to keep watch on his wife and her circle. Among the detective's documentary hauls was a code alleged to have been drawn up by Mrs. Foster and Beecham so that they could telegraph each other with impunity. Counsel read out the code, with glossary. Below are extracts from it. The Mrs. Wightman referred to was the caretaker at Redcliffe Square; Miss Taylor a lodger alleged to have been introduced at Mrs. Foster's instigation to compromise her husband.

CODE WORD	EQUIVALENT
Beastie	Mrs. Foster
Philanthropist	Mr. Foster
Fire	Mr. Beecham
Brangaene	Miss Heyman
Trick	Mrs. Nash
Weakling	Mrs. Wightman
Ortrud	Miss Taylor
Sunshine	Must see you
How	What news?
Hoorah	Good
Darn	Bad
Mouth, Tooth Threat, Bone Tune, Thrive Zone, Truly Threepence	Numerals from 4 to 12

Evidence of "familiarities" completed the petitioner's case. Counsel admitted that there was no direct evidence of misconduct, "but the jury will be asked to infer that it took place." Half a dozen compromising incidents, as the petitioner considered them, were mulled over. It was alleged that Beecham constantly visited Mrs. Foster at Redcliffe Square. That they were often alone in the flat. That on one occasion they locked themselves in. That on another they spent some time in the drawing room with the lights out. That Mrs. Foster commonly spoke of Beecham as "Boy", "Kiddy" or "Tommy". ("What of that?" inquired Beecham under examination. "I am pretty well known as 'Tom' or 'Tommy' to a very large number of people.") That once she was seen to put her arms around his neck and kiss him.

Later that summer, Foster's counsel continued, Beecham lent his cottage at Boreham Wood to Prince and Princess Bariatinsky. Among the Bariatinskys' guests were Mrs. Foster and Miss Heyman; also, according to one witness, "Mr. Pound, a poet." (The reference was,

of course, to Ezra Pound. The author of *Cantos* was an early Beecham
adherent. "In a long talk I had with him", he testified after one of their
first meetings, "I caught him thinking. By GAWD, a musician *thinking*,
straight off his own bat!") Beecham, although engaged throughout the
relevant period on a provincial conducting tour, contrived on several
occasions, the petitioner alleged, to rejoin his friends at Highfields for
the odd evening. One night he was glimpsed at the piano in the drawing room. Mrs. Foster stood behind him, her arms about his neck.
("How", Beecham later inquired, "can anybody play the piano when
somebody's arms are round his neck?") On the same night Mrs.
Foster, whose dress had been undone by her maid, was glimpsed in
conversation with Beecham at the door of the nursery, where he was
to sleep. On a third ocasion Mrs. Foster came down to dinner, Beecham
and Miss Heyman also being present, in nothing but a night-dress and
dressing gown.

(2)

Such, in brief, was the petitioner's case as outlined by counsel. It
was not an impressive one. To argue that propinquity, opportunity,
epistolary endearments and the occasional hug and kiss logically
involved adultery smacked more of the knowing leer than of equity.
A verdict against Mrs. Foster and Beecham on these grounds would
have been palpably unjust. They both went into the box and firmly
denied they had indulged in familiarities of any kind. The general
imputation put to the jury on their behalf was that the petitioner's case
was founded largely on the tittle-tattle of muddle-headed servants.

As to the charge that he visited Mrs. Foster at Redcliffe Square every
other day, Beecham said the thing was impossible. During the relevant
period he was occupied day and night with rehearsals for the *Mass of
Life*, which entailed a week of shuttling between London and Hanley,
and for *The Wreckers*, which he had to prepare in ten days instead of
the two months usually allowed. "I mention all this", added the co-
respondent, "to show that I had little time for visiting and philander-
ing." Similarly with the stories about his looking in at Highfields when
the Bariatinskys and Mrs. Foster were staying there. He produced his
engagement diary to show that, on the dates given by the petitioner's
side as the occasions of misconduct at Highfields, nothing of the kind
could possibly have taken place, since he was either conducting in
Torquay, Bedford and Great Malvern or travelling to those places.

Mr. George Elliott, K.C., for Mrs. Foster, and Mr. Henry Fielding
Dickens, K.C. (sixth son of the novelist), who appeared for Beecham,

alike scorned the notion that there was anything incriminating about Beecham's letters to Mrs. Foster, whom they depicted to the jury as a warmhearted, generous woman, concerned only to assist Beecham in his musical career and promote a reconciliation between him and his father. In the phrase "My love, my darling", Mr. Dickens saw nothing more than an expression of Beecham's indebtedness to Mrs. Foster on musical and filial counts. For her part Mrs. Foster thought Beecham had perhaps gone a little far in these endearments. Her counsel asked whether she had remonstrated with Beecham on the point.

"When I saw him", she replied, "I told him I would be much obliged if he would never again address me with such rubbishy nonsense, and he never has done." In cross-examination she argued that the success of *The Wreckers* and King Edward's interest in that production, which occurred around the time the letter was written, must have turned Beecham's head. "He would call anybody anything then", she explained.

The same line was taken by Beecham himself.

"The production of *The Wreckers*", he said in reply to his counsel, ". . . had been very successful. So much so that a special performance was commanded by the late King Edward which took place the day before I wrote that letter. It was exceedingly successful, and the late King complimented me personally on the work I had done. That would be a source of satisfaction to any young man. At the same time, these very anxious negotiations with my father were brought to a climax and ended very happily that day. I must frankly confess I was in a state of mind in which I was not absolutely responsible for anything I spoke or did. A wiser person might have been capable of indiscretions under such circumstances."

(3)

The alleged love code—both the respondent and the co-respondent insisted it was nothing of the kind—came in for a good deal of attention. Its author seems to have been Miss Heyman, the pianist. Four years earlier Miss Heyman had given two joint recitals with a male singer at Bechstein Hall. At the first of these she played Bach, Daquin, Scarlatti and Chopin. Her range was from *Le cocou* to the "Revolutionary" Study. She first met Beecham in 1903. At his concert for the Philharmonic Society in 1910 she endeavoured, according to Society's historian, "to make herself heard in Mr. Vincent d'Indy's *Sinfonia Montagnarde* but was badly beaten in the attempt by the percussion!" In the witness box she described herself as American-born. She had visited most of the capitals of Europe and was "prominently con-nected" with music in England.

Mr. Shearman, K.C., cross-examining, observed that the code name she had chosen for herself was "Brangaene". Miss Heyman's reply had a petulant ring. "All my life", she said, "I have been 'Brangaene', but not *your* 'Brangaene'." There was laughter at this.

Shearman: "Is Brangaene in *Tristan and Isolde* a lady who keeps watch while two people have a love scene together?"*

Witness: "I have been reminded in court of that function of hers, of which I have never taken cognisance. Brangaene is a type of friend-ship."

Shearman: "When you chose 'Brangaene' you didn't know she was a go-between for the protection of two people carrying on an illicit amour?"

Witness: "I have never regarded Brangaene as a go-between."

Mrs. Foster threw further light on the code. In the witness box she spoke rapidly and in a low tone. Judge and counsel repeatedly com-plained they had difficulty in hearing her. It was her evidence about the code and its provenance which gave a new turn to a case which, from the petitioner's point of view, had not seemed to be prospering.

The witness explained that the code was devised on the basis of opposites. "Philanthropist was used to represent her husband because he was "the meanest man I ever knew". Similarly, "Brangaene" was chosen because it was so absolutely untrue. "Mr. Beecham, Miss Heyman and myself", explained the witness, "were like three boys together, and Miss Heyman chose the greatest love story in the world to make it ridiculous." In any case the code had never been used by Beecham and herself for any communication, amatory or otherwise. She had used the code solely for writing to "the man Roche". Miss Heyman had written out the code, but there was no mystery about the affair—although Roche had tried to make it so.

(4)

This was the first mention in court of a mysterious and, it would seem, unsavoury personage who, though not called to the witness box, dogged the respondent and co-respondent to the end of the proceed-ings with dire consequences.

---

* The reference is to an incident in Act II of Wagner's music drama. While Tristan and Isolde sing of their passion for each other, Brangaene keeps watch from a tower over-looking the moonlit garden against the return of Isolde's husband King Mark. In the preceding Act, Brangaene has well-meaningly tricked Tristan and Isolde into drinking a love potion.

"Who", inquired the judge, "is Mr. Roche?"

Mr. Roche turned out to be a private detective. First he was hired by George Sherwood Foster to spy on his wife and Beecham and gather evidence for the divorce lawyers. But, while still in Foster's pay, Roche went to Beecham and said in effect, "I would like to spy for you instead."

Realising that a divorce petition was in the wind, with himself as as co-respondent, Beecham agreed to the proposal. He engaged Roche and paid him £236 for his services, which lasted two months.

"Did you appreciate", Beecham was asked in cross-examination, "that Roche was collecting evidence for someone else and that if you retained him he obviously could not use what evidence he had collected against you"?

"No, I did not", replied Beecham. "I was ignorant of these matters then."

"Did it not occur to you that to pay a person watching you was bribing him not to disclose the evidence he had obtained?"

Was he not aware, persisted Mr. Shearman, K.C., that, if Roche collected evidence of misconduct on the husband's part, that would put an end to the husband's petition?

Beecham replied that he knew nothing about the law. "Mrs. Foster represented herself to be unhappy, and I wanted to render her some service."

"In what way?" interposed Mr. Justice Bargrave Deane. "To help her to file a petition in answer?"

Witness: "Yes."

The "petition in answer", alleged Shearman, was to have been furthered by a plot against the husband. In cross-examining Mrs. Foster, counsel produced a letter to Roche in her handwriting. Did she know anything, he asked, about a plan that a woman should go into the same house, No. 24 Redcliffe Square, where Mr. Foster was?

Mrs. Foster: "Roche told me a Miss Taylor had been put into the house."

Mr. Shearman: "Was she put into the house to entrap Mr. Foster into misconduct?"

Witness: "I remember Mr. Roche had a lot of wild schemes."

Shearman: "Was that one of them?"

Witness: "Very likely."

Shearman: "Was she to get evidence by herself of misconduct with Mr. Foster?"

Witness: "Now you bring it to mind, Mr. Roche had some such suggestion, but it was Mr. Roche's suggestion."

Shearman: "Did you approve of it? Yes or no?"

Witness: "I may have done so, but the woman's name I do not know."

Shearman read an extract from the letter to Roche in which Mrs. Foster herself advised that "the lady" should insinuate herself into 34 Redcliffe Square as a person looking for rooms, thus obviating suspicion on her husband's part. When the "lady" had entrapped Mr. Foster into misconduct, suggested Shearman, that would be the end of his case against the respondent. Was that Mr. Roche's plan? . . . Yes, agreed the witness, that was Mr. Roche's plan.

Shearman: "And you were writing in that letter warning him how carefully he must do it?"

Witness: "I do not know. If a rogue like Roche suggests that sort of thing and I fall in with it—it was his plan."

Shearman: "And did you fall in with it?"

Witness: "Evidently, from my letter."

Shearman: "Did the lady actually apply to become the tenant?"

Witness: "I could not tell you, because we discovered Mr. Roche was a great rascal, and we had nothing to do with him."

In re-examination Mrs. Foster modified her position somewhat. The idea that her husband should be entrapped into misconduct suddenly seemed quite new to her. She was aware, she told her counsel, that Mr. Roche was anxious to have someone put into the house to watch her husband; nothing more.

Beecham in re-examination made the same point. The idea was, he said, that Miss Taylor should watch the husband, not trap him. In any case the idea was an absurd one. When it was put to him he refused to countenance it.

Beecham's general attitude on Roche was airy and dismissive. But Roche was the pivot of the case. If his dubious transactions had not been brought in, Foster's petition might well have failed.

(5)

The jury retired.

Outside Court 1, Probate, Divorce and Admiralty Division life went on multifariously. Various things of a non-legal sort were happening within a half-mile radius which affected at least three persons who had been in the witness box.

At the Kingsway Theatre the stage staff made ready for the opening that same night of Prince Bariatinsky's newly-translated play *The Great Young Man*. Princess Bariatinsky was to play the leading role, that of Princess Helen Noboltsky, a "good-hearted woman of the world". The play was understood to be about matrimonial problems.

At the offices of the Beecham Opera Company a handout was issued which said that Joseph Beecham had just bought the Aldwych Theatre, and that the Company intended to redecorate it against reopening in December.

On the stage of his almost completed London Opera House, Oscar Hammerstein told reporters, against a din of upholstering and carpentering, that his first season would open irrevocably on November 13th. Before he was through with the project, said Hammerstein, he would have spent £300,000 on it. And he was not at all worried. Rolling his cigar to the opposite side of his mouth, he expressed confidence that London would support him. Certainly, London had not seen anything quite like Hammerstein's folly—for that is what it proved to be. The theatre had an artesian well of its own, as though built to endure siege. There were *two* royal entrances—one for the King and Queen, the second for the Queen Mother. From the roof sprouted a "Marconi apparatus", so that opera lovers could book their seats "even six hundred miles out at sea".

*　　*　　*　　*　　*

The jury were out for fifteen minutes. When they returned there was a short dialogue between Mr. Widdicombe, Clerk of the Court, and the Foreman:

Clerk: "Do you find that Maud Christian Foster committed adultery with Thomas Beecham?"

The Foreman: "Yes."

Clerk: "Do you find that Thomas Beecham committed adultery with Maud Christian Foster?"

The Foreman: "Yes."

Mr. Shearman, K.C.: "I ask for a decree nisi, with costs against the co-respondent."

His Lordship: "Yes."

Utica Beecham had been among the co-respondent's witnesses. She testified that she had always lived on very affectionate terms with her husband, knew he was meeting Mrs. Foster from time to time, and encouraged him in an association which she thought would be helpful to him professionally.

The day after the case ended, she was telephoned by a musical duchess, who advised her to start divorce proceedings on her own account. "Why not", urged the duchess, "get ten or twenty thousand pounds alimony?"

"I do not believe in divorce," replied Utica.

CHAPTER THIRTEEN

BERLIN, PARIS, BIRMINGHAM

(1)

LATE IN NOVEMBER 1912 English newspaper correspondents in Berlin received a serial telegram from some Beecham publicity man inviting them to a forthcoming concert there by the Beecham Symphony Orchestra. The terms of the telegram were sketchy. When and where was the concert to be held? On these points no clue was given.

Telephone inquiries turned up a surprising piece of news. Unknown to the English colony, Beecham's orchestra were already in Berlin, having been engaged for a five weeks season (November 15th to December 20th) with Diaghilev's Ballets Russes, that new marvel and intoxicant of the Western world, at the Kroll Opera House. By an oversight which was presently rectified, the orchestra had not been identified on Diaghilev's bills or programmes. Before returning to London, said a belated advertisement, they were to give not one but two concerts at the Königlische Hochschule für Musik on Saturday December 16th (actually a Monday) and on Monday December 21st (actually a Saturday).

Beecham and his players were no strangers to the Diaghilev world. They had played for the Ballets Russes during their revelatory seasons at Covent Garden during the preceding summer and that of 1911 and were the only European orchestra who, at the time of the Kroll visit, had a working knowledge of Diaghilev's repertory, which was technically an exacting one. There were preliminary rehearsals under Beecham in the Soho waiters' club basement. Including eight orchestral wives, the party travelled via Harwich-Hook on a stormy mid-November night. Many were seasick. Encased instruments slid and bumped unregarded about cabin floors as the boat rolled and tossed. The arrangement was that Beecham should come along later for the Hochschule concerts. Meantime the orchestra were to be in the hands of Pierre Monteux, Diaghilev's conductor-in-chief.

The first night at the Kroll, which comprised the *Polovstian Dances* (Borodin), *Narcisse* (Tcherepnin) and *Cléopâtre* (a compound of Taneiev, Rimsky-Korsakov, Glinka and Moussorgsky) was ill attended. Later the theatre was jammed for gala performances graced by the

Kaiser and Kaiserin. Gorgeously uniformed and bemedalled, Wilhelm II paid three official visits. During the interval the entire audience stood with their backs to the stage and stared at him. Responsively the Kaiser showed off his profiles, preened his moustaches, looked dashingly handsome (on this all the orchestral wives were agreed) and altogether behaved with an aplomb that matched that of Diaghilev's dancers. It was not only on gala nights that the Kaiser came to the Kroll. He was there on other occasions, concealed from the general view—but not from certain strategically placed members of the orchestra—by a plush curtain. At least one of the programmes was re-ordered to flatter Wilhelm's taste, *Petrushka* being dropped to make way for *Cléopâtre*. "But naturally", comments Monteux. "The woman who danced Cleopatra was nearly nude."

In some ways the trip was haphazardly organised. Hence the B.S.O.'s threat of strike action half-way through the season. After half a century, memories of the contretemps are blurred and do not perfectly dove-tail. What appears to be beyond doubt, however, is that the players had not been paid for an extra rehearsal. Some of them were being pressed by Berlin boarding-house keepers and needed the money urgently. After bandroom meetings and a delegation to Beecham's tour manager, they were promised that they should be paid in full on a specific day. Before curtain-rise on the appointed night the money was not forthcoming. The men refused to go into the pit. After twenty minutes a Diaghilev emissary appeared. He said there would be a pay-out later that evening. The curtain went up at 8.30 instead of 8 p.m. At the first interval the pay-out began. There was not enough money to go round. Another strike threat. Another curtain delay. More money was promised at the second interval. Not all the players were satisfied even then. The performance should have ended at 11 p.m. It went on until midnight.

One B.S.O. veteran remembers seeing the Kaiser in the theatre that night; he was on one of his incognito "behind-the-curtain" visits. Especially because of this circumstance, Diaghilev's managers were extremely annoyed, although the delayed pay-out appears to have been wholly their fault. Their annoyance was shared by Beecham, whose first act on reaching the Adlon Hotel from London was to cancel a complimentary party arranged for his orchestra at a bohemian Berlin restaurant.

Yet the orchestra finished at the Kroll with greater professional prestige than they began. A thing that won them respect was their quick mastery of a new Stravinsky score, one of the three or four most

arduous and esoteric scores of the century so far: *Petrushka*. A handy
yardstick to their alertness was provided by the relative slowness of
extra woodwind players, Germans all, who had been recruited on the
spot.

For the Hochschule concerts the orchestra were seventy-five strong.
Their programmes included two Delius pieces, *Brigg Fair* and the first
Dance Rhapsody, Vaughan Williams's *In the Fen Country*, Balfour
Gardiner's *Shepherd Fennel's Dance*, Percy Grainger's *Mock Morris*
(which especially delighted the Berliners), Berlioz's *Carnaval Romain*
Overture, a Paisello overture and Mozart's *Haffner* Symphony.

After the first concert Sammons said to Ernest Hinchcliffe, the
second bassoon, "I never felt so nervous in my life." At this writing
Sammons had been dead for several years. "What", I asked Hinchcliffe, "made him say that?"

Hinchcliffe explained: "Like all of us, Sammons was tensed up.
Perhaps that is a good thing for the performances. I wouldn't know.
Beecham was an extraordinary man. He came into the same category
as Nikisch. All improvisation.We never knew what he was going to do
next. You could rehearse with him in the morning—but it didn't mean
you were going to get the same thing at night. You had to watch him
as a cat watches a mouse. That was especially the case at the Hochschule
concerts. We were all jumpy."

About the *Haffner* Symphony the local pundits hedged or wrinkled
their noses. One professor is credited with the judgment that it was
magnificent but not Mozart. Otherwise these concerts, Beecham's first
on the Continent with his own orchestra, caused something more than
the "mild stir" of which his biography modestly speaks. Independent
accounts tell of large audiences, stormy applause and flattering recep-
tions generally. Extracts were cabled to London from cordial critiques
in the leading Berlin newspapers. To anyone who knew the carping
and exacting temper of Berlin music criticism, it was evident that
Beecham and his players had scored a triumph.

The orchestra was agreed by the Berliners to be an élite body, one
of the best in the world, finely disciplined, not only subject to the
strong will of their *chef* but also delighting in the making of music for
music's sake. Where, marvelled *Die Signale*, the principal Berlin
musical weekly, did London find such magnificent young instrumentalists? The violins were credited with rich, noble tone, the woodwind with lustre, the brass, "which has not quite the dignity and
amplitude of our best German brass", with uncommon delicacy of
execution.

Much was written about Beecham's inborn gifts and idiosyncrasies. The *Vossische Zeitung* spoke of his "eccentricities of conception and expression" and mannerisms of gesture. "One smiles at first, and one laughs, too, perhaps. But in the end one falls under the spell of this sharply defined personality." Of *Brigg Fair* the *Signale* critic wrote that he had never heard Delius's score done by any conductor, even Nikisch, so spontaneously, with such conviction and wonderful shading. Undoubtedly, he concluded, the sacred fire burned in Beecham's bosom.

Altogether, the Berlin press cuttings made an agreeable bouquet. I have analysed them here not because ancient press critiques have intrinsic merit—ordinarily they make dull reading—but because this particular batch marks the beginning of an international conducting career which has had few parallels.

(2)

No enterprise in Beecham's career illustrated more strikingly the man's impulsive patriotism than the Denhof salvage operation of October 1913. The modestly framed references to it in *A Mingled Chime* do not tell a tenth of the story.

Ernst Denhof was a Swiss German who, from headquarters in Edinburgh, had put on touring opera in the provinces for three seasons with fair success and—as is shown by the inclusion of *Elektra* in his repertory—with some audacity. In September he set out for the Prince of Wales Theatre, Birmingham, the first halt on a tour scheduled to cover nine cities, with a company over two hundred strong. There was an orchestra of sixty-five which Denhof promised to increase to eighty-two for *The Ring*.

No English theatre outside London had ever seen an orchestra like it. Its players were drawn from the Royal Opera, London Symphony, Queen's Hall and Beecham Symphony orchestras. Denhof boasted that his orchestra alone cost as much as any typical travelling show lock, stock and barrel. The overall salary list stood at £2,600 a week equivalent to between £10,000 and £13,000 of 1961 money.

There were some who wondered where the cash was coming from. "From the box office, of course", replied Denhof. For the best seats at *Elektra* and *Rosenkavalier* (translated as *The Rose Bearer*), he proposed to charge a guinea. Why not? He was (he claimed) taking out productions up to Covent Garden standards. The public must pay accordingly. Either Denhof himself or someone close to him gave the singers and players to understand that the financial liabilities of the tour were covered by the subscriptions. As quickly appeared, such was not the case. The claim to Covent Garden standards proved equally illusory.

There were two conductors. Beecham was to have charge of certain *Ring* cycles, as well as of *Tristan*, *The Mastersingers* and *The Magic Flute*. The remaining operas—*The Flying Dutchman*, *Tannhäuser*, *Elektra*, *The Rose Bearer*, *Pelléas et Mélisande* and Gluck's *Orpheus*— were entrusted to a conductor from Frankfurt, Hans Schilling-Ziemszen, who had assisted Beecham at the Royal Opera some months earlier. The principal singers included a handful of foreigners. Among these was Hans Bechstein, an admired Mime in *The Ring*. The rest were recently established and, in several cases, first-rate English talents: Rosina Buckman, Carolyne Hatchard, Cicely Gleeson-White (who sang Elektra), Walter Hyde, Frederick Blamey, Frederic Austin and Robert Radford.

All the performances were in English. Beecham, whose translated productions were to have an immense vogue during the Kaiser's war, made no bones about his hostility to translation in principle. Qualities of accent and inflection, even literal meaning—all went to the wall, he complained. He pointed his teaching with an extraordinary story.

"My ideal of translation", he said, "is *Tales of Hoffmann*, as I produced it in London a year or two ago. Seated round a table at rehearsal, each artist decided for himself or herself the particular words he or she could vocalise most easily. These were the words actually sung at that production and at every subsequent production under my auspices."

Denhof and his staff had been planning the tour, or talking about it, since the beginning of the year. Certain of the Birmingham performances, nevertheless, had the air of last-minute improvisation. The scenery for *Pelléas* was not delivered from the railway goods yard until late on the afternoon of the performance. Anything in the nature of a scenic rehearsal was out of the question. Chaos reigned backstage. The eight scene changes, which are supposed to be bridged by Debussy's entr'acte music, were hopelessly prolonged. Often the music, which was half smothered by scene-shifting dins, petered out before the stage had been reset. To round off a sorry night, the Maeterlinck text, which always sounds gauche in English, however well translated, was further marred by the German accent of one of the singers. "Do nossin' more", "Mélisande, do not lean so var out of ze vindow", he sang, with a wealth of facial expression and dramatic gesture.

On the musical side some of the performances came in for high praise by the discerning. This applied especially to Beecham's *Tristan*.

The orchestral tissues and Beecham's handling of them, wrote Ernest Newman, were beyond anything hitherto hoped for or dreamed of by provincial operagoers. At this time Newman was in his middle forties; his sharp pen, as yet unmellowed, was immensely entertaining. His overnight notices of the Denhof season for *The Birmingham Post* are readable still—not only for their shrewdness and wit but also for their aggressive conservatism. This latter element came out noticeably in his Strauss critiques. In *Elektra* he responded to the honey of the Recognition Scene and kindred pages. Of the rest he wrote: "I make bold to say . . . that with all its genius *Elektra* contains more bad music, more futile music and more stupid music than any opera ever produced by a man of first-class reputation." What annoyed him particularly were its "strident drum-bangings and trumpet-screechings." In later years Newman substantially changed his line on the *Elektra* music. At the time of the Denhof tour its harmony and orchestral dynamics were to a large extent over his head.

On *Rosenkavalier* his obtuseness was startling. When Oktavian presents the Silver Rose, unrelated common chords, transparently and glitteringly scored, fall like stars in the orchestra. The page is one which most connoisseurs salute, including many who find the bulk of Strauss little to their taste. This is what Newman wrote of it: "The Silver Rose theme is ugly and meaningless in itself and . . . always just enough out of key with the rest of the orchestra to give the audience the general feeling that the players are making a series of mistakes. It may sound harmless enough in twenty years; at present it must be frankly called hideous."

(3)

Whether Denhof brooded over Newman's writings is doubtful. He had other things to think about. Throughout his Birmingham fortnight the theatre was rarely more, and often less, than half full. Halfway through the second week he cut his prices, with little result.

The second fortnight of the tour was scheduled for the Theatre Royal, Manchester. Here again attendances were woefully thin. Denhof looked at advance bookings for *The Ring* which, conducted by Beecham, was to occupy the second week. They weren't enough, he groaned, to pay for a musical comedy. He had lost £4,000 (equivalent to between £16,000 and £20,000 of today's money) in three weeks. Clearly the end had come. He publicly announced that the tour was to be abandoned.

The final show, as then scheduled, was *The Flying Dutchman*. As

Newman had pointed out, the portrait of Vanderdecken over Senta's door resembled Harry Tate, a renowned music-hall comic of the day, in a suit of mourning. But the back row of the chorus, who had once delighted in this, were amused no more. They and their colleagues were faced with the prospect of being stranded in Manchester after three weeks of a tour which was to have lasted fifteen. There had never been so resounding an operatic failure in English history. After the last curtain a smallish but compassionate audience shouted for Denhof. They wanted to cheer him for his good intentions. But Denhof was not accessible. Closeted with theatrical accountants, he was working out his salvation. The saviour was to be Beecham.

Due in Manchester to conduct the following week's projected *Ring* cycle, now cancelled, Beecham had been informed of the disaster by a telegram from one of Denhof's singers. Two days of telephoning followed between London and Manchester. Beecham had hoped to intervene in time to save the second Manchester week as well as the rest of the tour. He was five hours too late, however; the Theatre Royal management had already signed up a repertory company to put on *The Importance of Being Earnest* as a stop-gap.

On the Saturday afternoon Beecham and Donald Baylis, his general manager, travelled north. One hour after their arrival in Manchester they went on to the stage. The entire Denhof company were assembled there. Beecham's speech was brief and elating. He was prepared, he said, to carry on the tour as planned by Herr Denhof, with the same salary list and at his own risk. It was too late to do anything about the projected second week in Manchester. "But I propose, ladies and gentlemen", he said, "that we meet in Sheffield a week tomorrow." A great cheer went up.

Beecham was not greatly interested in the artistic aspect of the venture. This he made clear later. What did concern him was to rescue the chorus singers and orchestral players, especially, from their financial predicament and to restore the credit of English operatic management on the Continent, where the collapse, if not rectified quickly, would create "a lamentable impression."

Baylis got to work tensely. With a sheaf of papers under his arm—personnel lists, booking-plans and so on—he contrived to be in half a dozen places at once. After his fashion, he made as great an impression as his master. One who was present in the theatre that night testified years later, "We were all very glad to see Beecham, but when Baylis started fixing things we knew the tour really *was* saved. Our spirits had been drooping. He had an electrifying effect." The following day everybody went back to London, the chorus men and women and the orchestral players on rail tickets and a week's part-pay at the expense of the theatre circuit involved in the tour. A week later the company reassembled at the Lyceum, Sheffield, as Beecham had promised.

MR. THOMAS BEECHAM APPEALS TO THE SPORTING INSTINCTS OF THE SHEFFIELD PUBLIC TO SUPPORT HIM IN THIS GREAT EFFORT. So ran the newspaper advance advertisements. The idea was probably Baylis's. His feeling for public psychology, as Beecham acknowledged, was uncanny. With Schilling-Ziemszen, Beecham shared a six-piece repertory: *Tristan*, *Orpheus*, *The Rose Bearer*, *The Flying Dutchman*, *Elektra* and *The Mastersingers*. Business was twice as good as either the Birmingham weeks. But deficits persisted.

"Has grand opera paid in Sheffield?" Beecham was asked towards the end of the Lyceum run.

"Grand opera", came the reply, "will never pay. People have to get out of their heads that opera is anything but a fine art. It must be supported as picture galleries, parks and other things are supported that are supposed to give pleasure to the public. Music gives as much pleasure as collections of old pictures, most of which are bogus and bought at high prices."

As he passed from city to city on his errand of salvage Beecham aired his views with castigating relish. The North of England received many a whipping. It was to be feared, he said, that an ancient and irrational prejudice against the theatre lingered on there. "People who have busts and pictures of Beethoven, Mozart and Wagner in their houses and profess veneration for them shudder when it is suggested that they might go to a theatre to hear the works of these geniuses. And yet no one can possibly get an idea of the genius of the greatest composers outside the opera house."

On Beecham's own showing, the ingrained reluctance of the provinces to support touring opera was not surprising. How could they be expected to support a form of entertainment which, from the death of Carl Rosa to Denhof's advent, a period of twenty-five years, had been, to use his own phrase, absolutely mediocre at best and, at worst, marked by "downright Philistine barbarism"?

By the time his company returned to the Theatre Royal, Manchester, for a final and vindicating week, he had worked out, for that city at least, a scheme for a month's grand opera every autumn with the use of local orchestras—either the Hallé of Mr. Brand Lane's—at an estimated subsidy cost of £10,000 per season. He undertook to guarantee half this amount himself and to furnish stage settings from his own London stock into the bargain, provided guarantees for the other £5,000 could be found within the city itself. The conductorship (he tentatively proposed) should be divided between himself and Richter's successor, Herr Michael Balling, on the basis of equal status, and he hoped it would be possible to secure Sir Henry Wood's co-operation as well.

Never had Beecham been in such a mood of self-effacing benevolence. He even offered the local guarantors' committee casting-vote powers for use in the event of dispute on any vital point. But one thing he ventured to insist upon. The "representative moneyed men" of Manchester must do their part. "A Socialistic subsidy is not to be looked for", he advised. "Nor is that what we find in Germany. There the subsidy comes from the aristocracy. In Manchester it should come from the commercial men."

As will be seen, Manchester was to have its opera seasons on a scale and in circumstances which nobody imagined in 1913. But again, it was Beecham who bore the financial brunt.

CHAPTER FOURTEEN

TWO LIEUTENANTS

(1)

THE SALLIES TO Berlin and into the English provinces were undertaken in and among historic London opera seasons, or during preparations for them. Nineteen-thirteen was above all else a Strauss-Stravinsky year. The former's *Rosenkavalier*, which proved to be his most popular opera by far, came to London under Beecham's aegis after a delay of two years. Stravinsky's *Le Sacre du printemps*, which underwent preliminary rehearsal, through Beecham's good offices, at the Aldwych Theatre, where he was lessee, went forward to its hated and rowdy first night in Paris.

London had heard samples of the *Rosenkavalier* music in August 1911. At a Prom concert that month, Henry Wood put on a waltz suite from the opera which, as he reported later, "we all thought . . . a strange, lovely mixture of Mozart-like episodes, folk tunes and even the Romanticism of fifty years ago." From this opinion there were dissentients here and there. The composer of *Le Sacre* found *Rosenkavalier*, like all Strauss operas existing and to come, "cheap and poor" in musical substance.

In Lady Cunard's blue drawing room at Cavendish Square, Beecham played reams of the score from memory to Arthur James Balfour and George Moore among other listeners. Until the outbreak of the Kaiser's War, the *Rosenkavalier* waltzes were heard in every Belgravia ballroom. People actually danced to them. Most operagoers already had clearcut and wrong-headed ideas about the story of the opera. They had heard travellers' tales about the post-amour dawn scene in the Marschallin's bedroom and the pursuit of a stripling dressed up as a chambermaid by a lecherous baron. The general notion was of something sensual, perverse and depraved. We have the word of a shrewd contemporary observer, Arnold Bennett, for this.

Naturally, the first performance of the piece at Covent Garden under Beecham (January 29th, 1913) sold out ten days beforehand. The low prices for the season perhaps had a little to do with this; even in the grand circle the top price was only 15s. Two other Strauss operas, the inevitable *Salome* and *Elektra*, which Beecham made more deafening than ever, were included in a German repertory of five items

(*Tristan und Isolde* and *Die Meistersinger* were the other two) which, dovetailing with the Ballets Russes, ran until March 8th. Bearing in mind Strauss's swingeing performance fees, the prices were strikingly lenient. Kalisch, who gave explanatory talks about *Rosenkavalier* in Aeolian Hall and elsewhere, broke off to write an article in which he disclosed admiringly that, even if every seat were sold on every night, the season could not possibly pay for itself.

As in the case of *Salome*, *Der Rosenkavalier* came in for a mauling, although only a minor one, from the Lord Chamberlain. In the *cabinet particulier* of Act III, Mariandel (i.e., Oktavian "in travesty") pokes her head into the alcove and says, "Jesus Maria, steht a Bett drin, a mordsmässig grosses. Ja mei, wer schlaft da?" To which Baron Ochs lewdly replies, "Das wird Sie schon seh'n".* The Lord Chamberlain offered Beecham alternative courses. He could have the bed and no relevant words; or he could keep the words and have no bed. The second course was chosen. To what end? Few in the audience could make head or tail of sung German; even fewer the Viennese dialect in which much of von Hofmannsthal's libretto is framed.

The first night began at 8.20 p.m. (twenty minutes late) but, thanks to liberal cuts, was over by midnight. Beecham's slow *tempi* wrung the last drop of syrup out of the score's more emotional pages. At the end he was greeted by an explosive sort of shout when he appeared on the stage. The phrase is Arnold Bennett's. The Beecham fever had reached a point at which it mattered little what he played. To be in the man's presence was enough. Hofmannsthal's libretto, Bennett added "was certainly not understood by the stalls and the grand circle. What its reception was in the gallery I was too far off to judge."

At the end of the season Beecham claimed, surprisingly, that *Rosenkavalier* had attracted more attention than any previous work by Strauss. (My own impression after leafing through old newspaper files is that *Elektra* and *Salome* made a greater stir.) He conceded, however, that the Ballets Russes—for whom he had conducted the luscious *Thamar*—were "the most artistically complete and musically progressive entertainment-form of the age."

Another addition to Beecham's personal repertory was *Meistersinger*. His first intention had been that Richter should conduct all four performances. But history repeated itself. Richter was unable to appear. As at St. Helens in 1899, Beecham conducted in his stead. It

---

* Mariandel: "Jesus Maria, there's a bed, a great big one. Who sleeps in it?" Baron: "That you'll find out in good time."

was generally asserted, he complained later, that his *tempi* were too quick. Stop-watch timings, which he produced in refutation, showed that his *Meistersinger* performance (precisely which performance is not specified) was, on balance, thirty seconds longer than an unidentified performance of Richter's.

But overall timings of this kind prove nothing except average *tempi*, and, as is well known, the average *tempo*, like the average woman, does not exist. Six months or so later Newman heard Beecham's *Meistersinger* on tour. Newman found that Beecham's temperament, well suited to *Tristan*, did not guide him quite as surely in *Meistersinger*, running rather to vivacity, sensitiveness and lucidity than to the breadth and solidity which are generally held to be indispensable in this case. "Perhaps", added Newman, "one would not have minded even his most rapid *tempi* so much, only that they made it extremely difficult for the bass singers to articulate." Much the same thing may have happened at Covent Garden. The stage manager's stop watch was no assurance to the contrary.

(2)

From Covent Garden, Beecham moved in the spring to His Majesty's where, with the actor-manager of that theatre, Sir Herbert Tree, he gave eight performances of yet another Strauss-Hofmannsthal opera, *Ariadne auf Naxos*, preceded, as its authors originally intended by Molière's comedy *Le Bourgeois Gentilhomme*, the whole in a translation by Somerset Maugham. His next move was to the Theatre Royal, Drury Lane. His four weeks' season at this theatre in the summer of 1913 and his even more historic nine and a half weeks there in the summer of 1914 will be dealt with in a later chapter. Meantime, he had broken with Covent Garden.

One factor which led Beecham to resign from the board of the Opera was his colleagues' indifference to the reputation, now prodigious, especially in America, of Fedor Chaliapin. It is true that some years earlier the Syndicate had thought of giving Chaliapin a trial. An emissary in New York sounded the basso on the Syndicate's behalf. When Chaliapin learned what fee they were offering he lay back and laughed hugely. "That", he said, "would hardly keep me in cigarettes."

The Syndicate were unresponsive—and equally unrealistic—when Beecham proposed a month or two of Russian opera and ballet at Covent Garden, with Chaliapin as its mainspring, for the high season of 1913. A second estranging factor was the collapse of Oscar Hammerstein. The looming threat of the London Opera House had brought

Beecham and the Syndicate together. In effect, the London Opera
House was no more. Beecham and the Syndicate were free to go their
different ways.

It had taken a mere eight months (November 1911 to July 1912)
to bring Hammerstein low. During that time he had put on two
seasons, produced eighteen operas, resorted to patent makeshifts
(*Norma*, his third effort, sported bits of ancient Roman scenery and
furniture from Nougué's *Quo Vadis?* on the opening night) and
employed singers whose talents compared drably with the Melbas,
Tetrazzinis, Destinnovas, McCormacks and Martinellis of Covent
Garden. A devoted band of earls, dukes and barons who called themselves the Committee for the Welfare of the London Opera House,
toiled unsparingly in the Hammerstein cause. His newspaper advertising became flamboyant and tended to screech. Before the end of
his first season he cut his prices. Stalls came down from a guinea to
half a guinea. The earls and dukes got George V and Queen Mary to a
charity matinée. In the lobby, Hammerstein advanced to meet the royal
pair with outstretched hand, saying, "How are you, King?" The King
took Hammerstein's hand good humouredly and replied, "I am delighted
to meet you, Mr. Hammerstein. I admire your theatre very much."

Hammerstein's talents as a "card" served him no more than his
stratagems. His audiences became pitiably small. Massenet's *Don
Quichotte*, noted later as a Chaliapin "vehicle", accelerated the downward spin. On the first night only £85 was taken at the box office;
on the eighth a mere £51. On his last night (July 15th, 1912) Hammerstein talked to reporters. In eight months, he said, he had lost £45,000.
But there was no question of throwing in the towel. He proposed
to reopen for a third season of opera in November.

The truth is, he was beaten and knew it. Actually his losses ran to a
million dollars. He sailed home and put the theatre into his son
Arthur's hands for liquidation. Oscar Hammerstein had built his last
opera house and launched his last opera season.

What was to become of the theatre in Kingsway? Rumour spread
that Beecham was going to buy it.

"Not so", replied Donald Baylis. "Mr. Beecham has been thinking
for some time of building an opera house of his own in London."

(3)

One of Hammerstein's more remembered nights was marked by the
presence—and early departure—of one who was to be closely linked
with Beecham and his enterprises until the eve of Hitler's war.

Perhaps against his better judgment and as a *quid pro quo* to his committee of noble names, Hammerstein had been persuaded to include in his second season *The Children of Don*, first item in an operatic trilogy by Joseph Holbrooke named *The Cauldron of Annwen*. Founded on Celtic mythology, the "book" was by a moneyed (and open-handed) peer, Lord Howard de Walden. Great pains were taken with the production. The eminent Arthur Nikisch conducted. In his own sphere the stage director, Jacques Coini, was little less celebrated.

Hammerstein listened to the première from the wings as usual, sitting on a bentwood chair and smoking a cigar in defiance of theatre bye-laws. Next morning *The Times* described the work as "the most severe blow which the cause of struggling British opera has sustained for many years."

For the cause of British opera Hammerstein cared little. What concerned him was the blow to Oscar Hammerstein. His depression was turned to irritation, either on this night or at a later performance of the work, by continuous chatter from a stage box just above and wide of where he was seated. The box was occupied by Lady Cunard's party, which included the King of Portugal. The chatterer in chief, according to Hammerstein's biographer, Vincent Sheehan, was Lady Cunard herself. As the chatter went on Hammerstein's irritation became anger. Calling an attendant, he sent him to Lady Cunard's box with a message, "Mr. Hammerstein requests you to leave his theatre at once." The party promptly complied and never set foot in the London Opera House again: not that the theatre had much more to offer them.

At this time Lady Cunard was forty but looked—and, when it came to the point, claimed to be—five years younger. She was small, bright, fair and bustling, with a talent, as well as a passion, for pushing and controlling events and people. On the social side she was the great whipper-in, wheedler, contriver and bully at all the major opera and ballet seasons of the Beechams (for Joseph, too, was in the picture now) from 1913 onward.

It was she who dragooned titled people and the rich into sub-scribing for boxes they didn't really want. If any dispute arose as to which ducal party should sit in which box (and feuds on such matters could be acrimonious), it was Lady Cunard who arbitrated with bludgeon or velvet glove. At Covent Garden and at Drury Lane alike she could be seen on glittering Ackté, Chaliapin or Nijinsky nights with diamonds in her pretty hair, darting alertly from box to box, keeping her finger on the social pulse and seeing to it that everybody found the performance marvellous.

More than one good judge considered that, without her social impresarioship, the 1913 and 1914 seasons of Sir Joseph Beecham (he had been knighted in 1912) would have been not merely costly but financially impracticable. The rich people whom she chivvied into sitting night after night through entertainments they found boring have not had much thanks for their martyrdom. In the main their lot has been derision and abuse. In the charitable language which certain addicts of opera reserve for those who cannot see the point of it, Osbert Sitwell summed up Lady Cunard's approach thus: "She had grasped the fact that in the London of the time, in order to ensure the success of an art-luxury such as Grand Opera, it was absolutely necessary to be able to rely upon a regular attendance by numskulls, nitwits and morons addicted to the mode, even if they did not care in the least for music." For the greater glory of the Beechams and her own relish, Maud Cunard rounded up these lowly intelligences with astuteness and tenacity.

Daughter of a moneyed American family, Maud Alice Burke was brought up in New York and heard her first Wagner (an entire *Ring* cycle, apparently) at the Metropolitan Opera House when twelve. Of this experience she wrote later: "It was as if a new world had opened out, revealing a race of men and women very Titans of humanity, endowed with superb gifts, and the musical setting in which they were enshrouded made an impression on me that was to last as long as life itself." This is typical of Lady Cunard's prose which, at its ripest, is as good as a *Ulysses* parody. At twenty-one she was engaged to a Polish count and jilted by him. Two years later, in 1895, she married Sir Bache Cunard, second baronet of his line, grandson of the founder of the steamship company. Cunard was then forty-three, twenty-one years older than his bride. A less compatible pair it would have been hard to find. The husband was a great foxhunter. In Northamptonshire he set up his own pack and, as M.F.H., had engrossing quarrels with the Quorn Hunt about their joint boundary. A worker in silver, he turned out creditable altar pieces and rode to church every Sunday morning on a pony which he left untethered to browse among the tombstones.

His wife's passion for entertaining was little to his taste. The visitors' book at their home, Nevill Holt, was soon filled with gilded or noble names. After fifteen years Maud Cunard left Nevill Holt never to return or remarry, and settled in London, where her restless genius as hostess had more congenial scope. George Moore, the writer, promptly fell in love with her and remained devoted for the rest of his days. But in 1910-11, as we gather from the most authoritative of her memorialists, "another took first place in Lady Cunard's affections."

She met Beecham at one of Mrs. Charles Hunter's supper parties in London. Known behind her back as "Mrs. Lion Hunter", this insatiable hostess, a sister of Ethel Smyth, had as great an appetite for celebrities as Lady Cunard herself. Her mien was regal. Lady Cunard and Beecham often went down to week-ends at Hill Hall, the Hunters' place in Essex. One of the bedrooms there became known as the Beecham room. A dark-eyed troubadour whose bearded features were uncommonly like the maestro's dominated the wallpaper pattern. Beecham played tennis, talked intolerantly and amusingly and strummed Mozart by the hour to awed listeners. There was no music in the world, it seemed, that he could not play instantly on demand. He carried far more music in his head, said Ethel Smyth, than any music shop on its shelves. Mrs. Hunter's ear, although devoted, was less expert than her sister's. She once brought out a record of Delius's *On hearing the first cuckoo in spring* and, mentioning that she had made "heaps" of Delius converts with it, put it on for Beecham. He listened with patience, then mildly observed that it wasn't Delius at all but Moskowski's *Scherzo capricioso*. The *Cuckoo* was certainly there but on the other side; the labels had been transposed. Everybody laughed about this except Delius who, when told of it, flew into a pet.

Lady Cunard's salon on the eve of the Kaiser's war was at 20 Cavendish Square, a house of some grandeur, with baroque, stone-floored hall, wide, frescoed staircase, richly panelled dining room and long blue drawing room. Balfour, the former Tory Prime Minister, was often seen there. For years he went regularly with Lady Cunard to Wagner nights at the opera. His taste ran from Handel to the more accessible contemporaries. According to Beecham he was the only leading statesman of the day who had ever taken the slightest interest in music. In the opposite party camp Lady Cunard was on comradely terms with the reigning Prime Minister, Asquith, and his wife Margot.

The Cavendish Square salons were multifarious occasions at which not only cabinet ministers and bankers but poets, ballet-struck sub-alterns, shipbuilders, concert pianists and guests of a score other vocations jostled and bewildered each other. "How's business?" General Sir Ian Hamilton, future hero of Gallipoli, was heard to inquire breezily of a young composer. And, without waiting for an answer: "I heard that fellow Kreisler play a thing of yours the other night."

George Moore was another habitué. He tended to monopolise the tabletalk if given a chance. His arrogance had droll turns of phrase. Conrad's novels he described as the wreckage of Stevenson floating on the slops of Henry James. Sometimes he was shocking in a bizarre way. One night at Cavendish Square he asked a lady next to him at table, "Are you married?" "Yes", she replied.

"And how long have you been married?" pursued Moore.

"For nearly twenty years."

"And do you still love your husband?"

"Of course I do. I am devoted to him."

Moore wrinkled his nose. "How disgusting!" he murmured.

Sitting at Beecham's right hand, Lady Cunard served on operatic management boards, orchestral committees and festival executives. Sometimes they acceded, sometimes resigned together. At rehearsals she was active and ubiquitous and wore airs of authority. It was quickly evident to professionals that she didn't know much about music. Her limitations were equally evident to various non-professionals, among them Muriel Draper, a rival musical hostess of taste and tenacity. The rivals graciously exchanged visits from time to time. At one of Mrs. Draper's private chamber concerts in Edith Grove, Lady Cunard listened with shining eyes while a string quartet led by Sammons played Haydn. When it was over she said brightly to the players, "How about some Mozart?—that is, if Mozart wrote any chamber music."

"If he'd written any more", exclaimed Warwick Evans, the 'cellist, "he'd have bust his——"

"There, there, Warwick", Mrs. Draper soothingly interrupted, "never mind. . . ."

Lady Cunard said many things during her thirty years' social reign which people agreed tacitly not to mind. Hers was an exuberant and purposeful soul. Such are forgiven a good deal.

(4)

As Lady Cunard attended to the social side of Beecham's seasons, so did Donald Baylis to their harder practicalities. We have already had a glimpse, in the chapter on the Denhof rescue, of Baylis in his administrative element. His was an unusual career. It deserves a further note here. Baylis served Beecham for ten years, until his death at the age of thirty-seven, and was in many ways his *alter ego*. In times of crisis or crucial development the maestro tended to wrap himself in remote and godlike inscrutability. At such times Baylis spoke for him. He used his prerogative with the ease and relish of one accountable for his phrasing and emphases to none but himself.

It is doubtful whether the English theatre has known a comparable career. Certainly there has been nobody like Baylis in opera before or since. Like his master, he was bred, if not born, in St. Helens and was said in a local obituary notice (1920) to come of a family well known in the district "who have been much devoted to music." His real name was not Donald Baylis but Donald Herbert Goas.

With no education to speak of, he entered Joseph Beecham's pill works at the age of twelve, graduated from office boy to correspond-ence clerk and by twenty-five had become secretary to the general manager. He sang tenor in the parish church choir with such distinc-tion, according to publicity material either put out or sponsored by himself years later, that his superior drew Joseph's attention to his merits; and Joseph was so impressed that he arranged for him to be trained in singing, in music generally and in German diction.

At twenty-seven, having learned leading tenor rôles in Wagner, Verdi and Puccini, he forsook his desk at the pill works for good and joined Thomas Beecham at Covent Garden as a member of the chorus. The first opera in which he sang was *A Village Romeo and Juliet*. He had never set foot in a theatre before. Four months later he was leading Beecham's chorus in *Shamus O'Brien* at His Majesty's. This function he doubled with that of assistant acting manager. Made up as a revelling student (*Hoffmann*), a tie-wigged nobleman (*Figaro*) or a sidewhiskered roué (Fledermaus), he would pass the time between chorus calls coping backstage with a dozen administrative matters by typewriter, telephone and whispered talk in the wings. By 1913, Beecham and his father had made him the general manager of all their operatic and other musical enterprises. This happened three years after his first entry into the theatre.

At Covent Garden and Drury Lane, Baylis was henceforth the *éminence*, the right hand, the privileged intermediary. He lifted all burdens of detail from Beecham's back. As Beecham's commitments multiplied under the aegis, in coming years, of the Beecham Opera Company, so did the wrinkles of care on Baylis's forehead. If a third 'cello wanted to become principal 'cello, if an assistant conductor wanted to try his hand at *Tristan*, if a leading soprano wanted more pay or a Number One dressing room, if programme-printers or scene painters or wigmakers wanted bills paid, it was understood that Baylis was the man to see and that without Baylis's backing they would get nowhere.

He is remembered at the height of his power a few years later, that is to say, before the calamitous Beecham receiving order of 1919, as a slim, small, buck-toothed man in his middle thirties with thinning hair and a premature stoop. He was at the theatre daily from nine in the morning until midnight. Down the years he wore the same sort of undistinguished grey suit with "butterfly" wing collar. Indoors as well as in the street he always wore a green homburg hat. This was, indeed, as much a backstage symbol as Hammerstein's silk hat had been. He carried a silver knobbed malacca cane, probably because he thought it the right thing for a theatrical manager to do. Otherwise there was nothing whatever of the theatre about his appearance or, superficially, about his personality. He had an aversion to tails, dinner jackets and desk routine. He transacted much day-to-day theatre business between whiskies and sodas in the theatre bar, picking his teeth with a quill the while. A fledgling conductor who had not been paid for a fortnight (such oversights often occurred) would come into the bar, mentally cap in hand. "What are you having, old man?" Baylis would genially inquire, with a gesture to the barman.

"I just wanted a word about money."

"You haven't been paid?"

"No, Mr. Baylis."

"How much do you want?"

The fledgling would name the sum, and Baylis, taking a wad of banknotes from his hip pocket, would lick a thumb and pay out.

These bar sessions lasted on and off until curtain-fall or after. It sometimes happened that, by the time he called a taxi and left for his handsome house in St. John's Wood, Beecham's *alter ego* was in expansive humour. He would sing snatches of tenor aria in a voice which, as the years passed, became a croak owing to the throat affection that prematurely killed him. But whisky never impaired his lucid and and endless industry. His feats of organisation in 1913 and 1914 were prodigious.

CHAPTER FIFTEEN

RUSSIA AT DRURY LANE

(1)

SIR JOSEPH BEECHAM, now in his mid-sixties, was approaching the one abyss as well as the social summit of his career. He had thought to retire when he became old. But no. More than ever he was the harried captive of the pill business.

"I lead a rushing life", he complained. "I am constantly travelling to and fro, between St. Helens and London and between London and New York." He had crossed the Atlantic nearly fifty times and hoped to set up a passenger record. Already he was the biggest newspaper advertiser and the most lavish patron of music in the world. One thing consoled him for the perpetual pressure and scurry of affairs. Under his control the pill business had expanded to a degree that put its founder's achievements in the shade. "My father", he used to say, "thought he had reached the acme, but I knew very well that he hadn't." All in all, the family motto, *Nil sin labore*, fitted Joseph well.

He rarely found time to touch the organ which Pilling, builder of railways, had designed for the imposing mahogany music room at West Brow, Hampstead. Like the sister instrument at Ewanville, this had cost £3,200. On buying Turners, Morlands, De Wints, Coxes and Constables, Joseph had spent thousands more. Many of these master-pieces—which *The Connoisseur* for June 1914 described at stupefying length—were hung at West Brow in a gallery whose skylight was painted with purple Highlands mountains and a foreground of torrent and trees. This transparency could be illuminated at night. It must have clashed regrettably with the Constables.

West Brow was a thirty-room mansion near Hampstead top. Joseph had bought, gutted and internally rebuilt it in opulent *art nouveau* style during the early years of the century. He plainly intended that the house should have a dynastic air. His study, with wall tapestries in silver, brown and gold, was dominated by a carved panel over the fireplace which bore his monogram and the inaugural year, 1903. Carved, cast or embossed, the Beecham arms and crest—escallops, martlets, a swan's head—were on view in all the main rooms. An even more remarkable dynastic symbol graced the main stair leading from the entry hall to the upper floors. On the newell post at the foot, beneath a canopy upheld by spiral oak pillars, rested a globe of greenish mottled alabaster, one foot in diameter. This represented The Pill from which the dynasty's fortunes derived. That Joseph should have given The Pill a shrine argues irreverent drollery in either himself or, what seems likelier, in some adviser.

From the pill symbol one went upstairs to Joseph's picture gallery or downstairs to Joseph's strong-room. This had a green-painted door and a brass combination lock which stared like an eye. Behind the door was a steel grille with double lock; behind the grille, shelves stocked with documentary and other valuables. The most fateful documents ever housed in Joseph's strong-room had to do with his buying for two and a quarter million sterling of the Covent Garden Estate.

As will be told in due place, this was the transaction which brought anxiety and shadow in the wake of Joseph's triumph. From this anxiety Joseph never emerged for the brief remainder of his life. After his death the Covent Garden deal was to complicate and confound his son's professional career for over a decade.

(2)

Meantime Joseph's hour of glory had struck. In 1913 there was no hint of shadow. The man who had once played the harmonium at hymn-singings and would crawl the carpet in search of dropped half-pennies appeared before the world as an impresario, handing out contracts, handsome cheques (he paid Chaliapin alone £400 a night) and manifestos apparently of his own composition.

His first manifesto came out early in 1913. Fastidiously printed in heliotrope ink, it announced Sir Joseph Beecham's Grand Season of Russian Opera and Ballet, to be given at the Theatre Royal, Drury Lane, from June 24th to July 25th. In a message to the public Joseph explained that, like many musical amateurs in Britain, "I have always been an admirer of the wonderful Russian operas written during the second half of the last century, and it has been my constant desire to see them produced on the English stage. But"—and here came a dig at the directors of Covent Garden—"but, as season after season went by without witnessing even a preliminary step in this direction taken by those habitually engaged in theatrical undertakings, hope gave way to disappointment." Of course, conceded Joseph, he realised the difficulty entailed in transporting an entire company from St. Petersburg to London. Such an enterprise was doubtless well-nigh impossible of achievement during the course of a normal opera season.

"But quite recently there has arisen an opportunity which may not occur again for many years"—actually it recurred twelve months later—"of bringing some of these remarkable works to London, together with . . . artists best fitted for an ideal interpretation of them.' The opportunity referred to was the presence within practicable distance, namely, at the Théâtre des Champs-Elysées, Paris, of a company of Russian singers based on the Imperial Opera of St. Petersburg. This company had been brought to Paris by Serge Diaghilev, whose own ballet company was on the spot as well. "Of the quite unique claims to public favour on the part of this celebrated organisation", concluded Joseph, "I have very little to say except that I am sure the opening night will yield to the music-loving public an artistic sensation such as it has not enjoyed for many years."

(3)

That first Russian month at Drury Lane took in three Russian operas, all Chaliapin "vehicles"—*Boris Godounov*, *Khovantchina* and *Ivan the Terrible*—and fifteen ballets. As well as Debussy's *Jeux* and his controversially erotic *L'après-midi d'un faune*, the ballet repertory included a formidable new Stravinsky piece which had recently goaded Parisian firstnighters to riot: *Le Sacre du printemps*. For the operas there was a superbly trained and touchy chorus from St. Petersburg, who were accustomed to intrusive applause and encores in their own right. The orchestra was Beecham's. But Beecham himself did not appear on the conducting strength, which was entirely foreign: Monteux, Emile Cooper (Russian despite his name), Rhéné-Baton and Steinman. Beecham's main appearances were in this box or that; or even backstage when circumstances invited it, as on the occasion, for example, of the Chaliapin riot described below.

The season opened sluggishly; but soon the town took fire. Drury Lane became fashionable and obligatory. The crowned or coroneted heads who were intrigued or bludgeoned into the Drury Lane boxes by Lady Cunard drew at their heels crowds of snobs and starers. Furthermore there was a great hiving-in of intellectuals. Moussorgsky, Rimsky-Korsakov, Debussy, Stravinsky and the rest opened up iridescent and fevering new worlds. For the first time since the onset of Wagnerism in the 'seventies, entertainments which were predominantly musical in character excited if anything more support from outside strictly musical circles than from within. Chaliapin, Nijinsky and Karsavina nights drew poets, artists and dilettantes of every nuance. Not all the celebrities wore tiaras or the Garter sash. During intervals a curious figure was seen to stalk through the foyer. She wore a short corduroy skirt, a white silk shirt and a small hat perched on her massive head. Her name was Gertrude Stein. Miss Stein was usually attended by a young woman with melancholy eyes who wore oriental gauzes, enormous earrings and a tinkle of chains and bracelets.

This pair were, in a sense, a symbol of Joseph's new-found public. His two Drury Lane seasons introduced thirty or so operas and ballets either new to London or as good as new. No such wave of unfamiliar music, much of it aggressively novel in idiom, had ever overwhelmed the town before. In the way of concentrated revelation, nothing like it has happened since. Not more than three or four out of the thirty works could be called profoundly or decisively historic. Things seemed otherwise, however, to the cultivated dabblers of the day, who were inclined to salute a deathless masterpiece every time the curtain went up.

Certain aesthetic hallucinations of the time are reflected in the letters and diaries of Charles Ricketts, the artist and theatrical designer. A lifelong operagoer and musiclover, Ricketts was in some ways a shrewd judge as well as a talented writer. But today it is impossible to read without smiling indulgently his assessment of, for example, Rimsky-Korsakov's *Le Coq d'Or* which was first introduced to Drury Lane not as an opera, which it is, but as a quasi-ballet and mime show, which it was never intended to be. For Ricketts, *Coq d'Or* was "an outstanding revelation of the highest art . . . almost uncanny in invention, entrancing as music and of the utmost significance as a departure which may open a new life of art or hasten the decadence of that which exists. It is at once a return to the birth of tragedy and its end, and quite serious people are already discussing the possibilities of its method even in Wagnerian drama." Half a century later it is obvious that *Coq d'Or*, pretty though it be in a technically penurious way, made not a scratch on European musical thought.

Like a whole generation of his kind, however, Ricketts was stunned and bemused. The great Russian Visitation coloured and dominated the rest of many lives. Whether the judgments of Ricketts and his kind were sound mattered little at the time. What did matter was the fevered elation they experienced. It is to be surmised that no other generation has experienced anything quite like it.

(4)

There were, it is true, limits to contemporary appetites and perceptions. This was clear from London's response to *Le Sacre*.

There were three performances of Stravinsky's ballet under Monteux in 1913. It then dropped from Joseph's repertory without public lament or murmur. Most people loathed it. For all its limitations, which are fairly evident now that *Le Sacre* has become a concert repertory piece, the score endures both as a memorial and as an entity with sap in it. Not overnight, to be sure, but certainly during the next decade or so, it helped to change the face of an epoch, inducing new ways of conceiving music and listening to it. A retrospect of the London performances which Joseph paid for may not, therefore, be out of place.

Through Beecham's good offices, as has been said, the first piano rehearsals were held in the Aldwych Theatre. The dancers complained (erroneously) that the music had no tunes. Unable to memorise it, they laboriously counted out the beats and bars. They called *Sacre* rehearsals "arithmetic classes". Those who had the ear of Diaghilev and Nijinsky, who was producing, complained that the piece was unsuitable for dancing. The pair were unmoved. The riotous first night at the Champs-Elysées the following May is now as much a history book entry as the *Tannhäuser* fiasco at the Paris Opera in 1860. But the history books are not to be followed in every particular. Far from weeping over the "battle", as has been sentimentally reported down the decades, Diaghilev, who knew the value of publicity to the last kopek, was highly pleased. "Exactly what I wanted", he said.

The London première came six weeks later. Monteux was given eight rehearsals with the Beecham Symphony Orchestra as compared with eighteen for the Paris première, the difference being accounted for partly by the fact that the dancers were now on terms with their task and partly (as Monteux admitted later) by the English players' superior skill. The Drury Lane first night sold out weeks ahead. Ten minutes before curtain-rise Edwin Evans, the critic, appeared in the footlights and began to read a typewritten essay on *Le Sacre* as spectacle, symbol and music. Somebody started to clap ironically. Evans folded his typescript and bowed himself off. The tap of Monteux's stick was heard. Then came the first phrases of the Introduction. These phrases are for solo bassoon. Nothing more exposed or exacting had ever been written for the instrument. The solo went off without mishap, however. So, apparently, did the rest of the score. At the end a handful in the audience hissed; another handful tried to get up a cheer. The majority seemed politely neutral. But many who had checked their bile in the theatre let themselves go in the bar. Some complained that Stravinsky's music had given them a headache. Others cut in with, "Call that music? My God!" Ricketts said he had wanted to howl like a dog. "I thought of doing so", he added, "but realised nobody would hear me." The *Sacre* costumes and massed, angular dance movements were hated as much as the music. After the *tutus* and dreamlike languors of *Les sylphides*, which preceded the Stravinsky, the *Sacre* women in their scarlet and flaxen smocks, leg wrappings, bast shoes and daubed, doll-like make-up were considered an affront to taste and breeding.

At rehearsal next morning Monteux thanked the players for their handling of an immensely difficult score; they had been splendid, he beamed. This praise conveys nothing more, I fear, than that the externals of the music were well cared for. With the roots of Stravinsky's music, Monteux had no affinity at all. After first hearing Stravinsky play through the score on the piano at Monte Carlo, he drew Diaghilev aside and said, "I will never conduct music like that." Diaghilev persuaded him to swallow his revulsion. In old age Monteux told me, "I did not like *Le Sacre* then. I have conducted it fifty times since. I do not like it now."

In this, Beecham, Monteux and most of the critics, whose notices were outraged and apoplectic, saw eye to eye. Beecham's autobiographical reference to "this striking and interesting work" is brief and glacial, serving merely to point his preference for *Petrushka*. At Drury Lane and for evermore, he regarded *Petrushka* as "its composer's masterpiece", a phrase which excluded the rest of the Stravinsky canon.

(5)

On the eve of the Kaiser's war, Fedor Chaliapin was in his prime, noble of voice, overwhelming of presence.

His first entry as Boris Godounov, burdened with guilt and the crown of the Russias, or as Ivan the Terrible, crouched on horseback, with bloodshot eyes, was invariably the signal for a jubilant shout that shook the walls of Drury Lane. Ricketts marvelled especially at his twin impersonations in *Prince Igor*. In this Chaliapin was two entirely different persons: "a burly blackguard, every inch a prince—a very bad one—when he drinks on the stage, sings bawdy songs, threatens women with his brandished chairs, or kicks a door down. . . . In the same opera he transforms himself into a small, wiry yet genial Tartar —polite, cordial and strange, with something feline hidden in his expressions and gestures. He holds one spellbound, and the audience roars when he has merely entered the stage."

Chaliapin was charmingly attentive to young beauties. Diana Manners never missed a Chaliapin night. When taking his curtain, he would turn towards the box where she sat and bow to her "as he must have done to the Tsar." On nights when not singing, he would bring round flowers and offer them with all the gallantry in the world. He encouraged Lady Diana to dress up as a peasant girl or boyar's wife and sing in the chorus—which in any case usually included English reinforcements—for the fun of the thing. Hearing Chaliapin sing so near her was much more exciting, she found, than a seat in the stalls or in a box.

With subordinates of the Imperial Opera, Chaliapin's ways were not always so agreeable. He was inclined to settle backstage wrangles with his fist. On at least one occasion, the subordinates got together and retaliated in kind. The incident occurred on a blazing day in July 1913. Chaliapin had been commanded to sing an additional *Boris* before King George and Queen Mary. The performance was inscrutably advertised as "by desire". A ballet bill had been suppressed to make way for it. Disappointed balletomanes were invited to come and get their money back at the box office.

To mark the occasion, Chaliapin bought a grey top hat. As he walked to the theatre from the hatter's shop in the late afternoon sun, he admired himself in every shop window, as delighted as a child with a new toy. At the theatre he was met with scowls. The performance was to be a "benefit" for the chorus. Apparently the singers were dissatisfied with the pay arrangements and, for reasons which have never been clarified, put the blame on Chaliapin. Highly independent and perhaps a little spoiled, the St. Petersburg choristers seemed to sense the winds of a revolution which was still four years away. Their mood was assertively radical.

Massed on the stage, they took part stentoriously in the National Anthem, which opened the proceedings. In the royal box, with the King at her side, stood Queen Mary, majestic under a high tiara. After the Anthem, the chorus sang in the *Boris* prologue. Just before the Coronation Scene, however, they went on strike. With only English choral reinforcements on the stage, a famed spectacle misfired.

At the end, Chaliapin, gorgeously robed and crowned, came storming off through the wings. He began a shouting match with the chorus-leader, who had organised the strike, and ended, characteristically, by knocking him down. Instantly the entire chorus hurled themselves at Chaliapin, threatening him with the staves they had carried in the prologue, and bore him to the ground. According to one witness, Fred Gaisberg, his recording manager, Chaliapin would have been badly mauled—or worse—if the mezzo-soprano, Patrenka, had not covered him with her body. One account says he was rescued by stage hands, escorted to his dressing room and, as a precaution, locked inside it. Another version gives the credit to policemen from Bow Street who had been telephoned for by the stagedoor keeper.

When, after a tactical interval, Chaliapin emerged from the dressing room, he carried a loaded revolver in either pocket. The final curtain was followed by venemous harangues all round. Then Chaliapin uttered some appeasing phrase. The chorus hurled themselves at him again, this time to hug and kiss. The reconciliation was sealed by the appearance of Baylis with a bag of gold. He handed a sovereign to each chorister. Everybody stayed on in the theatre and drank tea until 5 a.m. Drury Lane had never known such an orgy of goodwill.

CHAPTER SIXTEEN

NINETEEN ACRES, 1914

(1)

NINETEEN-FOURTEEN: summer days of unflawed blue and gold. Before that summer was over the world had swung into the long night of war. For the moment, polite and moneyed society gadded and glittered on the assumption that the foundations and frills of civilisation would last with little modification for ever. For nearly ten weeks, Beecham's season at Drury Lane ran neck-and-neck with that of the Syndicate at Covent Garden. On scorching evenings half-an-hour before curtain-rise, the approach-streets serving both theatres were a tangle of motor-cars, with an occasional landau marooned among them. Watchers on the pavements glimpsed feathers, emeralds and imperious profiles through plate glass.

At Drury Lane, if you were rich enough, you hired a grand-tier box for the season at £136. For this you heard two operas in German (*Der Rosenkavalier* and *Die Zauberflöte*), one in English (Joseph Holbrooke's *Dylan*) and seven in Russian, including three productions new to London: *Prince Igor* (Borodin), *May Night* (Rimsky-Korsakov) and *The Nightingale* (Stravinsky). The season's fifteen ballets included Diaghilev's perversion of *Le Coq d'Or*, the *Josephslegende* of Richard Strauss (who conducted its entirely unmemorable first night) and another new score which has had greater success in the concert hall than in the theatre: Maurice Ravel's *Daphnis et Chlöe*. At Covent Garden *Parsifal* and Charpentier's *Louise*, *Samson et Dalila* and *Götter-dämmerung*, *Butterfly* and *Don Giovanni* rubbed elbows in a repertory that read like the inventory of a bazaar.

Covent Garden had the Great Voices. Melba, Destinnova, Caruso, McCormack, Martinelli and Scotti sang for the Syndicate that year. The Beechams could offer no such list; they relied mainly on middling or budding celebrities. Chaliapin again was their trump card. Apart from him and Frieda Hempel, whom they paid 150 guineas a night for her Königin der Nacht (*Zauberflöte*), nobody else in their lists either bestrode the world or had it in him to do so. The two houses were committed to tacit rivalry in the social field. Beecham opened with *Der Rosenkavalier*—as usual his orchestra drowned the singers much of the time—before King Manoel, Queen Augusta-Victoria and the

Prince of Hohenzollern. Maud Cunard, gowned in white, diamonds in her hair, looked forth from her box and was not as pleased with her social contrivings as she had hoped to be. At Covent Garden that night, Queen Alexandra, the Empress Marie of Russia, the Princess Royal and Princess Maud were listening to Melba in *Rigoletto*: a much more imposing list, it had to be allowed.

According to Mr. Baylis, however, it was wrong to assume that anything so crude as competition prevailed. A week before the Drury Lane opening, fortified by advance bookings of £30,000 and a daily queue at the box office, he said: "London is a very big place. It is absurd to suggest that there isn't sufficient room for both operas. Paris and Berlin maintain three operas each. People of taste and discernment will want to visit Drury Lane and Covent Garden alike. Not that we expect to make money on the venture. We stand to lose very heavily."

Beecham was originally scheduled to conduct fourteen operas or ballet performances. Actually the tally came to fifteen; and this is how. Monteux was expecting to become a father. For days he put in regular telephone calls to his home in Paris. One Saturday morning he went to Diaghilev and said, "It's a girl. I leave for Paris on the next boat train. I return on Tuesday."

"But", objected Diaghilev, "you are conducting *Petrushka* on Monday."

"I must ask you to find somebody else."

"But nobody else knows *Petrushka*."

"Sorry, Serge Pavelitch, my taxi is at the door."

Naturally, Diaghilev turned to Beecham. At that time Beecham, while admiring *Petrushka*, had no technical knowledge of it. He spent the week-end with his head in the score. On Monday morning he had a scratch rehearsal with such orchestral players as could be rounded up on what was supposedly a free morning for them. His conducting of the ballet that night is said to have been flawless. (In those days how many critics could be sure?) This may have been the occasion on which Nijinsky, by nature a humourless young man, uttered his only recorded pleasantry. Listening from the wings he said, "Comme l'orchestre dirige bien Monsieur Beecham çe soir."

Beecham's *Petrushka* gave a yet keener edge to his players' almost possessive pride in him. Already they were boasting to incredulous friends that he conducted *Rosenkavalier*, *Thamar* and Rimsky's *Scheherazade* without a note of music in front of him. Their pride was a necessary therapy. Without it they could hardly have coped with their Drury Lane burdens.

A certain Thursday and Friday were remembered with relish and awe. The whole of Thursday was spent rehearsing and, in the evening, presenting a new opera. Few of the players got to bed before midnight. Next morning they were back in the pit at 8.30 for the full rehearsal of a second novelty. This went on until 11 a.m. The orchestra were then evicted to facilitate the lighting and scenery rehearsal; they carried on in the theatre foyer. At 12.30 p.m. they were carted *en bloc*, music stands, instruments, band parts and all, to the Portman Rooms, Baker Street, where they continued until the time came to return to Drury Lane for the evening performance, starting at 7.45 p.m.

Days such as this called for uncommon musicianship as well as for uncommon stamina. Most of the music they had to play was hard to understand and technically tricky. The 1914 repertory presented the B.S.O. with masses of what then seemed freakish material. Feats of sight reading and assimilation were performed which have never been surpassed.

Whether all of Beecham's novelties were worth assimilating was a moot point even at the time. Consider Holbrooke's *Dylan*. Why Joseph and his son should have spent such money and pains on this work is among the minor puzzles of operatic history. Although they had little else to say in its favour, the critics found the scenic effects magnificent and more distinguished than anything ever before vouchsafed to English opera. The libretto called for flights of singing wildfowl which, when not simulated by plumed choristers, were projected on to a cinematograph screen, a film having been made expressly for the purpose on the Bass Rock. Beecham prepared the score with zeal. An orchestra of Wagnerian size overflowed into the stage boxes, where the percussion players, among others, were housed. At one point he stopped the rehearsal during a deafening *tutti* and said, "Gentlemen in the box! You are making an entirely inadequate din. Kindly play twenty times as loud!"

The lighting plot gave much trouble. A man in dungarees was constantly shouting up to the electricians' bridge, "Black out, 'Arry!" At one vital point the black-out did not occur. This was in a scene where ancient castle walls were supposed to be swept away by a tidal wave.

Beecham rapped the rostrum rail. Stroking his beard, he addressed the producer in his blandest tones. "Mr. Fairbairn", he said, "at the precise moment when your very formidable castle walls, contrary to the laws of gravity, rise into the air to enable vast buckets of rice to be poured on the stage in semblance of deluge and flood, may I suggest that it would be appropriate to have a black-out from our friend 'Arry?"

In backstage circles throughout W.C.2 "Our Friend 'Arry" was thenceforth immortal.

Dylan came and went. It puzzled its composer nearly as much as everybody else. In a curtain speech he expressed surprise that the audience had listened to his opera with so much patience, "seeing that it is so unlike any other opera ever written—especially Russian opera!"

(2)

Of all Chaliapin nights that season the one that made the greatest stir was the complete *Prince Igor*, with the Diaghilev troupe dancing the orgy scene in Act III and Chaliapin doubling Prince Galitsky and Khan Kontchak. At three on the Sunday afternoon preceding the first performance he walked on to the stage and, noting the apparent chaos which prevailed not only there but throughout the theatre, went to Baylis in tearful consternation. The situation was impossible, he said; the première would have to be postponed from Monday to Tuesday. Baylis replied soothingly. "Impossible" was not in Beecham's vocabulary, he said. The production would be ready on schedule.

That week-end was a Baylis masterpiece. On the Saturday night Frieda Hempel and Claire Dux sang in a memorable *Zauberflöte* which ended at 11.30 p.m. Immediately after the last curtain stagehands moved in and worked through the small hours, striking and stowing the *Zauberflöte* sets and bringing in the *Prince Igor* crates. At six they took an hour off for breakfast. Then they set to work on *Igor*. Packed in immensely long boxes, the *Igor* canvases had to be stretched, as required by Russian theatre practice, on frames built to fit at the last moment by the stage carpenters. Some of the canvases bore sketch designs merely. Again in accordance with the Russian technique, they were spread out on such horizontal surfaces as could be commandeered and finished off by painters who worked on all fours.

Amid hurly-burly and backlog, a general rehearsal began mid-afternoon. While one scene was being rehearsed, scenery and props for the next were being knocked together in corridors and other overflow workshops. The noise was uninhibited. The general rehearsal ended at half past two on Monday morning. Spurred by overtime pay, the stagehands swarmed on again. They set up the *Prince Igor* scenes, with the paint still wet on some of them, for a dress rehearsal beginning at 11.30 a.m. This ended seven hours later. The stage staff had seventy-five minutes exactly in which to reverse the sets in the scenery dock, the dress rehearsal having, of course, left them in back-to-front order.

Two hundred men had worked with little respite for seventy-two hours, kept cheerful by good pay and their sense of Baylis's efficiency. They had a facetious backstage language of their own. *Kovantchina* became "Scotch in China", *Daphnis et Chlöe* was "Daffy", *Scheherazade* was "Sherry Zad", *Thamar* (inevitably) "Tommy".

The *Prince Igor* curtain went up on the dot at 7.45. Not a brushstroke, not a Tartar's bowstring was out of place. The performance blew like a scented gale—and with a perfection of detail that suggested leisured weeks of preparation. Beecham, who was in front that night, acknowledged when ageing that never again, in any theatre, was he to hear so jubilant a tumult as the one that followed the scene in the Tartar camp. The last curtain fell at midnight amid spellbound roars. Nobody wanted to go home. The audience, reported *The Times*, would willingly have stayed on into the small hours to hear more.

(3)

The Tsar conferred the Order of St. Stanislaus upon Sir Joseph. The King made him a baronet. And Mr. James White proposed to put £50,000 into his pocket.

Sir Joseph had met White the previous winter while relaxing at the National Sporting Club. His new crony had pink cheeks, piercing blue eyes, thinning hair and what was to be known as a Charlie Chaplin moustache. He talked glibly and softly with an undisguised Rochdale accent. At the age of thirty-seven he could look back on a startlingly mixed career. Starting in his mid 'teens as a bricklayer's labourer, he downed the hod to build houses on his own account at cut prices. In his twentieth year he profitably sold a "twopenny circus" before buying it. This was a model for later operations on a bigger scale. In Matlock he ran a theatre which had unsuspected defects; during an entertainment for the Duke of Devonshire's tenants the floor gave way, throwing most of them into an empty swimming bath beneath. Surviving this setback, as well as a term with the British South Africa Police during the Boer War, he settled in London as a fight promoter. In the autumn of 1911 he announced a contest at Earl's Court between a British champion, Bombardier Wells, and the redoubtable negro heavyweight, Jack Johnson.

Earlier that year, at Reno, U.S.A., Johnson had battered and beaten a white boxer, "the once all-conquering Jeffries", in a spectacle that aroused acute racial feeling and disgust. Clearly Wells was no match for Johnson. The prospect was that Johnson would pulp him. Whatever the outcome of the fight Johnson was to get £6,000, Wells

£2,000. White and his associates stood to net thousands more from a gate-money exhibition in contravention of National Sporting Club rules.

When these things became known hostile clamour arose. There were protests from the Archbishop of Canterbury, Free Church leaders and that revered arbiter of sport Earl Lonsdale. As a result Mr. Winston Churchill, then Home Secretary, intervened. On information laid by the Director of Public Prosecutions, an injunction was granted which banned the contest as tantamount to a breach of the peace.

White had suffered a rebuff from the national conscience. It was the making of him. "Next morning", he used to recall, "I was a ruined man. I had three taxi-cabs full of writs served on me all at once. Everybody wanted their money back. I had spent it. But the publicity brought me to the notice of the millionaires. I went into high finance and never looked back."

As later events, culminating in suicide, were to prove, White was overweening and over-confident. On the subject of the Covent Garden estate Joseph listened to him open-mouthed. The estate was, it appeared, in the market. Covering nineteen acres (explained White) it took in four theatres—the Royal Opera House, the Theatre Royal Drury Lane, the Strand Theatre and the Aldwych; the Covent Garden market; Bow Street police station; twenty-six streets, from the Strand in the south to Long Acre in the north, Aldwych in the east to St. Martin's Lane in the west; and the National Sporting Club premises where the two of them were at that moment seated. Already a Mr. Mallaby-Deeley was in negotiation with the owner of the estate, the Duke of Bedford. White's idea was that he should negotiate on Joseph's behalf with Mallaby-Deeley and, having pinned down that gentleman, complete the deal vis-à-vis the Duke himself.

That, roughly, is how things fell out—on paper, at any rate. The purchase price was agreed at £2,250,000. Joseph paid Mallaby-Deeley and his associates £250,000 at once. The remaining £2,000,000 was to be paid to the Duke in instalments, the entire transaction to be completed by November 11th, 1914. The Duke's first two instalments would amount to £250,000. Joseph had already paid a like sum to Mallaby-Deeley. That meant a total "first stage" outlay of £500,000. Already Joseph had arranged to get this money back and more. Before signing with the Duke, he agreed to sell the benefit of his contract and instalments to a Manchester stockbroker, Alexander Lawson Ormrod, for £550,000. He would thus be £50,000 better off than when he began.

There was no prospective benefit for the tenants; the contrary, in fact. They were to have an opportunity of buying the freeholds outright or of entering into long leases—at the new owner's prices. Altogether, the deal which White propounded to Joseph and in large part negotiated for him, has the look of a naked take-over, an exercise in the art of buying cheap and selling dear without intermediate community service.

Admittedly Joseph's spendings on music were in themselves enough to salve his social conscience. He overflowed with beneficent plans. That his two Drury Lane seasons had cost him dear was an open secret. Yet they were in no sense to be isolated experiments. Dates were already pencilled at Drury Lane for the summer of 1915. Not only that; there was to be an Independent London Opera House, a building that should be a credit to the city, with a stage and appurtenances "especially designed for the presentation of modern operatic works." Joseph did not say in so many words that he was going to build this theatre himself, but it is clear from various indirect references that such was his intention.

His son, too, had plans. After the 1914 season he would rest for a month or so, then take his orchestra to Germany for three weeks, visiting Berlin and other cities. Probably they would go on to St. Petersburg and halt in Paris, on the way back. . . .

An odd thing happened on June 22nd. This was the first night of Strauss's *Josephlegende*. During the afternoon Diaghilev received a telegram from Count Harry von Kessler, joint author with von Hofmannsthal of the scenario. Sending his best wishes for the première, von Kessler regretted he could not be present and mysteriously expressed fear lest Diaghilev's projected autumn season in Germany, which was to parallel that of the Beecham orchestra, might not after all take place. After puzzling for a moment over Kessler's foreboding, Diaghilev tossed the telegram aside, saying, "The dear Count must be ill. Why shouldn't my beautifully planned tour take place, I should like to know?"

The season ended to a clamour of curtain calls. Joseph was half coaxed, half dragged on to the stage where Karsavina had just danced the Ballerina in *Petrushka*. He looked pathetically small and nervous. Somebody handed him a gilded bay wreath. Nobody seemed quite to know whether this came from the dancers or from the galleryites. It was to the galleryites, in any case, that Joseph addressed himself. "Many years ago", he said, "I remember paying a shilling, at a time when shillings were not too plentiful with me, to come into the gallery of this theatre and listen to opera. I cannot tell you how grateful I am to have had the privilege at last of doing something more tangible in the cause of music."

The crowd went home reluctantly, just as after *Prince Igor*. Dust sheets were drawn over plush and gilt. A swarm of singers, dancers, players, sceneshifters, machinists and wardrobe hands dispersed on holiday.

Ten days later Britain was at war. There were some in the Diaghilev troupe who remembered von Kessler's telegram. The Count stood close to Court circles in Berlin. Now all was clear. His intention had been to warn Drury Lane of the Kaiser's war nearly five weeks before it broke out.

BENEVOLENT AUTOCRAT

(1)

SWARMS OF GERMAN musicians disappeared at a stroke from pits and platforms throughout the land. Freed from a notorious incubus, British players felt they had come into their own at last, breathed more freely than for decades—and, in the case of many of the younger among them, promptly threw away everything they had gained. By March 1916 two or three thousand registered orchestral players had enlisted in the Services. The number was soon to be swollen by the call-up of married groups under Lord Derby's voluntary enrolment scheme.

During the early months of the war, a time of daze and dislocation, there seems, nevertheless, to have been much under-employment in the profession. Beecham decided something must be done about this.

In the spring of 1915, while lunching at Pagani's, he saw Landon Ronald enter the restaurant and waved him over. In a public speech at Manchester a few months earlier he had railed derisively at the impotence, as he saw it, of England's music colleges. Landon Ronald happened to be the principal of one of these, the Guildhall School. About this institution Beecham had been especially withering. London's music colleges in general, he had said, were useless institutions. He had the most profound contempt for the lot of them. He wouldn't dream of auditioning any of their singing graduates. He knew perfectly well beforehand that they'd all be bad. The Guildhall School of Music was the worst of all. "A great bazaar", he called it.

It is not surprising to learn from Ronald's memoirs that, in his opinion, Beecham was by nature "inclined to be supercilious and contemptuous." Certainly he had reason, on entering Pagani's, to be aloof and wary. Within a matter of seconds Beecham had charmed him into a state of glowing comradeship. He explained that he needed Ronald's help. Indeed, British music at large needed Ronald's help.

Britain, pursued Beecham, had thousands of orchestral players. What were the majority of them doing? Nothing at all. Of those in employment the bulk were engaged in musical occupations unworthy of their talents. The flower of our instrumentalists were playing in music-halls, "legitimate" theatres, cinemas, cafés, restaurants. The vulgarising effect of such occupations was incalculable. The Government could have obviated this sorry state of affairs by co-operating with the leaders of the profession to direct the activity of our players into more regular and honourable channels. The Government had done nothing of the sort. It was up to resolute individuals to take action! Would Ronald join him in a season of summer Promenade concerts at the Albert Hall? . . .

Ronald accepted with delight; he even agreed to contribute some of the guarantee capital.

Of course there was to be no music of enemy origin. The country was newly in the grip of irrational aversions. On the outbreak of the war Henry Wood's weekly Wagner nights at the Proms had been dropped and replaced by French and Russian programmes lest patriot mobs should break up the proceedings. Musical leaders here and there piped up with cautious reservations. Henry Coward, the choral conductor, suggested that a ban should be imposed but confined to German music written after 1870, the year German aggrandisement began. Under this lunatic proviso Brahms's D minor Piano Concerto would have been impeccable; his B flat major Piano Concerto a thing of the devil.

Beecham for his part drew up a prospectus in Ronald's name as well as his own which asserted that they had long had the joint desire to give a series of concerts from which there should be a complete absence of Teutonic music. Their wish to omit such music was due quite as much to artistic as to "other considerations". A season devoted to non-Germanic music only could be of the highest artistic attraction. Looking back towards the end of his life, Ronald exclaimed, "Imagine programme after programme without one work by Bach, Beethoven, Haydn, Mozart, Mendelssohn, Schumann, Brahms, Wagner! We were asking for trouble—and we got it."

Some of the trouble was unsought. In an Albert Hall not more than a third full, most of the audience having paid sixpence a head, Beecham conducted, as his share of the inaugural programme, music from *Prince Igor*, a *Fire Bird* suite and the *Sigurd Jorsalfar* music of Grieg. Two nights later Zeppelin L.28, commander Hauptmann Linnarz, dropped eighty-nine incendiary bombs and thirty "grenades" on North-East London, killing seven persons and injuring thirty-five. Nervous gloom overtook the town. Next morning Beecham and Ronald tried to convince each other that Prom attendances would not suffer.

"On the contrary", argued Beecham, "the Zeppelins will *drive* people into the Albert Hall not only as a musical resort but also as a shelter from the bombs!"

The public took a different view and stayed away. Ronald lost the money he had staked. Beecham insisted on continuing the season at his own cost but soon had to admit failure and close down. Bombs were not the only deterrent. The prospectus listed a dismaying amount of music by living British composers, not more than four of whom—Elgar, Sullivan, Edward German, and Coleridge-Taylor—had any popular following. (During the early war years the public suffered—or were invited to suffer—a great deal in the cause of chauvinism. A body called the War Emergency Entertainment Committee boasted of producing 200 new British compositions at 200 concerts.)

Beecham still had money to spend. There seemed no limit to his bounty. The London Symphony Orchestra began to founder. He gave their 1915-16 concert series substantial financial backing and kept their overdraft within reasonable limits. (Half-way through this season he became Sir Thomas Beecham. He received his knighthood in the New Year honours of 1916 at the age of thirty-six.)* Earlier he had thrown out a lifeline to the Royal Philharmonic Society. When, in 1914, the Society proposed to put its orchestra on half pay he sent them a cheque; as a result the players continued to get full fees.

One of his concerts for the R.P.S. coincided with a widespread rumour that 80,000 Germans had landed in Kent, armed to the teeth. Clubs, theatre lobbies and restaurants that evening were full of woe-begone faces. Cyril Scott was at the Queen's Hall to hear Beecham conduct his *Two Passacaglias for Orchestra*. He found Beecham completely unperturbed. His was one of the coolest heads in London that night.

Nearly two years later the Royal Philharmonic Society, hard-up again, decided to suspend concertgiving for twelve months. Once more Beecham came to the rescue. He advised the board of the Society to let the 1916-17 season proceed as arranged; he and Baylis would be "finally responsible" for the financial outcome. Not only that; he undertook also to conduct the Society's concerts for five years, with the option of a further five and to raise a guarantee fund of £10,000.

The conditions which Beecham attached to this offer smacked of autocracy. He was to be elected a director and to be chairman of every meeting he attended, while Baylis was to become honorary-secretary. Between them they were to have entire control of the programmes, the

---

* Over forty years were to pass before his name next appeared in a Royal honours list. In the summer of 1957 at Buckingham Palace, he was invested by the Queen with the insignia of the Order of the Companions of Honour.

orchestra and the concert arrangements generally. In short, he proposed to put the Royal Philharmonic Society, once the patron of Beethoven, in his pocket. Being in no position to bargain, the directors unanimously agreed to terms which, as the Society's historian, Robert Elkin, acknowledges, deprived them of control over its affairs.

(2)

From London Beecham turned his benevolent gaze to the provinces. Early in 1917 he decided that Birmingham would benefit by a little stirring up. Descending upon a meeting of influential citizens presided over by the Lord Mayor, he undertook to enrol and train a permanent local orchestra, composed mainly of regional players but led by first-rate musicians from outside, and maintain it for a probationary period of three years. He spoke in a vein of patronising irony.

"In Birmingham", he said—and, reading his words, one can hear the drawl, see the circling motion of the nose tip—"in Birmingham you do not know very much what an orchestra means and what it would cost. An orchestra is something of a bogey to you. It is the simplest thing in the world to have an orchestra and to run it. It entails no great responsibility and little liability; and after you have listened to it a great deal you will find it a very nice thing to have. By the time the orchestra is able to play well you'll be quite proud of it."

It was, he admitted, a pity that Birmingham lacked a good concert hall. Some of his hearers inwardly bridled at the implicit slur upon their famous town hall auditorium, which they regarded as little less than a national sanctuary. Had not Mendelssohn conducted the first English performance of *Elijah* there in '46? "Your town hall", Beecham went on, "has architectural merit; but it is one of the last places in the world anybody would wish to sing or play in. Everything is wrong about it except the outside."

At this sally the citizens chuckled uneasily, as citizens the world over always did for half a century whenever Beecham affronted their susceptibilities. At the end of the meeting they busily set up a committee. The enrolment of players began. Then, for one reason or another, the project staled. In the spring of 1918 Beecham came back to Birmingham and, at a crowded meeting in the University, addressed the influential citizens again, this time as if they were backward children. He said, "A year has gone by since I addressed you on the subject of an orchestra for Birmingham. And of course you have done nothing!" Again the citizens laughed guiltily. Soon afterwards the town hall was requisitioned by the Food Controller. Having, according to Ethel Smyth, spent £2,000 on the project, Beecham postponed it indefinitely. By that time Beecham was nearing the end of his financial tether. Grants for the City of Birmingham Orchestra, founded in 1920, came from the municipality, an organ which Beecham had in the first place implicitly snubbed. "For an enterprise of this kind", he said in his original speech, "the energies and directing influence of one individual are needed rather than those of a collective body such as the city council. . . ."

Manchester, too, came in for its portion. The war had put its blight on the Hallé, as upon most other orchestras. "The public", complained Beecham, "has during the past two years [1914-15 and 1915-16] shown an increasing indifference to the Hallé Concerts Society, for which I am responsible artistically."

From the summer of 1916 onwards he used the Hallé Orchestra for his mammoth opera seasons at the New Queen's Theatre, which will be touched on later. Between the bouts of opera he would return to the theatre and, helped by subaltern conductors, give three weeks or so of promenade concerts, with seating removed from the ground floor and all levels packed with one-and-tuppennies, four-and-threes and the like. (The new entertainment tax had given theatre prices a capricious look.) What with the Proms and the opera season, the Hallé Orchestra played in 1917 for thirty-two weeks continuously, as compared with a maximum of sixteen weeks in normal times.

Again Beecham footed the bills. The Hallé Society gratefully conceded that without his financial help the orchestra could not possibly have survived. One way in which he had helped was in conducting the Hallé Orchestra for nothing. It was added that he paid the full fees of all conductors who appeared at Hallé concerts when, though billed, he was unable to attend.

Such may have been Beecham's general intention. The intention did not always work out in particular cases. I have heard one of Beecham's junior conductors of the period say, "From 1916 onwards Tommy was periodically in financial difficulties. As a result he was often prevented from making personal appearances. It was Baylis who 'did' for him in such situations. (Beecham himself was very aloof.) He would say, 'Sir Thomas would like you to take a concert in such and such a town on such and such a date.' Usually one got precious little notice. Sometimes scores were provided. Sometimes you had to scrabble around for them. In Manchester I conducted several modern suites—*Fire Bird*, *Thamar* and *Sadko*, for example—without rehearsal and, in some cases, without technical study. For such jobs we—myself and other junior conductors, that is—got a small expenses fee only. The reward was prestige."

(3)

Neither then nor at any other time did Beecham regard the symphony orchestra as an end in itself. For him the concert hall was little more than an adjunct to the opera house; a place where one listened to orchestras when they were not more validly engaged.

"It is difficult", he told an interviewer, "to have a vital executive branch of the art when the creative branch is declining all the time. Thirty years ago there was produced almost every month an interesting symphonic work by Brahms, Dvořák, Tchaikovsky, Rimsky-Korsakov, Grieg, Saint-Saëns. . . . For the last five or ten years those who give concerts have had the greatest difficulty in obtaining one interesting new work a year. This points to a gradual exhaustion in that form of music."

The future, then, was not with symphony but with opera. "In the course of a few years", he forecast on another occasion "we shall find that Liverpool, Glasgow, Birmingham and Manchester will each have its opera house in full going order, with opera in the mother tongue." The first three cities on this list, it was gathered, would have to do their own opera-house building. So far as Manchester was concerned, the charge would be upon him. In October 1918, after months of hintings and comings and goings, the Lord Mayor of that city received an electrifying letter. In it Beecham entered into undertakings as follow:

"1. I will build in Manchester an opera house that shall be of size and importance not less than those of any other opera house in London or any Continental towns with the exception of Paris and Petrograd.

"2. I will commence building at the first moment conditions of labour and readjustment in prices of materials make it possible after the conclusion of peace.

"3. When the opera house is built, I will maintain and manage it for a period of ten years.

"4. At the expiry of ten years I will present the building as a gift to the city."

Sir Thomas added that he made the foregoing offer subject to these conditions:

"The City Corporation shall find and provide a site for the opera house of not less than 45,000 square feet.

"Although the building at the end of ten years shall become the absolute property of the city, I reserve to myself during my lifetime the right to appoint in connection with the control and management of the building all those persons that comprise the staff, business and artistic.

"That it shall be for me to draw up a constitution for the future government of the opera house.

"At the expiration of the ten years period, although I am to remain in control during my lifetime, yet all persons connected with the opera house shall be considered as servants of an organisation which shall consist of an association of the city authorities and myself."

The City Council recorded hearty appreciation of the offer, and remitted it to a special committee. Little more was heard of the matter. Seven months later one of Beecham's creditors successfully petitioned for a receiving order which turned Beecham's Manchester opera house and other grand projects into outdated dreams.

For the time being, however, grand opera, as Beecham heard and saw and understood it, was among the prime and germinal realities; a token that, amid the miseries and calamities of war, the collective mind was gradually turning to enduringly serious things. The masses, he declared, were thinking less about the tango and the turkey trot. Even musical comedy and revue (a more formidable mass distraction) were beginning to lose their appeal. The essential things of civilisation, grand opera among them, were taking their true place at last in the scale of social values.

Through what experiences had Beecham acquired these convictions? To answer this question we must glance back at the summer of 1916.

CHAPTER EIGHTEEN

DUCKS AND THE THUNDERSTORM

(1)

No MAN IN the public eye bothered less than Beecham about making his pronouncements square with one another or with his actions. Of all the self-contradictions he committed, none was grander or more fruitful than his founding of the Beecham Opera Company.

In the course of his railings against English musical academies, uttered at the yearly meeting of the Manchester Royal College of Music on December 4th, 1914, he permitted himself the following thought:

"Out of all the singers in England today, I should have the greatest difficulty in getting together a first-rate opera company. . . . In the first place, English singers cannot sing. There is only one I know who can walk on the stage with any grace. The others come on like a duck in a thunderstorm. I know only one of whose singing a word can be heard."

No sooner were the words out of his mouth than he set about disproving them. During a month or so of the following year, without any great difficulty—or any difficulty at all, apparently—he assembled some forty principal singers, trained them (in many cases from scratch) in operatic ways and employed them continuously, often to brilliant effect—and under the crippling circumstances of war—for four and a half years.

Of these forty only five were of foreign blood or extraction. Sixteen had been trained in those very schools, colleges and academies whose singing graduates he had said were not worth listening to. Many of them had never worn grease paint before. Theirs had been a world of starched fronts, white gloves, dress coats, *Messiah*, *Hiawatha* and *Elijah*. They were called on to shed what Beecham called the baleful inhibitions of cantata and oratorio. "Once the English singer is put into opera", he jested, "he becomes an ordinary human being like everybody else."

The company's first season, cautiously announced as by Messrs. Thomas Beecham and Robert Courtneidge (Courtneidge acting as producer,) began at the Shaftesbury Theatre on October 2nd, 1915

It lasted for ten weeks instead of the six originally planned and took in seventy-six performances of Gounod's *Romeo and Juliet* (chosen for the opening night), *Butterfly*, *Hoffmann*, *Bohème*, *Faust*, *Tosca*, *Figaro*, *Magic Flute*, *Carmen*, *Cavalleria Rusticana* and *Pagliacci*. There was a shilling gallery, and the performances were in English. Although London was under dim-out because of the Zeppelin raids, the theatre was packed night after night. The audience was increasingly dotted with soldiers on leave from Flanders or the training camps. *Bohème* and *Butterfly* nights brought in groups of girl clerks from the vast Government offices of the neighbourhood, where some of them were putting in a twelve-hour day.

Business continued thus during the following year, which brought almost non-stop seasons, first at the Shaftesbury, then at the Aldwych Theatre. Taking into account a five weeks' foray to the New Queen's Theatre, Manchester, during the spring, Beecham and five assistant conductors had by the end of 1916 conducted some 350 performances. To the original repertory were added, among other works, Puccini's *Manon Lescaut*, *Trovatore*, Stanford's *The Critic* (after Sheridan), *The Boatswain's Mate* by Ethel Smyth, Verdi's *Otello*, *Tristan* (which instantly became a hit), *The Seraglio*, *Samson and Delilah*, *Aïda*, Charpentier's *Louise* and Beecham's own stage adaptation of Bach's *Phoebus and Pan* cantata.

Such were the bare bones of a creative achievement which was—and is—without parallel in English opera or opera in English. To the bones let us add the flesh of atmosphere and incident.

(2)

The Shaftesbury and the Aldwych were small theatres; much too small for grand opera. Until the Theatre Royal Drury Lane became available in 1917, Beecham had to make the best of cramped, rowdy quarters. At both theatres it was necessary to lift out a row or two of stalls to admit an orchestra of forty or fifty which, initially, was a scratch affair, a wartime round-up from the L.S.O., the former Beecham Symphony Orchestra and the former Royal Opera orchestra. Hitting off the right sound balance as between stage and pit was tricky at best. Sometimes the conductors threw up their hands in despair.

In the *Aïda* triumph scene the chorus men ("none eligible for military service", it was patriotically claimed—which suggested a high proportion of crocks and elders) were regularly smothered by Beecham's highly trained and extrovert stage trumpeters. Parts of *Tristan* were a confused tumult. Even after the transfer to Drury Lane, Arnold Bennett complained of "horrible competition between the band and the singers" in Act I. On Puccinian climaxes Manon and Des Grieux (*Manon Lescaut*) were seen to open their mouths, but little could be heard; the vocal line was lost beneath the orchestral wave. Sometimes imbalance was the other way round. Of a *Samson and Delilah*, *The Times* reported that the singers seemed to forget that the Aldwych wasn't Covent Garden. The High Priest, indeed, seemed to think he was at the Albert Hall.

Beecham marshalled around him a dozen aides. At the head of them of course, was Donald Baylis, now a degree more lean, lined and sallow. The war brought him problems of a new order. Having waved off six truck-loads of scenery and eighty skips of costumes for a season at Birmingham, he belatedly learned that the theatre there was without stage staff. Seventeen labourers were hired from the local employment exchange. None of them had worked in a theatre before. They were rapidly licked into some sort of efficiency by the intent, all-knowing stage-manager, George King.

King's knowledge of the technical niceties was unrivalled. He had learned his scores as a chorus man and small-part singer with touring opera companies. No finger was cooler on the control button. In Manchester a tenor of genius drank much whisky before and during *Samson and Delilah*. As blind Samson, he made a tottering entry in the last scene, supported rather than led by the usual small boy. He rose splendidly to his top B and wouldn't come off it. King was watching like a lynx. With impeccable timing he blacked out and brought the curtain down. Half a second later the tenor made a grab at the temple pillars, which he was supposed to pull down. Missing them, he fell on his face. King's intuition had saved the show.

He first worked for Beecham, as assistant stage director, during the 1910 *comique* season at His Majesty's. At times of backstage tension he treated him as an equal, sometimes as a rather imperfect equal. During a *Parsifal* performance, with some other conductor on the rostrum, Beecham who, as occasionally happened, was prowling the theatre for no particular reason, came up through the pass door and into the wings. The Knights of the Grail had assembled and were awaiting the cue for their offstage chorus before solemnly filing on. The moment was crucial. King whipped round and said, "Will you please go, Sir Thomas?" Good-humouredly Beecham tiptoed away with exaggerated precaution. On a later occasion Beecham, by prearrangement with the orchestra only, began *Prince Igor* without the overture.

The curtain rose on a crowd of soldiers and boyars in startled disarray. King was the only person who reproved Beecham for his caprice—or mischievousness. He said to him, "Well, Sir Thomas you might have warned us. It's we who have to run the stage, not you."

First among the subordinate conductors was Percy Pitt, at this time in his middle forties, a bland, adroit ball of a man. Beecham's publicity, which had moments of unusual candour, said that both at the Shaftesbury and the Aldwych, Pitt's knowledge, judgment and experience had more than once saved an awkward situation "and prevented the audience from suspecting the imminence of any hitch in the performance." Julius Harrison, composer-conductor, graduated to Beecham from Covent Garden, where he had conducted two *Lohengrins* and, with a young man called Adrian Boult, used to play the Montserrat bells backstage in *Parsifal*. Before that he had memorised innumerable scores while correcting in red ink faulty punch holes on player-piano rolls at two pounds ten a week.

It is typical of the happy-go-lucky yet strenuous circumstances of the times that Harrison was privileged to double conducting and other duties for Beecham with a lieutenancy in the Royal Flying Corps. He was often seen on the rostrum in khaki. Baylis, too, served in the R.F.C. on a tacitly part-time basis. It was common talk that both he and Harrison had been awarded their commissions and conveniently posted to the R.F.C. depot in Regent's Park as a result of Whitehall string-pulling by Beecham.

What of Beecham's own vulnerability to call-up? In November 1916 an honourable and gallant Tory M.P. asked in the House whether, since Sir Thomas Beecham was of military age, Members could be informed what tribunal had exempted him from military service. A Government spokesman replied cryptically that inquiries were being made. In their unaccountable way, the Commons, or some of them, laughed at this. Nothing more was heard of the matter.

Another composer-conductor on the strength was Eugene Goossens. At a Wartime Emergency concert Goossens left his desk in the second fiddles of the Queen's Hall Orchestra to conduct a Symphonic Prelude of his own composing. Having conducted, he took up his fiddle again. Beecham was in the audience that night. At the end he sent round a message. Would Goossens see him at Cavendish Square next morning? Receiving the young man (Goossens was only twenty-two) in mauve silk dressing-gown and pink pyjamas, he explained that he was to have conducted *The Critic* and *The Boatswain's Mate* at the Shaftesbury but that, feeling tired, he had decided to go to Italy for a holiday instead. (Actually the "holiday" was a wartime cultural mission, on behalf of the Government, to Rome, where he conducted two orchestral concerts at the Augusteo. At the first concert, during Delius's *Paris*, he stopped conducting and stalked off the rostrum because the audience were inattentive.) Would Goossens take over for him? Goossens jumped at the chance. Sitting up until three the following morning he mastered enough of Stanford's score to take a first rehearsal at 10 a.m. He had finished with orchestral playing for good.

During the next four or five years Goossens conducted sixty or seventy operas, mostly for Beecham—forty or more of them without orchestral rehearsal. At the Shaftesbury, the Aldwych and Drury Lane theatres conditions were excitingly precarious. Disaster was invited but never supervened. Goossens once told the writer:

"There was no prompt box in front and no prompt in the wings. If a slip had occurred King would have put in a word. He knew his scores backwards. But slips didn't happen. It never occurred to anybody that a singer could go on the stage and forget his words or music. There's no such confidence nowadays." The period was one of scurry and improvisation. For Beecham's big Manchester season in the spring of 1916 the chorus were put on the train without proper rehearsal for the opening piece, *Boris Godounov*. "The tenors and basses", wrote Goossens, "actually rehearsed in a large 'saloon' car *en route* from London . . ., much to the astonishment of the passengers and crowds on the platforms at Rugby, Stafford and Crewe."

(3)

In an earlier chapter reference is made to the odd or freakish talents within Beecham's orbit. Thomas Chapman was more out of the ordinary than even James Whewall, the clairvoyant chorus master from Hanley.

A big-boned man with a hooked nose, tousled head and greying, evangelical beard, Chapman joined Beecham as a repetiteur at His Majesty's in 1910 and stayed with him until after the war. At the rehearsal piano he was omniscient, responding with somnolent promptitude to any and every demand made upon a memory which must have been the equal of Beecham's. These talents made him, after his fashion, indispensable. But there was also an eccentric squalor and humility about the man that invited patronage and perhaps a little contempt.

All the year round, August and January alike, indoors as well as out, he wore an enormous black greatcoat down to his heels, its pockets stuffed with half-eaten sandwiches, newspapers, unopened pay packets —he is said to have carried anything up to £150 around with him habitually—and a couple of vocal scores, say *Figaro* on one side, *Butterfly* on the other. Underneath the greatcoat was a suit which, in the phrase of one who worked with him, looked slept in and a century old. He had a watch that was fantastically fast and called for esoteric calculations; as likely as not, 2.20 a.m. meant 9.13 the previous night.

Where did Chapman live? Nobody knew for certain. There were rumours of a one-room lodging at Earl's Court: a big room with a gas-cooker and stacked newspapers bristling with date tabs which enabled him to turn up opera notices for years back. Most mornings he arrived late at rehearsal.

"Chapman", Beecham would accuse, "you are late again."

Puffing and blowing, Chapman would mop his brow and neck with a grimy handkerchief and say he was sorry, sit down at the rehearsal piano, set up a vocal score and address himself to what, as he understood it, was the business of the day. Then:

"What on earth is that you're playing, Chapman?"

"*Tannhäuser*, Sir Thomas."

"But it's *Tristan* I want."

Without hesitation or flurry—and also without score—he would start on *Tristan* at any point indicated. Presently his head would nod. It is claimed by more than one old Beecham singer that "Tommy" Chapman could play while dozing and that he awoke only when asked to repeat a passage or when he played a wrong note. Wearing some sort of rumpled dress suit he used to sit in the orchestra pit at the Aldwych and sleep unsnoringly through the first third of *The Magic Flute* and recover consciousness, without having to be nudged, exactly in time to play Papageno's "magic bells" on the celesta.

There was a night when Beecham, on giving the celesta cue, saw that Chapman was not in his place. Handing the baton to his leader, Wynn Reeves, he wriggled quickly to the celesta and filled in the part himself. Chapman had a cubbyhole under the Aldwych rafters. Falling asleep there instead of in the pit, he had remained dead to Papageno and the world. This is the only lapse recorded against him.

All who remember Chapman agree on his unique skill and application as a coach. If a singer had days instead of weeks to master a new part, Chapman could be depended on to get him safely over the technical hurdles and give him confidence on the night. With obscure, invaluable drudgery of this kind he was well content. Julius Harrison found a phrase that placed him perfectly. He was one of the "patient oxen of music".

(4)

There were others in the Beecham circle of gayer and more assertive temperament. Some of them we have met already.

Ethel Smyth conducted the first night of *The Boatswain's Mate*, which Goossens had prepared, and took an additional rehearsal at the last minute with blouse sleeves rolled up above the elbow, "so that the gentlemen of the orchestra can see the beat plainly"—not always an advantage, murmured her enemies, when the erratic Ethel was on the rostrum. One imagines *The Mate* to have been hearty but lowering entertainment. Based on a W. W. Jacobs' story, it had villagers who played banjos and mouth organs, a policeman who searched for a non-existent corpse to orchestral "quotes" of the Fate theme in Beethoven's Fifth Symphony, and a pub, The Beehive, which, at the Shaftesbury, was built on a daisy-dotted mound so high that most of the action took place half-way up the proscenium arch.

Miss Smyth's handling of the *première* was thought by some in the company to have been inept. Miss Smyth thought she had been splendid and was cock-a-hoop about everything. How great a man was Beecham! "I fancy he may tread other paths later on," she wrote. "It would not surprise me in the least if he were to die Astronomer Royal, Prime Minister, or even the Archbishop of Canterbury."

On a *Seraglio* night, with provocative scenery by a young Beecham protégé, Adrian Allinson, whose foible was to make trees look like snakes, Arnold Bennett sourly noted a number of "too well-dressed women holding court in their boxes."

The most regular court-holder, and perhaps the most conspicuous one, was Maud Cunard, to whom the war had brought new occasions for bustling and ordering about. She had Beecham conduct two *Manfred* matinées (words by Byron, music by Schumann), the first for the Duchess of Marlborough's "children's jewels fund", the second for Lady Islington's day nursery in Bethnal Green. She prevailed on Lord Derby to speak at a matinée for munition workers' comforts at which a hotch-potch of single acts from *Carmen*, *Butterfly* and *Romeo and Juliet* was offered.

Her great night of glory, however, was a *Seraglio* conducted by

Beecham and paid for by his father in aid of the six small children of Enrique Granados, the Spanish composer, who, with his wife, was drowned when the liner in which they were coming home from America was torpedoed by a German submarine. The box fronts were draped with Spanish shawls, and the programme sellers were girls of high degree in Spanish costumes. An equally picturesque audience, who included the Grand Duke Michael of Russia and a string of ambassadors and cabinet ministers, took such a time getting to their seats that the performance began twenty minutes late.

There is an amusingly etched picture of a wartime luncheon party at Lady Cunard's in Goossens's *Overture and Beginners*. Among the guests at Carlton House Terrace were A. J. Balfour (later Earl Balfour), "Eddie" Marsh (Sir Edward Marsh, as he was to become), private secretary to Winston Churchill, and Frederick Delius, who had fled to England when his home at Grez-sur-Loing was threatened by the advancing German armies. The querulous voice of Delius, which always dominated a general conversation, was heard inquiring why the British showed such abysmal ignorance of opera as compared with other European peoples. "Don't talk like that", advised Beecham. "Just you wait till we produce *A Village Romeo*. That will disprove what you say!"

"Bah!" retorted Delius. "The public here doesn't know a note of my music and cares less."

"Perhaps", put in Marsh, "that's because they don't like it."

"Don't like it, don't like it?" spluttered Delius. "Tell me what they *do* like!"

There was a moment of constrained or amused silence. Lady Cunard used it adroitly. "Dear Mr. Balfour", she put in, "*do* tell us how the Lloyd George coalition is working."

An awkward conversational corner was safely turned.

(5)

The Treasury's wartime restrictions on capital issues increasingly bedevilled the Covent Garden estate deal. Committed to paying vast and unobtainable sums which in peacetime he could have raised without difficulty, Sir Joseph Beecham worried, took sleeping pills, was often feverish and fatigued. Although he did not know it, his heart was extensively diseased.

In the Aldwych Theatre offices, which were his London headquarters, he and Thomas had repeated ways-and-means conferences with the ebullient James White, who played an expanding role in the

Beecham fortunes. White having obtained conditional promises of fresh financial backing, Joseph's lawyers were enabled to draft a "standstill" whereby all parties involved would agree to postpone completion of the Covent Garden transfer until after the war.

On Sunday October 22nd, 1916, Joseph paid one of his familial calls at Hamilton Terrace, where his wife and Utica and the children were living. As usual, Utica and the boys motored back with him to Hampstead. In the music room he played the organ. Eleven-year-old Adrian sat by him on the organ bench. He put a hand on his grandson's shoulder and said, "This little boy is going to be a great musician one day." (A musical setting by Adrian Welles Beecham* of Shakespeare's *The Merchant of Venice* was presented by Utica and Sir Frank Benson at the Duke of York's Theatre on November 22nd, 1922.) Before Utica left West Brow, Joseph said, "Get yourself a new dress. You are coming with me to *Samson and Delilah* at the Aldwych tomorrow night."

At lunchtime the following day a woman telephoned Hamilton Terrace and spoke so agitatedly that Utica did not gather her name. "I've just heard from Martin's Bank that Sir Joseph has died", said the voice. Utica could not take in the news at first. "What are you talking about?" she protested. "I'm going to the opera with him tonight."

Joseph had been found dead by his butler at breakfast time. That morning he and others were to have signed the Covent Garden "standstill". The funeral service was in St. Helens parish church, with music by Widor, Mendelssohn (an operatic contralto sang *O rest in the Lord*), Beethoven, Sullivan and Spohr. There were wreaths from opera singers, the opera chorus, stagehands, Lady Cunard, the Lancashire United Tramways and many more.

Joseph's death turned the Covent Garden affair, already complex enough into a fearsome maze. Actions and counter-actions multiplied. Five K.C.s and seven junior counsel went into Chancery Division, not to have these processes settled, which appeared hopeless, but merely sorted out and "consolidated". As a result an order was made for the administration of Joseph's real and personal estate. His art collection was stripped from West Brow and put up at Christie's. The Turner drawings alone fetched 23,330 guineas. The total for two days was £97,067.

Directly or indirectly, this infusion of cash had immediate bearing

* Now Sir Adrian Beecham, having succeeded to the baronetcy.

on the opera company's wellbeing. New productions were as lavish as war-time labour shortages would permit. Some of them, indeed, were lavish by any standard.

At Drury Lane an exultant gag circulated. "Baylis", it was said, "is nailing up new scenery with gold tin tacks."

CHAPTER NINETEEN

"AN AIR RAID IS ABOUT TO TAKE PLACE"

(1)

Along with the gold tin tacks went touches of callow experimentalism. Archie Camden, the bassoonist, remembers a symptomatic morning in Manchester. Beecham came down to the theatre for rehearsal and found scenery for a new production on the stage. Beecham stared at the scenery, and the company stared, apprehensively, at Beecham. The frown and the dilating eyes promised an explosion. Instead of exploding he put on his drawl.

"What's all this?" he asked King.

"It's the new scenery you ordered, Sir Thomas."

"Take it away."

"What shall I do with it?"

"Throw it in the Ship Canal."

The most innovatory designs were Allinson's for *Tristan and Isolde*. The curtain went up on a ship with salmon coloured spars which was on the point of being overwhelmed by gigantic waves in chocolate and plum mosaic, with foam like sugar icing on a cake. This and other effects of Allinson's made audiences gasp. After the first *Tristan* run the offending backcloth was replaced by a sea in assertive green. But Wagner's music was the thing, not its visual trimmings. With Rosina Buckman and Frank Mullings in the name parts *Tristan* always packed the Aldwych and became, indeed, a Saturday matinée attraction. Scores of letters came from soldiers at the front, after the initial performances, asking that it should be retained in the repertory. The animus against Teutonic music had gone. Beecham added *Tannhäuser* and *The Valkyrie* to his bills with impunity.

Mozart was closer to his heart, however. *The Magic Flute* occurred early in his wartime repertory. Beecham turned the spoken dialogues into sung recitatives, *secco* style, with offstage accompaniment by a small string band. "The trouble with English singers", he explained, "is that they don't know how to speak on the stage."

Either his singers' diction improved or he decided that his *secco* interpolations were musically ineffective. Not only did he use spoken dialogues in his next Mozart production, *The Seraglio*; he also had them garnished with topical gags on the lines of Christmas pantomime.

Wartime houses giggled at anachronistic references to meatless days, medical boards, sugar rationing and "Wait and see", a phrase jeeringly attributed by his critics to Mr. Asquith as Prime Minister. For *Figaro*, which came on at Drury Lane in the summer of 1917, he chose his cast as much for appearance and acting ability as for singing talent. Over a period of five months, he sent them on free days to a noted "legitimate" producer, Nigel Playfair, for diction lessons. Frederick Ranalow (Figaro), Miriam Licette (the Countess), Désirée Ellinger (Susanna), Frederick Austin (Almaviva) and Bessie Tyas (Cherubino) were gifted and, by this time, fairly seasoned artists. Again in reversal of his *Flute* policy and of Mozart's express intentions, he had them speak instead of sing all the *secco* recitatives, a procedure which would be found unpalatable in any English opera house today.

In Beechamite circles there were infatuated exclaimings over the sets and costumes. These were designed by Hugo Rumbold, a talented, stammering dandy who lived in one of the great houses on Piccadilly. In theatre lofts, among paint cans and turpentine bottles, he perched on stepladders, retouching his flats with happy absorption. He never wore a smock. His immaculate suits were three-guinea misfits or rejects which he bought from a Covent Garden dealer and had re-tailored for next to nothing. After the production's first, heady impact, people began to wonder whether Rumbold's designs were not, per-haps, on the exuberant side. It was complained that one half of the Countess's boudoir was exquisitely of its declared period, 1789, but the other half too much like a cover from *Vogue*, and that the ladies' hooped skirts were unhistorically cumbersome, the one worn by Miss Licette outvying anything in the wardrobes of Queen Elizabeth or a Velazquez Infanta. During a *Figaro* interval Bennett met Bernard Shaw. Shaw grumbled about the performance. Nor was he the only grumbler. For Beecham's touch seems to have been widely variable.

Ethel Smyth, who had been enraptured by one of his *Figaro* per-formances, fled from a second at the first interval because his new whim was to take the music at such a pace that "the singers, unable to act, sing or enunciate could only bubble and squeak." According to her *Beecham and Pharaoh*, she later took Beecham to task for this. He explained that his development had been unequal and that he occasionally thirsted to experimentalise. He added, however:

"What with this heavy responsibility and that insoluble difficulty and the perpetual inrush of one thing on top of another, I was often in such a state of exasperation that I neither knew nor cared what I was doing. As for Mozart, ... don't you know how, when you are in that state, if the porter or the postman or some quite neutral person comes in, you can be quite civil and self-controlled. But if somebody you are fond of pokes a head round your door, you'd like to murder that person! Thus with Mozart. In such cases my feeling would as likely as not be 'Damn and thrice damn Mozart.'"

(2)

Then the Russian repertory.

Remembering Chaliapin and the great seasons of 1913 and 1914, Beecham had the original sets and costumes of *Boris Godounov* exhumed at Drury Lane and remounted in Manchester. There and elsewhere the revived opera was first sung in French, because the only available Boris, Auguste Bouilliez, a Belgian artist, knew it in no other language. On the first night in Manchester, Ernest Newman heard a woman on the row behind him complain at the end of the second act that the only word she had understood was "toujours". Yet the enthusiasm was enormous. *Boris*, wrote Newman, was going to be the most popular opera in England. Its conquest of the British public, despite the handicap of a foreign tongue, had been "immediate and absolute." Presently *Boris* was Englished. Robert Radford and Robert Parker alternated in the name part before hushed, over-flowing houses. Neither was a Chaliapin, but that did not seem to matter greatly; people came to hear Moussorgsky rather than his interpreters.

After *Boris* translated versions were produced of three other Russian operas which had been heard at Drury Lane before the war: *Ivan the Terrible*, *Khovantchina* and *Le Coq d'Or*, the latter no longer danced, as under Diaghilev, but sung and acted as its authors intended. A little inconsistently, Beecham entrusted the *Coq* production to an eminent ballerina, who concentrated on the processions and incidental dancing and let the principals and chorus take care of themselves. The outcome was appalling inco-ordination.

After a chaotic morning of rehearsal, Baylis and Percy Pitt, the conductor, prevailed upon Beecham to take over the stage management himself. On the very day of the performance, at half past ten in the morning, a new start was made. With piano accompaniment, the whole company toiled steadily until two o'clock. After a half-hour break for sandwiches, work was resumed. It continued until six. Seven hours' emergency rehearsal instead of seven hours' rest sometimes works as a first-night tonic. The curtain went up at 8 p.m. on one of the smoothest and gayest premières in the company's history.

A fourth Russian opera was prepared by Beecham, *A Life for the Tsar*. Lady Cunard found him an artist who had seen Glinka's opera produced in what was soon to be known as Petrograd. Rehearsals began at the Aldwych. Advance snippets appeared in the newspapers. Beecham conducted excerpts from the score with his opera chorus and three of his principals at a Royal Philharmonic Society concert in December 1916. A few months later revolutionary ferment overspread Russia. Far from wanting to lay down their lives for their Tsar, the Russian people, or most of them, concurred when Nicholas II was dethroned and did not intervene when his ministers had him arrested. A corresponding coolness to the Romanov dynasty was felt in Allied countries. Whether for this reason (as some alleged) or (as he claimed) because of material shortages, Beecham dropped Glinka. In the King's Bench Division he contested the scenic artist's bill. Losing the case, he was required to pay the plaintiff an extra £100.

(3)

In anybody of less steely constitution, the ceaseless grind and ramifying of musical and business affairs would have induced alcoholism or nervous collapse. Beecham flourished under multiple stresses. After an early session at the Beecham estate office in the Strand, he would drive to rehearsal in a motor-car fuelled, because of the petrol shortage, from a gasbag on the roof. He exuberantly demanded ever greater avalanches of sound. Halting a *Faust* rehearsal in Manchester, he inquired of the bass trombone.

"Mr. Hoyland, are you producing as much sound as possible from the quaint and antique drainage system which you are applying to your face?"

"I am playing it as loud as I can," replied Hoyland.

"Well, then", rejoined Beecham with a large gesture, "roll it about on the floor!"

When it came to more delicate sound fabrics he was equally intent and demanding. At Birmingham one night intruding latecomers caused a disturbance while the strings were playing their exquisite *pianissimo* music in the *Aïda* overture. Stopping the music, he ordered the doors leading to the stalls to be closed and kept closed until the end of the act.

Often at the Aldwych he rounded off rehearsals by giving auditions. A tenor would sing the "Flower Song" from *Carmen* or Tamino's first aria from *The Flute*. If satisfied Beecham would murmur, "A very good voice. You should have an excellent career. Thank you, Mr. So-and-So." Then he would vanish, leaving Mr. So-and-So in a state of excitement and uncertainty. On such occasions Baylis emerged from the shadows with a contract form in his hand, saying, "Now Mr. So-and-So, we must give you some work." The salary range was erratic. There were conductors at £750 a year. During the tentative seasons at the Shaftesbury in 1915-16 a leading tenor was taken on at five pounds a week. It is said, on the other hand, that Frank Mullings at the height of his celebrity got sixty guineas for a single Tristan and forty guineas for a brief comic role, that of Midas in *Phoebus and Pan*. (I must add that Mullings's noblest achievement, one that is stamped for ever on the memory of a privileged generation, was not Tristan, however, but a Verdi role, that of Otello.)

Once the company was well launched, Beecham played fast and loose with his own billings. Singers were never quite sure until actually on the stage who was going to conduct on any given night. There was, for example, a Saturday at the Aldwych when, having conducted *Faust* in the afternoon, he decided to replace Pitt, who was to have conducted *Aïda* in the evening. At times he was in the grip of a daemon. The need to saturate himself in iridescent sound was imperious; it could keep him at the rostrum from morning until near midnight. In other moods he would hand over the baton to some subordinate an hour or two before a performance for which he was announced and, as likely as not, take a couple of off-duty singers to the Waldorf or the Savoy for a drink. Talk was one of his great relaxations. Some of his pronouncements left his hearers puzzled and questioning. Did Tommy always intend to be taken seriously? Holding forth about Gounod's *Romeo and Juliet* to Julius Harrison and Baylis, among others, he said, "I have, as you possibly know, sufficiently sensuous a nature to think that the spirit of Shakespeare is greatly enhanced by music such as this." Without elucidating the point, he once told his assembled company that, generally speaking, they were deficient in a sense of Original Sin. Revered operas for which he had no personal taste were amusingly castigated both in talk and in print. When told what a pity it was that he had missed a student performance of *Dido and Aeneas* he dismissed the handiwork of Purcell and Nahum Tate as

". . . . something which may be played by a gifted company of musical amateurs or mellow professional singers for their own amusement. It is absolutely the last thing in the world to give a company of unsophisticated students. One does not engage as leader-writer on a paper a man who is able to write only in the style of Chaucer. The manager of a concert society would never dream of engaging a pianist to play, say the Grieg Concerto, who had spent his time practising on the spinet. How, then, in the name of goodness, can anyone expect a singer to be engaged for any opera written during the last fifty or hundred years who has been brought up exclusively on such toast-and-water musical fare as *Dido and Aeneas*?"

Purcell's score had, he allowed, undeniable beauties of a kind but was "absolutely acrhaic in feeling and has as much to do with practical operatic work, classical or modern, as the games played in Noah's Ark or the exhibition of virtuosity given by old Jubal in his patriarchal domestic circle have to do with performances of *The Ring* at Bayreuth or a cycle of opera at Covent Garden or Drury Lane."

Another theme was the crowded and fervent support for opera which had sprung up in the provinces. He took his company for fortnights or months—or even longer—to Sheffield, Leeds, Bradford, Manchester, Birmingham, Glasgow, Edinburgh. Everywhere the rule was cordial pandemonium and Beecham-worship after final curtains. In Manchester not only the *Carmens* and the *Bohèmes* but such rarities or novelties as Bizet's *Fair Maid of Perth*, Verdi's *Falstaff* and Puccini's *Girl of the Golden West* played to capacity, or near it, in a house that seated over 3,000. In seven weeks early in 1918, according to Baylis, the company played to aggregate houses of 99,761—far more, exulted Beecham, than attendances during the same period at the Manchester art gallery. He talked seriously of making Manchester his operatic headquarters. Enthusiasm there was always on the boil. In London he had to stoke it up anew before each season.

There was a factor which he either overlooked or was prevented from mentioning by the current censorship. London was wincing under a terror that reduced not only operagoing but all other forms of public entertainment: the Gotha raids.

(4)

To an inured generation the bombings of the first World War seem a small matter. In thirty Zeppelin or aeroplane raids on London, 670 persons were killed, 1,962 wounded. To those under its immediate shadow the affliction was real enough.

The first raid on London's theatre district occurred on an October night in 1915. In *Faust* at the Shaftesbury, Robert Radford was singing Mephistopheles not in red, according to English tradition, but, after Maurel's fashion, in black. During the first act Zeppelin L. 15 hung over the roof of the Waldorf Hotel, coned in searchlights, a pretty spectacle against the stars. She dropped nineteen bombs, many of them on Joseph's nineteen acres. One of them made a crater outside a theatre of his, the Strand. There were 127 casualties in central London, including thirty-two killed. The Shaftesbury went unscathed. But the attendance at *Romeo and Juliet* the following night was poor. Lulls followed. Business revived. It was the Drury Lane seasons of 1917 and 1918 that bore the brunt.

First by day, then by night, the city was bombarded by the Kaiser's "giant" Gotha planes. As many as 300,000 a night sheltered in Tube stations. But there were more distinguished retreats. One of them was the cellars of Wimborne House. Lady Cunard arrived there with Lady Randolph Churchill during a night raid in October 1917. Both, wrote Lady Diana Cooper to her husband, were a little tipsy and talked wildly: "They had been walking and had got scared and stopped for a drink. Maud had a set purpose to go to the opera because, is being raid night, the public required example. She really, I expect, wanted to die with Thomas Beecham if [Drury Lane] was to be hit. So we let her out at ten."

Mobile anti-aircraft guns parked near the theatre during a *Pagliacci*. Their fire made counter rhythms to the bass drum beats which herald the strolling players' entry. Shrapnel rattled on the stage roof. Baylis urged the singers to carry on. They needed no urging. Blanche Marchesi, who had sung for Beecham on the Kelson Trueman tour fifteen years earlier, considered their heroism rash and the management's attitude cruel. Theatres were on a telephone warning circuit. The threat of sudden death was met with professional courtesy. During a *Tristan und Isolde*, with Mullings, Rosina Buckman (name parts) and Edna Thornton (Brangaene) on the stage, James Elliott, the assistant stage manager, suddenly appeared among them in dress clothes. Advancing to the footlights with upraised hand, he said to the audience, "We have just been informed that enemy aeroplanes have crossed the coast and that an air raid is about to take place. I would like to tell you that the walls of this theatre are seven feet thick, but I don't think it's too good for you in the upper and grand circles I suggest you all come down into the stalls."

Even with the entire audience assembled there, the stalls were only half full. The raids were killing business. So Baylis resorted to "papering" tactics. He gave free passes to all R.F.C. officers at the Regent's Park depot, among others. Beecham was losing £500 to £1,000 a week. In expectation of an ultimate yield from his father's hampered estate, he was obliged to run his company on borrowed money at swingeing interest rates. From this stage on, failure was inevitable.

CHAPTER TWENTY

DÉBACLE—AND DELIVERANCE

(1)

With the return of peace the masses, or most of them, turned away from those higher values to which Beecham had thought them permanently converted. Frivolous distractions were on the upgrade Opera declined in favour. His 1919-20 seasons were the last flare-up of a candle which, even before burning down, guttered capriciously.

There was a brief reconciliation with the Grand Opera Syndicate. Beecham now called himself the Sir Thomas Beecham Opera Company Limited. Jointly with the Syndicate he put on two international seasons, the first from May to August 1919, the second from May to July 1920. Both were pale, confused echoes of pre-1914. A score or so homebred singers from Beecham's own company mingled with the Melbas, Destinnovas, Edvinas, Annseaus, Dinh Gillys and Martin-ellis. Out of nearly forty productions Beecham conducted only nine —*La Bohème*, *Roméo et Juliette*, *Tosca*, Gluck's *Orfeo*, Verdi's *Un Ballo in Maschera*, Bizet's *Pêcheurs de Pêrles*, Massenet's *Manon* and *Thaïs*; and *Naïl*, by the London-born Isidore de Lara.

Defined by Beecham as a simple, kindly and manly fellow who, almost to the end of his life, boxed and bicycled daily, de Lara composed nine operas, all as transient as snowflakes. *Naïl* concerned life in the desert, complicated by daggers, poison, jealousy and nautch girls. When *The Times* found the music fluently platitudinous, nobody demurred. "*Naïl*", said Julius Harrison, "is the last nail in the coffin of English opera." Beecham rehearsed and produced it at exhausting pressure in nine days. During that time Charles Ricketts, the designer, had to get the scenery and two hundred dresses finished. "Everybody else", he complained, "had gone to sleep." The final rehearsal was still going on at 6 p.m., two hours before the performance was due to begin. Non-singing supers threatened to strike over a costume change in the last act. Forty dresses went astray. Sunsets occurred in the middle of the night; there were insanely quick dawns; limes played on unmarked spots. Some observers ascribed these and other mishaps to backstage "Bolshevism". No, said Ricketts: it was merely fatigue and temperament run riot. He added that the managerial staffs deserved no mercy. They couldn't even sweep a crossing properly.

Obviously the situation was one that called for the Baylis touch. But during the 1919 season Baylis was laid low by laryngeal tuberculosis. A week after the 1920 season opened he died.

Between the international seasons of 1920 and 1921, Beecham's English company wintered at Covent Garden. From November to December 1919, and again from February to April 1920, they sang 103 performances of twenty-six operas, adding to their repertory, the despised *Naïl*, *Susanna's Secret* (Wolf-Ferrari), *Meistersinger*, *Djalimeh* (Bizet) and a revival of Delius's *Village Romeo and Juliet*. These were the last seasons in London of Beecham's company as then controlled and constituted. Since the experimental season at the Shaftesbury in the autumn of 1915, they had sung forty-three new productions. Principals and chorus alike had acquired techniques and a feeling for ensemble hitherto unimagined in English opera. Under the administrative stress and confusion which followed Baylis's death, however, the company's alert efficiency began to crumble. The *Village Romeo* and *Djalimeh* productions were lengthily postponed, and a series of Sunday concerts at Covent Garden was scrapped altogether "owing to the impossibility of freeing the stage from rehearsal." Under Baylis such muddles had been unthinkable. Like *Naïl* and *Le Coq d'Or*, the new *Parsifal* was in rehearsal on the day of the opening. The rehearsal is said to have lasted six hours. Albert Coates conducted that night. Some of the actors, we are told, did not know what notes to sing or when, Amfortas and the male chorus were out of tune, the female chorus dragged, the Flower Maidens had a ridiculous *tremolo*, and the Montserrat bells produced weird notes. Thus *The Times* critic. At a later performance the swan killed by Parsifal hit and stunned a super, and the spear hurled by Klingsor from his sinister battlements stuck half-way along its invisible wire, completing its flight in jerks.

Gradually, however, the season became stabler and ended with distinction. There were great *Otello* and *Tristan* nights. The orchestral playing under Beecham in *Meistersinger* induced raptures. His gallery following became clamorously affectionate. After final curtains they took to chanting "Tommy, Tommy, Tommy!"

Tommy Beecham may not have given the masses an enduring taste for grand opera. He had certainly given them a taste for Tommy Beecham.

(2)

With the well-off he was no longer a compulsory vogue. But he had come to the end of his financial tether. He had no choice but to look to the well-off for support. English opera was no longer a matter for individual funding and nursing. From this stage on, he preached the doctrine of artistic oligarchy. "To make opera a success in England is the simplest thing in the world", he would say. "All you have to do is interest about a dozen very rich people who would be willing to spend for the next five or seven years not less than £50,000 a year. It has been done in America. Why not here?"

The very rich did not respond. He was driven to other money-raising devices.

Lady Cunard interrupted the winter season at Covent Garden to organise a Grand Opera Ball in support of a £10,000 endowment fund for the production of English operas. A dance floor was built over the stalls; two princesses, the Aga Khan and droves of duchesses supped in boxes and retiring rooms; and Lord Loughborough led a ceremonial procession that included most of the officers in the Brigade of Guards. These and other diversions were watched from the upper levels of the theatre by humbler social infatuates who had paid ten shillings for the privilege. Fancy dresses were disinterred for the occasion which had been moth-balled since great occasions of the 'nineties. Looking majestic and palely reproving as usual, Clara Butt, whose contralto had become a national institution, wore oriental draperies in orange and gold. Lady Diana, hooped and flounced in the fashion of Queen Anne, threw pennies from her box to a young man dressed as a beggar. Hundreds of necks were craned when a couple from the Diaghilev troupe danced *Le Spectre de la Rose*. As the dance floor was at stage level, few could see what was going on. Lady Cunard had collected prizes for a five shilling draw: pearl pin, china vase, ruby ring, tickets for aeroplane flights over London, and so on.

The royal box had been reserved for the Prince of Wales and Prince Albert. It was hoped that the two future kings would come on from the Carpentier-Beckett fight at Holborn Stadium. Several dancers reported around midnight that one or the other of them had arrived, wearing a domino. The report was erroneous. Having accompanied *Le Spectre*, Beecham's orchestra retired. For general dancing there was a new thing called a jazz band.

From grand tier boxes, noble dowagers looked down on the new age and did not find it to their taste.

(3)

Faced after the war with cumulative losses on his operatic enterprises of £104,000, including £40,000 interest charges on loans, Beecham was compelled to realise his assets. The scenery, props and wardrobe of the Beecham Opera Company were delivered into the hands of a liquidator. No sooner had this happened than he began negotiating with the liquidator to get these properties back and use them further at a weekly rent of £200, subject to a deposit of £1,000. Twenty-five or more productions were involved. They had cost Beecham £150,000.

The rental basis having been negotiated—solely with a view to keeping his artists employed—he scheduled a six-months tour which was to last until April 1921, taking in Birmingham, Edinburgh, Glasgow, Leeds, Bradford and Liverpool. At the same time he talked of sending ahead Mr. Robinson, his new general-manager, as a financial emissary. The idea was that Robinson should talk to influential people in these cities and secure their practical support for the formation of a new opera company. The project having been prematurely publicised, Beecham angrily cancelled his instructions. He wrote to Robinson: "The extraordinarily muddled account of the proposed opera company which appeared this morning in the Press —how, Heaven alone knows—complicates things vilely. It may be necessary for me to disclaim any connection with it. I want you to profess little or no knowledge of it until I give you the word. . . . A great blunder has been commited that may wreck the enterprise. The Press is the most damnable of institutions and will kill anything if it gets the chance."

Throughout his life Beecham cultivated the Press adroitly. Un-doubtedly he owed much to it. That this note of rancour should have escaped him is evidence of the acute tensions he was under-going. The company's Birmingham season, billed for a month, opened at the beginning of October 1920. At the end of the third week, William Dennis Hunt, the company's manager, received a telegram from Beecham asking them to return to London at once. Hunt hastened to Carlton House Terrace, where Beecham was staying. "Hello, Hunt", said Beecham, "I've just sent you a wire to bring back the company." "I know", replied Hunt, "—and it can't be done, it mustn't be done!"

From what Beecham said then and later it is clear that he realised he could finance the tour no longer. Two hundred pounds a week rent was too much for him. He did, however, tell Hunt that, if he were relieved of the rent and the £1,000 guarantee, the company might continue the tour in his name. One of his tenors, Webster Millar, put up the money. The artists held a meeting in Birmingham and pluckily decided to carry on as a "commonwealth", with a certain pooling of financial responsibility. Some months later they took over Beecham's operatic assets and, as the British National Opera Company, survived—most of the time precariously—for another seven years.

(4)

Meantime, the receiving order of May 1919, made on the petition of a moneylender, had been published to the world in *The London Gazette*. In consequence Beecham's affairs were protractedly examined (the hearings lasted until March 1923) at creditors' meetings, in the London Bankruptcy Court and in the Court of Chancery.

Reduced to essentials his predicament was as follows. Under Joseph Beecham's will, Thomas (like his brother Henry) was to enjoy a life interest only on 46 per cent of the income derived from the pill business. If there had been no complication, Thomas would, from 1919 onwards, have been drawing £90,000 a year as his share. But Joseph had confided the administration of the estate to a body of trustees; and the trustees were reluctant to pay beneficiaries under the will until the massive liability of the Covent Garden estate had been dealt with. On this transaction £1,750,000 was still owing. "Jimmy" White, increasingly in the public eye as a buyer of racehorses and cotton mills, was doing what he could to rid Beecham and his brother of their encumbrance.

At one of the creditors' meetings, Beecham's lawyers (there were two of them in attendance) told the Senior Official Receiver that a friend of the debtor was willing to sign a cheque for a sum which would pay Beecham's debts down to the last penny. They could not, they were afraid, divulge the friend's identity.

"He is a person", boasted one lawyer, "who could sign a cheque for six figures without knowing it."

"If £50,000 or £100,000 were needed", put in the other, "it would be forthcoming."

After further coyness, a third lawyer, Mr. Sharp, who represented Mr. X, handed Mr. X's name to the Senior Official Receiver on a bit of paper.

"You will see", suggested Mr. Sharp, "that my client is well able to find the money."

The Senior Official Receiver waved the suggestion aside. "You must not assume I can tell that from his name", he said testily. "I am not well acquainted with people who are accustomed to dealing in hundreds of thousands of pounds."

The same night White let it be known that he was the anonymous benefactor in the case. He was not, however, quite as open-handed as the lawyers had made out. "It is incorrect", explained his secretary, "to say that Mr. White is finding Sir Thomas Beecham £100,000. Certain negotiations are pending for the sale of some of the Beecham estate properties. If the transaction is complete, Sir Thomas will receive about £100,000 out of it." White's good offices, it seemed, were merely those of a middleman.

During the proceedings in the Court of Chancery—which were concerned with Beecham's interim income from the trustees under Joseph's will—it was stated that, instead of the £90,000 a year which he would have inherited in normal circumstances, Beecham was getting only £20,000 a year, the balance going, by arrangement with the trustees, to reduce the Covent Garden estate debt. By way of further contribution towards the settlement of his affairs, he had limited his household and personal expenditure for three years to £5,000 per annum.

The proceedings in Chancery were presided over by Mr. Justice Eve, then sixty-five, who has long been remembered for a singularly unhappy philistinism. For Beecham, Mr. Frederick Maugham, K.C., pleaded that his client had spent a fortune in advancing music.

Mr. Justice Eve: "And what good does that do anybody?"

Mr. Maugham: "That is a question on which opinions may differ."

Mr. Justice Eve: "They do."

In an amended statement of affairs, which took into account the Covent Garden incubus as well as his operatic debts, Beecham calculated his gross liabilities at £2,131,571 and estimated that his assets would yield a surplus of £74,724. With the concurrence of the Court of Chancery, the trustees under Joseph's will were authorised to hand to the Official Receiver a portion of the business income which had been amassing in Beecham's name for five years. At a session of the Bankruptcy Court in March 1923, Beecham's lawyer said he was prepared to give the Official Receiver at once a cheque for £44,200 which would discharge Beecham's debts in full. The Registrar approved and rescinded the receiving order which had occasioned all the legal commotion.

As he was at pains to insist later, Beecham was never adjudged bankrupt. He always claimed that he paid his 1919 creditors twenty shillings in the pound, in accordance with his undertaking. There were, to be sure, some creditors whose bills, during the years that followed, he contested—usually without success—in the King's

Bench Division. A baritone, a tenor, a conductor and an operatic manager were between them awarded some thousands of pounds for breach of contract and broken engagements.

.   .   .   .   .

Because of his business and legal preoccupations, Beecham was exiled from music from the summer of 1920 to the spring of 1923. During these years, as director of a family company he sat in the estate offices at Covent Garden and sold enough of the properties under his control, while increasing the revenues from the rest, to cancel what had once been a nightmare.

His return to music was grandiose. At the Albert Hall (April 8th, 1923) he conducted the combined London Symphony and Albert Hall orchestras. Two hundred players were before him. Dame Clara Butt sang out of tune and was reluctant to stop. About to start on a third "extra" after her second printed number, she was deterred by a galleryite who shouted, "I came to hear the orchestra!"

The concert ended gloriously with *Ein Heldenleben* and *The Ride of the Valkyries*. Beecham was at the rostrum again. It could not be said that all was well with the English musical world. But at least some spark and hope had been restored to it.

CHAPTER TWENTY-ONE

"SLIGHT HIATUSES"

(1)

THE FOLLOWING YEAR, like an imp catapulted from outer space, he made a token return to opera. It is true that the return, if not the manner of it, had been prearranged. Sagging already and sorely in need of the stimulus which his name alone could give, the British National Opera Company had pleaded with him to conduct at least one performance during their summer season (1924), at His Majesty's Theatre. Having listened to the company's emissaries with the impassivity of an appeal court judge, Beecham agreed to conduct a *Mastersingers* in the middle of July. It was arranged that on the preceding Sunday he should take a run-through with the orchestra, followed by a session with the principal singers.

The Sunday dawned blue and blazing. In the afternoon a small knot of B.N.O.C. directors awaited his arrival at the stage door. Like most people who waited for Beecham, whatever their age, quality, talents and deserts, they were excited and apprehensive. The orchestra had been twittering and tootling in the pit for half an hour. Suddenly a flip-flop of swing doors was heard at the back of the auditorium. A tiny figure in a white suit with white tie hurried down the aisle. Stripping his jacket and folding it neatly on the orchestra rail, he climbed over to the rostrum and picked up his baton. Almost before the players could get mouthpieces to lips or fiddles under chins, he had unleashed the C major opening chord of the *Mastersingers* Overture.

The mighty sound was heard by the reception committee out on the sun-scorched pavement. They started and stared at each other in consternation. Their first thought was that some impious subordinate had usurped the rostrum for a lark. A gibbering messenger came to them and explained. Although prompted in good time about the reception arrangement, Beecham had come in through the front of the house and had started the rehearsal without a word to anybody. In some agitation, the directors crept into the stalls and listened tensely.

During a run-through of the accompaniment to Pogner's Address, with its prominent horn solo, Beecham rapped the rail. "Where's the horn?" he asked with a kindly inflection. In the lamplit dimness a man put his hand up and said, "Here, Sir Thomas." "Very nicely played", conceded Beecham in the same soothing tone. Then, frowningly, with a characteristic downward thrust of the clenched fist: "But don't be afraid of the damned thing!"

The listeners in the stalls, some of whom had sung or worked in other ways for Beecham since the Shaftesbury-Aldwych seasons and earlier, leaned their heads together and agreed that retirement had not changed him by a hair's-breadth.

The Walther was sung by a bull-necked young tenor from the North with a voice of bar silver and no instinct whatever for the stage, on which he moved, whether as Radames, Siegfried or Rodolfo, like a jaunty warehouse foreman. During Walther's wooing of Eva, Beecham put an impaling question.

"Have you", he asked, "ever made love, Mr. X?"

Mr. X (sheepishly): "Yes, Sir Thomas."

Beecham: "Do you consider yours is a suitable way of making love to Eva?"

Mr. X: "Well, there are different ways of making love, Sir Thomas."

Beecham: "Observing your grave, deliberate motions, I was re-minded, Mr. X, of that estimable quadruped, the hedgehog."

An instant of frozen embarrassment in the pit and on the stage was dispelled by Mr. X himself, whose extrovert nature turned the gibe into a joke and dismissed it with a boyish laugh. Not all the artists against whom Beecham's shafts were levelled took them as well as Mr. X. What, to take one case, were the secret writhings of the *Walküre* soprano of whom he said—and was widely known to have said—that her singing reminded him of a cart coming downhill with the brake on? Or, more than a quarter of a century later, those of the girl brought in as relief harpist at a rehearsal of the Royal Philharmonic Orchestra? Presumably unnerved by her first assignment with Beecham, she consistently bungled the harp entries. Looking stonily over her head across the rehearsal floor, Beecham asked one of his assistants, "What is this young woman doing here? And who, may I ask, brought her in?"

It is hard to resist the conclusion that he enjoyed the humilated flurry that resulted from cruelties such as these. With every nerve around him overstrung, he would utter some jocose aside; nerves would suddenly relax and the rehearsal re-flow. These easements were timed with mastery. Without them, more than one Beecham enter-prise must have foundered through smart and despondency among his subordinates.

His tongue could be ruthless even in his late seventies. Sentimental observers had begun to diagnose a mellowing in him. He delighted in showing them how wrong they were. At an *Otello* rehearsal in Latin South America little more than two years before his death, he exclaimed "Horrible, horrible!" through the orchestral tumults at one of the women singers. Finally he stopped the music and, addressing nobody in particular, shouted, "Take that woman off the stage and bring me another soprano!" Supported by backstage factions, the singer stood her ground both then and on the night. Like Mr. X, but after a different fashion, she was psychologically armoured against Beecham's strokes. After a jubilant final curtain she left the theatre muttering imprecations against him in Italian.

. . .

Beecham's token *Mastersingers* at His Majesty's Theatre in 1924 was no beacon performance. Too few strings scraped competitively against an over-insistent brass section; and the singers, some of them newcomers to opera or as yet unseasoned in it, were so busy staring at Beecham in a trance-like way that they forget to act. These and other deficiencies pointed to a disorder more fundamental: a chronic want of funds. The B.N.O.C. perforce led a hobbled, hand-to-mouth existence. Early in 1926 Beecham vowed that until English opera was put on to a satisfactory basis, he would never set foot or show his face in an English operatic theatre again.

No further operatic largesse was to be expected from his own pocket. Again he was deeply involved with moneylenders. During 1924 and 1925 alone, his borrowings amounted to over £50,000.* Most other men would have found such a burden paralysing. Beecham hardly noticed it. In November 1927 he went to the country, as pamphleteer and stump orator, with a scheme which offered opera at "tuppence a week" under the aegis of the Imperial League of Opera, a brain-child of his own.

There was in Britain, he reasoned, an opera-loving minority which, in sanguine mood, he put at 250,000 and, when conservatively inclined, at 150,000. He proposed that these devotees should subsidise Beecham-directed opera with a pound down and annual contributions

---

* He admitted as much during complex (and sometimes faintly squalid) actions involving his liabilities and indebtedness in Chancery Division, King's Bench Division and the Appeal Court. These proceedings reached their climax after the second receiving order of Beecham's career, dated December 5th, 1930. This was discharged at the London Bankruptcy Court on July 13th, 1932, when, faced with estimated liabilities of £172,000, he undertook to pay a composition of ten shillings in the pound "as the first step towards a payment in full of all legitimate claims".

of ten shillings. Hence the catch phrase of "tuppence a week". Like most catch phrases, this told only part of the story. Having paid their tuppences, subscribers were to buy their tickets on top.

With the support of highly reputable trustees from the City, spotless lawyers, technical advisers and artistic aides, the League set up house in New Bond Street, had itself legally registered, printed contribution forms, and waited for the money to come in. Apart from the two-pence a week members, there were donors. Among these Lady Cunard put herself down for £5,000. Only one other person gave as much: Sir Joseph (later Lord) Duveen, the art-dealer. Time's graver had begun to make its mark upon Maud Cunard. That is clear from Virginia Woolf's ruthless word portrait, which dates from the Opera League's brief prime. Ridiculous, small and "parokeet faced", a "stringy hop o' my thumb," she showed the writer her bedroom, with its flower paintings, its triangular canopy of rose-red silk, its pair of gold slippers with gold stockings laid neatly upon them, and its two giant musical boxes (an echo of Ewanville?), both in playing order. In essence, judged Mrs. Woolf, a coarse, usual and dull woman—but how competent in "the commerce of life"! In the Opera League Lady Cunard found tasks of a sort that delighted her brisk, intent soul. She had views of her own on the art, not very coherent ones, it is true. She aired them in publicity articles for the League.

"Opera", she assured the world, "is not only great music but music set to epic poetry, written by some of the finest men of the age, and the setting has a value, for it immortalises national stories and old legends and sagas and epochs in history. . . . [For singers,] a superb voice is not sufficient; there must be creative genius, divinely be-stowed, for opera is a test of extreme musical ability, involving the elimination of everything that is frivolous and inessential . . ., an intuitive perception, creating a bond of unity between the singers, and is as though the vital spark of genius came like an angel of inspiration, waiting for the elusive moment to present itself. . . . The singer's vocation is no light one. However, there are compensa-tions for divine song, which seems to inspire the green and golden wings of thought, while the melting voice breathes a finer know-ledge, like poetry wringing music from the soul of things."

Perhaps because Lady Cunard's singular prose frightened potential contributors off, Beecham could not, campaign as he might, enrol more than 44,000 members out of the hoped for minimum of 150,000. After seven years the League wound-up in the Court of Chancery. A small proportion of the contributors opted to leave their money in the hands of trustees for possible future use in the cause of opera. The rest opted for their money back.

(2)

During the years between his re-emergence and his founding of the London Philharmonic Orchestra (1932), his chosen instrument at home, for want, as will presently appear, of a better, was the London Symphony Orchestra, which he periodically conducted at the Albert Hall, took out on tour, paraded at great provincial festivals and, when it was short of money, nursed and coaxed and helped over stiles.

In LSO ranks new tales were added to the old about the marvels of his memory. There was one prototype story which bred several variants. Returning from the Continent with hardly time enough to change into a white tie, he appeared in the pit at Covent Garden without a glance at his engagement book or the day-bills. Raising the baton, he turned to the leader and inquired, "What are we playing tonight?"

"*Figaro*, Sir Thomas."

"My dear fellow", he returned, "you amaze me!"

The performance from memory which followed (so runs the story) was pointed and polished in the ultimate Beecham manner; that is to say, in a manner without precursor or legatees. No man could have phrased Mozart with Beecham's wit and grace if his eye had been perpetually rooted in print. After one such scoreless, exquisite night, the Budapest-born conductor Fritz Reiner sought him out in his dressing room. "I wanted to thank you", he said, "for a wonderful night with Mozart and Beecham." Beecham rotated his nose musingly. "Why drag in Mozart?" he inquired.*

Outside Mozart and other preferred composers, his memory occasionally failed him. With no score on the desk to set him right, he usually resorted when in a musical fog to vague circling motions with both arms, like a swimmer doggedly doing the breast stroke. Virtually conducted by the first violin and other section leaders, the performance would either limp untidily along to full-close or, in extreme cases, peter out miserably. Veterans talk of his concert at the Queen's Hall with Selma Kurz, the Viennese coloratura soprano, who was ebullient in temper as well as of voice. With her obbligato flautist standing alongside, Miss Kurz had practised her main air, *L'Allegro, il Penseroso*

---

* The cadence recalls another pleasantry. At a function to mark his seventieth birthday, the chairman enumerated a dozen or so congratulatory telegrams from eminent people in many countries. Beecham listened with visible boredom, then inquired, "What, nothing from Mozart?"

ed il Moderato (a setting by Handel of a text after Milton), for most of
an afternoon in bed in the Langham Hotel, luxuriously propped among
pillows; and she was not disposed to put up with any nonsense. Half-way
through her performance, Beecham's beat went awry; the orchestra
came to a full stop, and Miss Kurz had no choice but to do the same.

Turning to the audience, Beecham said, "Ladies and gentlemen,
there has been a slight hiatus"—a thing they could not have failed to
notice. "We will start again." At the second attempt he lost touch
again. This time, happily, the leaders having been alerted, the "hiatus"
did not recur. It was a near thing, however. As soon as she reached the
artists' room, Miss Kurz wiped off the honeyed smile with which she
had accepted rounds of vociferously sympathetic applause andemitted
a chain of high-pitched oaths in German.

A more startling breakdown occurred during one of six *Prince Igo*
performances by an émigré Russian company which he conducted in
the early summer of 1931 at the Lyceum Theatre.* During the opening
scene his beat hopelessly tangled with the chorus. There was nothing
for it but to stop and make a fresh start. As the occasion was not a
Press night, no word appeared about it in the newspapers next dayn
but the incident is mentioned in the Gaisberg memoirs; and, according
to private information, it was witnessed by the conductor Robert
Heger, from Munich, who was having a free night from the concurrent German season at Covent Garden. At a *Ring* rehearsal a day
or two later, Heger described what had happened to at least one member of the orchestra. He concluded, "No conductor, however wonderful his memory, can afford to conduct opera without a score. It
is much too dangerous."

Heger's warning applies equally to piano concertos. At a concert of
the Royal Philharmonic Society early in 1930, Beecham launched upon
Beethoven's No. 4 in G major. Alfred Cortot was his distinguished
soloist. Flustered, apparently, by a conductor without score and (a
considerable aggravation) without baton, he lost his way in the finale
and, looking up at Beecham, exclaimed "Ah, ah!", as who should
say, "I told you so!" It was Cortot who, after whispered consultations
with the conductor and the orchestral leader, got the finale moving
again from an agreed point. As reported by Gaisberg, Beecham afterwards gave a facetious account of the incident. He maintained that a
lapse of memory had derailed the finale long before the overt

* It was during this season that Chaliapin reappeared on a London operatic stage under
Beecham's baton for the first time since 1914. At some of the performances he sat in the
stalls and, at each curtain, toweringly led ovations for Beecham. As Kontschak and
Galitsky, roles which he doubled only once, he showed much of his old power.

breakdown. For a while Cortot and he manœuvred to recover position, each trying all the concertos he knew, but were unable to hit upon a common musical denominator. "We started", he averred, "with the Beethoven, and I kept up with Cortot through the Grieg, Schumann, Bach and Tchaikovsky, and then he hit on one I didn't know, so I stopped dead.'

(3)

From time to time, the occasions being widely spaced, he would try his hand at some contemporary score. Generally speaking, musical styles and idioms outside those in which he had revelled from 1906 onwards, tended to irk and hamper him. The concert suite from Stravinsky's *Apollo Musagetes* ballet offered painful proof of this.

Beecham was prevailed upon to conduct *Apollo* at the Leeds Triennial Festival six months after the world *première* in Washington. The performance was so sketchily prepared that there was doubt until the afternoon of the concert whether it would be practicable. It is said that in this case again, Beecham lost the thread and escaped disaster only through the vigilance of his leader who, when matters came to a crisis, raised his bow for all to see and boldly signalled the players to a full-close which Stravinsky never intended. Whereupon Beecham tossed his baton on to the desk with a calculated gesture of contempt. There were faint hisses from the audience. It is a disturbing thought that these were intended not for the conductor but for the music which he had so sceptically and incompetently handled.

Throughout his life Beecham was chary of discussing in public other great musical names of his day. In private he was under no such inhibition however. A few years after the *Apollo* incident, but without any direct reference to it, I raised with him the general issue of Stravinsky's merit. As I had foreseen, his praise, like most of his musical acts, stopped at the pre-1914 ballets, especially *Petrushka*. "*There's* a work of genius!" he exclaimed. I shall never forget the first performance of *Petrushka* in Paris. 'Thank God', I said, 'here's something new at last!'"*

Had he, I pursued, nothing good to say about Stravinsky's later works? His reply was implacable.

"The later stuff", he said, "no longer bears Stravinsky's image. He has lost his image and cannot find it. You may search among the later

---

* This judgment was noted immediately after our conversation. When I quoted it to him over twenty years later he frowningly denied having said or thought anything of the kind. It was as though the shade of Delius had jealously intervened with bared teeth.

works in vain. When you hear *Brigg Fair* you know you are listening to Delius. When you hear recent Stravinsky it is hard to know what you are hearing. Some years ago I gave his *Apollo* music at Leeds. Poh!"—here he shrugged and waved a hand resignedly. "There was nothing in the music, nothing."

Thus it remained to the end. There was no unsaying and little undoing. With only minor and expedient or experimental deflections his career ran clean against the Stravinsky-Bartók axis which, at this writing, seems likely to dominate European musical history over the first half or more of our century. Apart from Delius, the only composer among his contemporaries to whom, a little belatedly, Beecham responded roaringly and consistently was Jan Sibelius, the Finnish sage and seer, as many deemed him.

Among the Sibelius scores which, especially in the 'thirties, he conducted with defiant relish was Symphony No. 4 in A minor. As heard by one school of critics—and by many concertgoers—the A minor was bleak, blizzard-swept stuff. This view seemed nonsensical to me. To my ear the A minor spoke partly, if not all the time, of sunlight, flowers and Mediterranean laughter. After a Beecham concert I wrote an article in this vein for the newspaper which I then served, in the provinces. Nine months later I met him in the mean conductor's room of a northern theatre where a company of his from Covent Garden were singing *La Bohème*.

"Yours", he announced imperially, "is the only sensible notice of Sibelius's Fourth Symphony I have ever read." He addressed the compliment not to me but to circumambience, as though the pink-painted brick-work had been a deferential, star-and-gartered audience. Against the view that the Fourth was chill and austere, he inveighed, gesticulated, frowned and puffed until his cuffs came down over his knuckles. That people should write with such uncomprehending folly about so magnificently romantic a work . . . !

In thirty years, the brassy, brooding *œuvre* of Sibelius has crumbled or dwindled to some extent in the estimation of many early adherents. In a field of shifting evaluations the post-hoc rightness or wrongness of Beecham's judgment is not of great moment. A more striking thing was the heat and dynamic of his admiration. When in full cry he spouted molten rock. He was the first volcano English music has ever known and may well be the last. For a parallel one must cite another age and country. In more than one aspect, Beecham was Hector Berlioz reincarnated and transplanted.

(4)

The years at which we have been glancing (1924-1932) were something of a trough in Beecham's life. They were a time of accidents, chronic ill-health and recurrent lameness; angry frustrations; running battles with claimants and creditors; busy professional schemings that came to nothing. Above all, they were a time of grand, withering pronouncements. Once or twice his tongue stooped to peevish rudeness. As they watched him limp on to the platform, or conduct from an invalid chair, or heard of concerts cancelled on doctor's orders, some must have wondered at times whether he was not perhaps sick in mind as well as body.

He told the concertgoers of Nottingham that they looked as if they had lived on grass for three years, like the king in the Bible; on the whole he would prefer to conduct for people in deepest Africa who beat tom-toms and lived on nuts. Of the gramophone which, within a decade, was to disseminate his art prodigiously, he spoke with barbed contempt. "Improvement in the gramophone is so imperceptible", he announced, "that it will take quite 5,000 years to make it any good." Music on the "wireless", as people then called it, was "the most abominable row that ever stunned and cursed the human ear, a horrible gibbering, chortling and shrieking of devils and goblins." Nor were his diatribes confined to music. From time to time he pronounced witheringly on national and international politics. The Bolsheviks were a pack of impudent Asiatic mongrels. Britain had gone soft in the head about them. The British Labour Party preached a gospel of thieving and stealing; they were as much the enemies of the English people at large as the Germans had ever been. For long the laziest nation in the world, we were now becoming positively comatose. For these and other reasons he meant to uproot his fortune, or what was left of it, settle as a conductor in the United States and stay there until extreme old age or never come back at all.*

What was the key to these furies and verbal out-flingings? The answer is simple. Without an orchestra within the hollow of his hand, an orchestra which, like the BSO of 1909, should be clay for his vivifying breath, he was suffering the gnaw and rancour of deprivation.

---

* This threat was made vehemently and without qualification at a Press conference convened on his behalf, with promises of "a sensational announcement", on November 4th, 1926. At the end of the year he sailed for New York in the *Aquitania*. By the middle of February, 1927 he was back in England, to all intents and purposes for good. In retrospect, his Press conference was seen to be an unpleasant mixture of bluff and humbug.

CHAPTER TWENTY-TWO

SECOND THRONE

(1)

As an intermittent guest conductor during the 'twenties and early 'thirties, Beecham came into contact with great or worthy permanent orchestras in the concert halls or orchestra pits of Berlin, New York (where his fee was £500 a concert), Philadelphia, Boston, Paris, Rome, Prague, Budapest. London had no orchestra which could compare in certain essentials with even the middling ones he conducted abroad. English musicians were admirable; there were, he insisted, none finer in the world. But our orchestral standards were a different matter. Especially following the world slump of 1929, tepid public support led to lack of funds and chronic impermanence. The perpetual question at the back of players' minds was: "Shall we be in corporate existence next year or, if it comes to that, next month?" Such fears, aggravated by limited concert schedules and scant rehearsals, sapped *ensemble* at the root.

As early as 1928 Beecham had outlined the status and functions, as he saw them, of a truly efficient and permanent orchestra. Already he provisionally called his vision the London Philharmonic Orchestra. The players would be under contract at fees ranging from £500 a year for the rank-and-file to £1,200 for principals. During eleven months of the year they would give about 110 concerts at the Queen's and Albert Halls, in the provinces and in various London suburbs, as well as taking part in opera seasons at Covent Garden. The twelfth month would be a holiday, during which the players would be bound not to take any professional engagements whatsoever. Such a basis, Beecham stressed, would exclude the deputy system, which had for so long been the bane of London music.

It would also entail some form of subsidy. He estimated that the great American orchestras were aided by private munificence to the extent in typical cases of not less than £25,000 a year. At one time, despite his foam-flecked abuse of broadcasting, he hoped the great provider in this country would be the B.B.C. During the late 'twenties there were uneasy negotiations between him and B.B.C. officials for the joint founding of "a first-rate permanent orchestra." Beecham was to be in supreme artistic control. The B.B.C. were to have charge of the business side. After fluctuating for two years, the negotiations had lapsed, the B.B.C. resolving in the end to launch a permanent symphony orchestra without Beecham's co-operation. With the B.B.C. sealed off, where could Beecham turn for sponsorship and a ready cheque book? An answer came in 1931. It was given by an energetic conductor of the younger generation, Dr. (now Sir) Malcolm Sargent.

Endowed with uncommon social as well as professional talent, Dr. Sargent had been enabled through the generosity of Mrs. Samuel Courtauld, wife of the rayon millionaire, to found an annual series of symphony concerts which commanded a big and guaranteed audience at reduced subscription rates. An isolated case of financial elbow room in a constricted orchestral world, the Courtauld-Sargent concerts were served by the London Symphony Orchestra on the basis (rare) of three rehearsals per programme. Like Beecham, however, the Courtaulds hankered after something more polished and dependable. Disturbed by the L.S.O.'s shifting constituents, they asked Sargent if he would be interested to found a permanent orchestra with a stable personnel which should always be available for their concerts. They were, they said, prepared to spend £30,000 on the new orchestra as a send-off grant and to subsidise it further as need arose.

Sargent went away and pondered. At this time he was in his middle thirties. He had a nature in which prudence tempered ambition. Deciding that he was too young to undertake the Courtaulds' project single-handed, he laid the matter before Beecham, with a suggestion of his own that the new orchestra, if formed under Beecham's leadership, should combine various concert series which were more or less independently managed. Sargent's own contributions to this pool of engagements would include, as well as the Courtauld-Sargent series, two others which he directed—the Robert Mayer children's concerts and those of the Royal Choral Society.

Beecham said the idea was wonderful and promptly took it under his wing. He speedily set up an administrative board which reflected a new tendency to plutocratic patronage based as much on taste and idealism as upon money bags. Of the four directors, Courtauld (now a widower) not only bought Renoirs, Manets, Cézannes and Van Goghs for the nation; he also wrote poems about them for the delectation of chosen friends. Neat, courteous and self-effacing, the man who once wore managerial overalls in family weaving sheds and dyehouses wrote fluent letters about painting, music and prose. An unpublished commentary of his on Meredith's *Modern Love* was cited respectfully by familiars at his Robert Adam mansion in Portman Place.

Courtauld's three fellow directors were Mr. (now Sir) Robert Mayer, Baron Frédéric Alfred d'Erlanger and Oliver Sylvain Baliol Brett, third Viscount Esher. Trained as a concert pianist, Mayer, who was born in Mannheim, had settled in London at the age of seventeen. To strengthen his wrists and refine his touch he used to practise for hours with newspapers tucked under his elbows. Abandoning music as a vocation on his father's advice ("Let music be your solace, not your money-getter"), he went into the City and made a fortune out of copper. On children's concerts and other musical causes he was to spend over £100,000.

D'Erlanger was an even more striking instance of commerce and the muses reconciled. At this time he was in his middle sixties, a benign soul with traces of foreign accent, as befitted his Parisian origin and his half German blood. As partner and, later, as head of a banking house in Moorgate, he financed infant railways in South Africa and department stores in Latin South America. Parallel with this ran a loftier career. D'Erlanger was a composer. The caller at Moorgate was as likely to surprise him at work on a twenty-stave orchestral score as on a balance sheet or company prospectus. From boyhood on he tirelessly produced symphonic music, concerted music, choral music, music for the theatre. At the Queen's Hall in 1903, Kreisler played in a quickly forgotten violin concerto of his. In the 'thirties his two ballets, *Les Cent Baisers* and *Cendrillon* were produced by Nijinska and Fokine respectively. His *Requiem Mass* (1931) is said to have been a pious echo of Verdi's. He wrote three operas. Adopting a pseudonym, Frédéric Regnal, for the occasion, he had one of them, *Inez Mendo*, produced at Covent Garden. One critic found the music, or some of it, vivaciously pretty. Another wrote that it achieved "a dead level of monotony." Judging by the untroubled silence which promptly fell on d'Erlanger's scores, the second of these judgments seems to have been the sounder.

In becoming a patron-director of the new orchestra, did d'Erlanger hope that Beecham might be induced to father his neglected concert scores? If he entertained any such thought, it was only incidental to his main motive—a disinterested love of fine orchestral playing. Such, at any rate, is the opinion of one of his old associates.

The special talent of the remaining director, Lord Esher, was for sitting on or presiding over unexceptionable committees and trusts. Vintage churches, museums of many sorts, speech training and assorted theatres—memorial, national, provincial and Shakespearian—were among the objects of his advisory zeal. Esher, it was reasoned, had a finger in so many pies that his presence on the L.P.O. board was indispensable.

What of the project's technical side?

At the outset it was decided by Beecham, with the enthusiastic co-operation of Sargent, who became its auxiliary musical director, that the new orchestra should be a reshuffled version of the London Symphony Orchestra, which was still a self-governing company with a directors' board made up of playing members. "Reshuffle" was a polite term for weedings-out and replacements. During the negotiations of Beecham or his spokesmen with the L.S.O. board, the latter agreed in principle that the orchestra's quality would be materially improved by a wide range of personnel changes. Among other appointments the leadership came under debate. At that time the principal violin and leader of the L.S.O. was the highly esteemed W. H. Reed, who had been at the first desk since 1912. During a railway journey on one of the L.S.O.'s unprosperous post-1929 tours,* Beecham and Reed hob-nobbed as was their wont.

"About this new orchestra of yours", propounded Reed, "I'm getting on, you know. [He was fifty-five.] Perhaps you'd prefer to appoint someone else as leader?"

"My dear Willie", averred Beecham, "the L.S.O. would be unthinkable without you."

On the strength of what he took to be a pledge, Reed turned down a lucrative offer of seven months' examination work later that year in South Africa for the Royal Academy and the Royal College of Music. Staying on in London, he confidently awaited the call to Beecham's first desk.

Other prominent players were buttonholed on Beecham's behalf by his agent Lionel Powell, who conjured up visions of a "super orchestra" which would enjoy a near monopoly of high quality concert-giving in London. Some players responded cautiously. A few made it clear from the start that they were not interested. Their attitude is summed up thus by a veteran L.S.O. player who remembers Beecham from the pre-1914 days: "Everything Beecham had touched since his big opera crash fizzled out. Take the Imperial League of Opera. He positively promised a 'preliminary season' with a repertory of six operas—he named them all—for the summer of 1930. Choral rehearsals had been fixed. Augustus John was designing sets for one of the star

---

* A tour early in 1932 took Beecham and the L.S.O. to Edinburgh, Glasgow, Liverpool, Dundee, Aberdeen and St. Andrews. Despite Beecham's prestige, the door takings at one of these centres were under £100. Business was disappointing all along the route.

productions, Berlioz's *Damnation of Faust*. What happened? Not a thing."

Rightly or wrongly, many musicians had lost faith in Beecham. Nor did his arrogant speeches help matters. Commenting on his begging campaign for the Imperial League, Sir Hugh Allen, director of the Royal College of Music, assessed the situation drily. "There are some people," he said, "who slap you in the face and ask for half a crown. Sir Thomas slaps you in the face and asks for a five pound note."

Opinions of this kind undoubtedly hampered Beecham's own endeavours and those of his friends.

(2)

Gradually the L.S.O., without having anything tangible to work on, became aware of a certain cooling-off on Beecham's part. Personal access to him was harder than ever to arrange. On the voyage back from Dublin after another L.S.O. foray, two player-directors solved this problem by knocking without prearrangement at his cabin door. Wearing pyjamas and dressing-gown (always his preferred habit when off the platform), Beecham received them mellifluously.

One of the directors asked, in a tone that betrayed misgiving, "You *do* want the L.S.O. as your new orchestra, don't you, Sir Thomas?"

"My dear man", replied Beecham, "if I didn't want the L.S.O., why should I be wasting your time as well as my own?"

Events soon proved, however, that the cooling-off was real enough. An insurmountable difference developed between Beecham and the L.S.O. board as to which players should be retained and which replaced. Beecham drew up one list, the board another. It is alleged in Beechamite circles that Beecham's list was unacceptable to several L.S.O. directors because it would have meant their own dismissal not only as directors but also as playing members. Not unnaturally, they were reluctant to give themselves the sack.

The negotiations limped on protractedly. At an early stage Lionel Powell died. He had been a musical impresario on the grand scale, boasting of branch concert agencies in twelve capital cities and of travelling round the world twice and to America forty times in pursuit of great box-office names. To the general astonishment, he left an encumbered estate with no assets to speak of and professional commitments which others shouldered out of goodness of heart. (Beecham and Mayer were the principal guarantors of a tour which he had scheduled for the Berlin Philharmonic Orchestra under Wilhelm Furtwängler.) Powell's former partner, Harold Holt, picked up the threads. In the summer of 1932 a meeting was convened in Holt's office of various interested parties, including L.S.O. spokesmen. The latter did not put in an appearance. When asked why, somebody in the L.S.O. offices explained on the telephone that, as Beecham was out of the country, there seemed little point in attending.

Sargent at once put in a call to Munich, where Beecham was conducting operas and concerts with sweeping success. Over the line came a sputter of fury. Then: "Very well, we'll form an orchestra of our own."

Negotiations with the L.S.O. board were at an end. This did not preclude negotiations individually with the cream of the L.S.O. players. Although he declared that the orchestra no longer commanded the confidence of the public, Beecham was still bent on capturing the players on his select list. Early in September, the orchestra met in Worcester to play at the Three Choirs Festival. On the first two days telegrams showered upon the Festival bandroom. Old hands vividly remember the green baize notice board with buff envelopes stuck under its criss-crossed tapes. Signed by Holt, the telegrams asked some two dozen members of the orchestra if they could accept an engagement with Beecham starting that autumn. In a flurry of consternation at a manoeuvre which threatened to split and kill, the L.S.O. directors called a general meeting at which those who had been telegraphed were passionately urged, for the sake of solidarity and corporate survival, to reject Beecham's offer. But initial doubts as to Beecham's trustworthiness had dwindled. Most of the players concerned ignored the directors' appeals and went over. Their secession and the almost mortal gap it opened in L.S.O. ranks left a trail of bitterness. In the years that followed there were charges, none of them documented, of broken faith, even of treachery.*

One undertaking, if it amounted to that, which Beecham overlooked or dropped concerned the leadership. That summer a telegram was delivered on Llandudno Pier for Paul Beard, first violin of the City of Birmingham Orchestra, who was leading an ensemble in the pier pavilion as a vacation engagement.

"Can offer you", telegraphed Beecham, "the leadership of my new orchestra. Please wire me by return."

Beard's reply was prompt. "Accept with great pleasure", he wrote. "Am packing my bags."

* See the relevant chapters of *London Symphony* by Hubert Foss and Noël Goodwin, and *Philharmonic Decade* by Thomas Russell.

Some days later W. H. Reed casually opened a newspaper. In it he read for the first time of Beard's appointment. No one having dropped any hint that Beecham intended to discard him, he was surprised and pained.

At one point Beecham or his board wavered on the title of the new orchestra. A suggestion was put up that they should purchase the title of the L.S.O. which, after twenty-eight years, was ingrained in English music-making. When this came to the ears of the L.S.O. board, Gordon Walker, the noted flautist—he was one of the few members who had rejected Holt's overtures—momentarily scandalised his fellow directors by saying, "I think we ought to sell Beecham our name." There were shouts of remonstration. Walker added, "We ought, of course, to ask him £100,000 for it."

Thus the proposal was quashed by *reductio ad absurdum*. The title adopted was the one which Beecham had spoken of four years earlier: The London Philharmonic Orchestra.

(3)

The 106 newly-enrolled players included a handful of youngsters straight from music college, or like Beard, established young players from provincial orchestras. Some of the newcomers were auditioned at the Abbey Road studios of the Gramophone Company (now E.M.I.), with whom Beecham had already contracted to make a minimum number of recordings each year. The days were gone for ever of his railings at the gramophone as a toy or parasite which could be written off for another 5,000 years.

"Those of us", he was to write a few years later, "who, since the beginning of the century, have been occupied with the making of music realise, perhaps more than others, what a revolutionary invention the gramophone was and how we should have been eternally grateful if it had appeared on the scene 200 years earlier."

For the opening concert, Beecham scheduled thirteen rehearsals—six for full orchestra, seven for orchestral sections. Most of them were held on a parquetry dance floor in the basement of a pillared insurance palace in Bloomsbury Square. Nothing as thoroughgoing or intensive had ever been known in English musical history. The works listed for the inaugural concert showed that in twenty years his prime musical allegiances had not expanded much. They were: Berlioz's *Carnaval Romain* Overture, Mozart's Symphony No. 38 in D (the *Prague*), Delius's *Brigg Fair* and Strauss's *Ein Heldenleben*.

Before the start of the rehearsals proper he called some of his leaders and principals, separately or in small groups, to his flat in Abbey Road. At the piano he ran through much of the programme from memory while they fragmentarily played their own parts, remoulding their phrasing as he directed and absorbing something of his slants and fervours.

Special attention was paid to *Heldenleben*, which Beecham spoke of off-handedly as "this old piece." As a master of the orchestra, he maintained, Strauss could not hold a candle to Puccini, who had everybody "licked." He went on: "I once spent a couple of days in the train with a German friend of mine. We amused ourselves by discovering how many notes we could take out of *Heldenleben* and leave the music essentially intact. By the time we finished we had taken out 15,000." These disparagements masked an unwavering taste for a work whose highly coloured heroics corresponded with much in Beecham's own spirit.

Heldenleben and the three other scores he "edited" for the occasion, pencilling in his own phrasing marks, which were afterwards transferred to the band parts by a relay of copyists. The working out of fingering and other details was delegated to the section leaders.

A new concentration and seriousness was noted in him. For the first time in his career he arrived morning after morning on the dot for rehearsals. Stripping off jacket and tie, he would plunge at ten a.m. into the business of the day. After lunch he occasionally appeared with a cigar and used that instead of a baton.

. . . . .

The London Philharmonic Orchestra made their début at the Queen's Hall, under the aegis of the Royal Philharmonic Society— who, for many years thereafter, used no other orchestra—on the night of October 7th, 1932.* Before going on to the platform, Beecham said to Beard, "Come on, Paul, let's show 'em what we can do." He knew that the hall was not full but showed no present anger.

Carnaval Romain exploded with a brilliance, fire and pressure which startled the players themselves. Although promising much, the final rehearsals had promised nothing quite like this. At the end of the Overture, the audience went wild, some of them standing on their seats to clap and shout. Their rapture was a foretaste of dazzled notices

* Principals and sub-principals that night were: violins, Paul Beard and B. Reillie; second violins, George Stratton and A. Hopkinson; violas, Frank Howard and J. Dyer; 'cellos, Anthony Pini and J. Moore; double-basses, Victor Watson and J. H. Silvester; flutes, Gerald Jackson; piccolo, L. Hopkinson; oboes, Léon Goossens; clarinets, Reginald Kell; bassoons, John Alexandra; horns, Francis Bradley; trumpets, J. H. Cozens; trombones, E. Garvin; tuba, W. Scannell; timpani, J. Bradshaw; harps, Marie Goossens.

in the newspapers next day. The years of fumble and frustration were over. Beecham was out of the trough at last. He had fashioned himself a second throne. He had given the world an orchestra whose like, according to long memories, had not been heard since the Beecham Symphony Orchestra of 1909. According to others whose memories were equally long, its like had never been heard at all.

But there were the empty seats. From the platform it looked as if the hall was not more than three-quarters full. At the interval Beecham strode and stamped and stormed in the conductor's room. The thing was, he shouted, a bloody disgrace to London. He went on storming for days. He would never bring his orchestra to the Queen's Hall again, he threatened. During his career Beecham made several such threats. He excommunicated particular concert halls and cities with imperial loftiness—and went on playing in them much as before. During the next eight years, the London Philharmonic Orchestra appeared nearly a hundred times at the Queen's Hall for the Royal Philharmonic Society alone. Over half of these occasions were conducted by Beecham himself.

CHAPTER TWENTY-THREE

COVENT GARDEN AGAIN

(1)

THE GREYING BEARD began to look like something mellow and dynastic out of Van Dyck. There was now a hint of portliness, a new inflation of manner, an affability which—when he chose to exercise it —warmed like the autumn sun.

The old foot trouble plagued him intermittently, however, entailing injections, a minor operation, spells of milk diet and the occasional tart outbursts. Was it gout? Or a chronic sprain? Outside the consulting room nobody was sure. One night at Covent Garden—whither he returned in May 1932, staying on as artistic director and later as supreme controller for eight years in all—the gallery intrusively applauded Lotte Lehmann, who was singing Leonora in *Fidelio*. Beecham whipped round, his face twisted with fury, and shouted "Shut up, you b——s!" In the concert hall he accepted pelting crescendos of applause with an ironical smile up one side of his face, or sucked a tooth quizzically. The Editor of *The Musical Times* accused him of treating his public with manifest contempt.

His more seigneurial gestures were talked of with relish. When strolling with Lionel Tertis in Regent Street on a spring day, he called a taxi-cab and flung his greatcoat inside, saying airily to the driver, "Follow me, my man."* In the opera pit he could be relaxed, genial— and irreverent. Often he gibed at Wagner, of whose *Ring* he chose to conduct seven complete cycles in the 'thirties. During a rehearsal of the colloquy between Brünnhilde and Wotan in the second act of *Die Walküre*, with two great personalities on the stage, Frida Leider and Rudolf Bockelmann, he puffed expostulatingly and exclaimed, "Isn't Wagner an old bore!" On a *Götterdämmerung* occasion, the Curse motif having recurred (not for the first time), he bawled, "We've been rehearsing for two hours—and we're still playing the same bloody tune!"

Although most of them were young and eager as greyhounds, the LPO players were tested and troubled, just as the Beecham Symphony Orchestra had been a quarter of a century earlier, by the implacable

---

* Such an incident may have happened more than once. There are accounts of it dating back to the days of the hansom cab. The present version is authenticated by Mr. Tertis himself, at that time (the mid-'thirties) adviser to Beecham on the LPO string departments at Covent Garden.

round of long nights, late curtains and morning rehearsals that stretched into the afternoon. Half-way through one *Ring* cycle, Beecham came down to the theatre at ten a.m. and found himself flogging not the dynamic and fiery LPO but an assembly of jaded packhorses. Halting the rehearsal, he sent his valet Smith, a blue-serged, bowler-hatted bull-terrier of a man, across to the Nag's Head for champagne and stout all round. Beecham had a name of his own for this agreeable mixture: Nigger's Foot. So that they could drink at their ease, the orchestra moved from the pit to the stalls. "Not much rehearsing was done the rest of *that* day", remembers a survivor.

(2)

The illustrious singers who converged in troops on Covent Garden for Beecham's international seasons were for the most part of strictly traditional background and training. At least one, however, brought with her scents and flourishes from a very different world.

Grace Moore was a radiant, high-spirited American blonde who had made her début at nineteen as ingénue lead in an American musical, *Suite Sixteen*. What she called her hip-swinging feats in her leading number, "First you wiggle, then you waggle", was a notable hit in "college towns"; the boys in the front rows, she remembered with some embarrassment, used to whistle endlessly for encores. A career nurtured in revue and the film studios culminated, after bouts of singing lessons, in soprano leads at the Metropolitan Opera House, New York. Her opulent smile flashed from a thousand hoardings. A learned society gave her a gold medal for furthering the cause of good music through the cinema. She was voted one of the world's ten most beautiful women.

While on her way up to these vertigos, Miss Moore made a trip to Europe and found herself one night at dinner aboard a yacht off Cannes with Lady Cunard as the hostess. Just as at Drury Lane before the Kaiser's war, "Emerald" Cunard was Beecham's untiring and ingenious henchwoman. Her status was now official. She had a seat on the Covent Garden board and a stage box with her name in gilt on its door. She whipped in subscribers as ebulliently as before. Her catering reforms were radical. In the foyer she installed the longest theatre buffet in London. Under her supervisory eye, newfangled trolley-bars trundled the grand tier corridor during intervals, peddling caviare, chicken and champagne to box subscribers. From what happened at Cannes it is clear that her writ extended to casting policy. On hearing of Miss Moore's early, though as yet untrumpeted successes in opera and the concert hall, she said impulsively, "You must come to London to sing. I will launch you there." To which Miss Moore replied, "This isn't the moment for it. Later on I will."

The moment came in 1935. Miss Moore's bright blonde charm and her soprano talent reached their apogee in the film *One Night of Love*, in which she played a hard-up, delectable singing student in Italy. *One Night of Love* swept the cinemas of the world. It was obvious that henceforth Miss Moore was going to be good business in the world's opera houses as well. At this time Beecham was not supreme at Covent Garden. Alongside him, as managing director of the current syndicate, worked Geoffrey Toye. The *rapport* between them was imperfect. Through Toye's initiative, as we gather from Harold Rosenthal's *Two Centuries of Opera*, which is based in part on Covent Garden archives, Miss Moore was invited to sing three Mimis (*La Bohème*) at £300 a night—twice the fee paid to such celebrities as Lehmann and Elizabeth Rethberg. Accepting the invitation, she expressed, through her agent, the hope that her début would be on the most fashionable night of the week and that the King and Queen would attend one of her performances. At Dover she was met off the boat by civic dignitaries, cheering thousands and an escort of "fans" on bicycles. In loftier circles these demonstrations were judged distasteful. Operagoers of the kind who habitually look down their noses at everybody and everything deplored that Covent Garden had sunk to the level of a cinema.

Arriving at the theatre for the dress rehearsal, Miss Moore was introduced in a corridor "to a man whom Toye explained was Sir Thomas Beecham. A hurried how-do-you-do was the extent of his greeting, and he brushed past us abruptly. I looked after him in surprise. The welcome I had found in other opera houses had usually been traditionally courteous. . . . This was the most brusque I had ever encountered."

A crowded and cordial first night ended with sixteen curtain calls and a swarming of friends to Miss Moore's dressing room. In the wings she almost collided with Lady Cunard, who turned her back and ostentatiously failed to see her.

"The day after . . ." wrote Miss Moore* "I learned what was eating [her]. When the announcement was made of my contract to sing at Covent Garden she flew into a rage and said she didn't want a moviestar there. . . . My advance sale had taken Covent Garden out of the red for the first time in twenty-five years. She was infuriated that

---

* In her posthumous autobiography, *You're Only Human Once*, which came out in 1947, after her death in an airline disaster.

Geoffrey Toye was taking the responsibility and getting the credit for launching me in London, where she was so accustomed to ruling the operatic roost. If I had been a failure, she would have been courteous and consoling, no doubt. The success was more than she could bear."

According to Rosenthal, the tension between Beecham and Lady Cunard, on the one hand, and Toye and his supporters, on the other, was carried to breaking point by the Grace Moore episode. Towards the end of 1935, Toye resigned. For the next four years Beecham was king. His rule at Covent Garden was as it had been for brief spells in 1910: absolute in fact if not by statute.

(2)

With another soprano who came into prominence during one of his 1935 seasons, Beecham's dealings were gayer and more enduring.

Dora Labbette's name weaves in and out of the Beecham record for fifteen years or more. She often sang for him in the concert hall. As early as 1926 she had taken part in one of his great assaults (in the eyes of most Handelians over forty, his racy tempi amounted to no less) upon *Messiah*. As late as August 1940 she sang for him in Haydn's *The Seasons* at Sydney, Australia. He thought highly of her talents and made much of them. In the late summer of 1935, however, she had not set foot on the operatic stage. Precisely how she contrived her début is more piquant than any account printed at the time.

For September-October 1935, Beecham scheduled a brief German-Italian season at Covent Garden, followed by a lengthy provincial tour.* It came to Miss Labbette's ear that auditions had been convened for a *Bohème* revival. Putting on a bright blonde wig and a plain black dress which contrasted markedly with her usual wear, she wrote AUDITION on an envelope, presented it at the Covent Garden stage door, pretending to be a foreigner without a word of English, and was ushered without question or delay into the wings. There she joined six young women who were waiting to be heard as Mimi or Musetta. An upright piano tinkled sedulously in the opposite wing as a bass lugubriously coped with *Vecchia zimarra*.

Miss Labbette was third in the Mimi queue. When her name was called she walked on to the stage in a tremor. From under her false curls she identified a vague blur in the second row of stalls as Beecham. Neither he nor any other acquaintance in the theatre recognised her. She was identified merely as Number Three. Listening to her own

* British casts with a stiffening of Italians sang *Ballo in Maschera, Barbiere di Siviglia, La Bohème, Freischütz, Koanga* (Delius) and *Siegfried*. The Covent Garden season and the subsequent tour were financially guaranteed from the rump of Opera League funds.

voice in the big Mimi arias, she found it riding the theatre's spaces more easily than she had expected. Percy Heming, who as well as singing baritone parts for Beecham helped him managerially, had posted himself in the amphitheatre. At the end of the audition he hastened down to tell Beecham that, from where he had been sitting, Number Three was the pick of the morning. Beecham instructed him to speak to Number Three and find out something about her, with a possible offer in mind.

When Heming went into the wings, Number Three was nowhere to be found. Immediately after her last top note she had scuttled from the stage and its precincts as fast as her feet would carry her. She went to her agent, Harold Holt, and told him what she had done.

"Why did you do it?" asked Holt.

"For a bit of fun," she replied. "I wanted to pull Tommy's leg."

"Well," said Holt, "now that you've pulled Tommy's leg we'd better see about getting you into his *Bohème* cast." He telephoned Beecham and invited him to luncheon at the Café Royal, mentioning that he would bring along with him an unknown but promising young Italian soprano. After the invitation had been accepted, a thought struck Miss Labbette. "What are we going to call me?" she asked. Holt leafed through a heap of discarded publicity material. After a while he said, "Here's a name. What about 'Lisa Perli'? Must have been dead for years. 'Lisa Perli's' just the thing."

As Lisa Perli, then, Miss Labbette, still sailing under her false hair, was duly introduced to Beecham next day. She did not attempt to keep up the masquerade. Her neatly placed allusions to mutual experiences on the oratorio platform confirmed a suspicion which had already dawned in Beecham's mind. Identifying Miss Labbette with a shout of delight, he took the party under his own wing and ordered champagne. It was agreed that, as Lisa Perli, she should sing Mimi. Within a week her pseudonym was in bills and publicity hand-outs. Acuter than Beecham had been at the audition, some old hands who attended her début identified her long before Act III. The first night was on a Saturday. On the Monday morning millions of newspaper readers learned that Lisa Perli and Dora Labbette were one and the same party.

Beecham had entered into the hoax exuberantly. His intimates were greatly diverted by the cold, stern expression he put on when refusing to answer reporters' questions. For days after the hoax had been exposed, he tried to convince himself that it was still a splendid success. During an interval in a later Perli performance he asked the conductor,

Clarence Raybould, "Do you think they [the audience] have any idea who she is?" Raybould laughed. "Really, Sir Thomas," he said, "what do you take us for?"

At Covent Garden and in family quarters hopeful attempts were made to keep up the jest. One spokeswoman earnestly explained that Dora could not possibly be Lisa, because Dora was in Paris on the night of Lisa's Covent Garden début. To elude interviewers, and also on account of a minor infection, Miss Labbette spent most of her *Bohème* season in a Welbeck Street nursing home, leaving her bed for each performance and returning to it immediately afterwards. Later she rationalised her "bit of fun" with the following formula. Opera was her new career. A new career calls for a new personality. And a new personality is helped by a new name.

A point she overlooked, apparently, was the innate and automatic preference of the London musical public, more marked then than now, for foreign names in all contexts and circumstances.

(3)

On concert platforms up and down the country, as also in Nazi Germany, which they toured in November 1936, the LPO served Beecham superbly. He let it be known that they were one of the finest orchestras in the world. The world cordially agreed. Yet at home the LPO did not always command capacity houses. One of the most brilliant musical organisms of the century was threatened by the canker of public indifference. One adverse factor, as has been pointed out by Thomas Russell, who later became secretary and business manager of the LPO, was that the frequency of Beecham's appearances tended to detract from his box office value.

On various levels the patron-directors at LPO headquarters had much to worry about. The benign Baron d'Erlanger gave up in despair after a tenure of one month. In the words of a colleague, "Administering an orchestra headed by Beecham turned out to be a task not at all to his taste."

The original understanding was that the orchestra should never promote concerts on its own account. It was to play only as and when engaged by outside promoters. These restrictive conditions seem to have irked Beecham, who took to arranging concerts and committing his players without consulting the LPO board. His independent ventures were not always successful financially. Sometimes the players had to wait for their fees. Sometimes their fees were not paid in full. Sometimes they were not paid at all. After four years the

overtime backlog threatened to become intractable. Under this head-
ing sums of up to £300 were owed to individual players, some of
whom, after much agitation, were offered one-third in settlement.
On the surface the LPO was all zeal and brilliance. Under the surface
there were currents of unease and resentment, laced with talk of County
Court writs.

The patron-directors did what they could to cope with the arrears
problem. During one crisis, at a board meeting called overnight, a
small group of benefactors, with Courtauld and Mayer at their head,
put £8,000 on the table at a few hours' notice so that immediate
salary demands could be met. For these and kindred first-aid measures,
Beecham showed his gratitude in a singular manner. Speaking at successive annual meetings of the Hallé Concerts Society, Manchester, he
said (1935) that the LPO was unique among the world's orchestras in
that it cost nobody a penny, and (1937) that the LPO had no support
from the State or from anybody else; it was a self-supporting institution.
Not until 1940 did he publicly admit that "sources no longer available"
had expended a very large sum on the LPO during the preceding
seven years. Courtauld and Mayer had ceased to be available as
"sources" in 1936. How much they spent on the orchestra has not been
disclosed. Their resignation was followed by the formation of a new
company, the London Philharmonic Concert Society Ltd., of which
Beecham and his lawyer were the sole directors.

(4)

There were other withdrawals from the Philharmonic scene.

Many players felt that the glory of serving Beecham hardly com-
pensated for pay-packet uncertainties and the annual spells of slave-
driving in the Covent Garden pit.* Among the first violins alone only
four out of the original sixteen players were still at LPO desks after
four years. The resignation which caused the biggest stir was that of
the leader, Paul Beard, who, in 1936, went to lead the B.B.C. Symphony Orchestra. "I felt," said Beard to his new conductor, Sir Adrian
Boult, "that just one more Wagner day at Covent Garden, ten in the
morning until midnight, would be the end of me."

It was Beard's resignation and its aftermath that first brought Sir
Henry Wood's anti-Beecham psychosis into the open.

That Wood could be touchy about his brilliant junior (by ten years)
was common talk on the musical grapevine. In 1933, Beecham having

---

* During the early years there were rehearsals even on Sundays. The players had no free
time. Under a subsequent reorganisation, a five-day-week was introduced.

cancelled a conducting engagement at a South Coast musical festival, the committee invited Wood to step into the breach, offering him lavish expenses on top of his fee. Wood's reply was a terse postcard with one italicised line, from Appletree Farm, his retreat in Hertfordshire:

"Very well, I will do it for you, but if you ever want me again during my conducting life, don't forget that I am the doyen of British conductors, and as such I think I ought to be consulted about the free dates *before everyone* (sic) *else is finally fixed*. Please excuse card."

The widespread notion that Beecham had a special sort of rostrum magic made him especially testy. One night the LPO were conducted by a junior English baton. Next morning a critic reported that they had played "with some proportion, at any rate" of the quality they usually reserved for their permanent conductor. In the spirit of prosecuting counsel, Wood took the matter up at the first opportunity with a famous LPO section leader. In what way, he asked, could an orchestra keep quality in reserve for any conductor whatsoever? The leader's reply, triumphantly quoted by Wood in *My Life of Music*, was, "That's no compliment to any orchestra. I know that when I am in good form I play well; if I'm not, no conductor can make me play any better. I always give my best; we *all* do."

This damned the critic. But it also put Beecham in his place.

Although his attitude to its founder was one of simmering hostility, Wood had no objection to the LPO. Early in 1936 he was under contract to conduct it the following October at the Sheffield triennial festival, of which he had been the musical director and general hero for many years. When the festival contracts were signed, Beard was still LPO leader. On learning that Beard had resigned and that David McCallum, from the Scottish Orchestra, Glasgow, had replaced him, Wood said in effect, "But this will not do. I have never worked with Mr. McCallum. At Sheffield I must have a leader who knows my ways and methods, just as Mr. Beard did. If I cannot have a leader of my own choice I may have to resign."

At one point in the subsequent negotiations, Beecham humoured Wood to the extent of provisionally putting in Bernard Andrews, sub-principal of the LPO, as leader for the duration of the festival only. Descending from the heights of injured protest, Wood let it be known that, after thinking matters over, and although he felt annoyed, he was willing to accept the Andrews compromise, since Mr. Andrews had worked with him and knew his mind.

Meantime the dispute had been leaked to the Press, by Wood himself among others. Beecham seized upon this as a reason or pretext for going back on the Andrews solution. At Sheffield, he announced, David McCallum and none other was going to be leader. There would be no substitution. Unless led by McCallum, the LPO would not go to Sheffield at all.

The exchanges that followed—mainly through the medium of newspaper interviews—were lively and unedifying.

Insisting that he should be "arbiter in the choice of leader", Wood denounced Beecham as a dictator. With a characteristic wink and sparkle of the eye, he added, "I have no intention of bowing the knee to him."

In reply Beecham scoffed at Wood's "fantastic" pretensions, arguing that if all conductors were allowed to pick their leaders the outcome would be chaos. "For instance", he posited, "suppose Toscanini and myself were invited to conduct at, say, Munich, and then said, 'Oh yes, I should be delighted, but I must have my own leader. He is a very capable and good fellow'. The authorities would very properly reply 'Very well, stay away'."

In an unreflecting moment Wood cited his professional seniority. Beecham's rejoinder was shattering:

"Sir Henry refers to his forty-two years' experience as a concert conductor and is polite enough to suggest that, compared with this, my own experience of orchestras is negligible. I can only reply that ... for the past thirty-four years I have been before the public of this country, not only as a conductor of concerts but also of opera, the latter branch being an infinitely more arduous matter than the former. So far as orchestras are concerned, I have been privileged to found no fewer than four new ones in this country.* The suggestion of Sir Henry that I am not competent to express an opinion on this matter passes from the zone of the fantastic to the less agreeable one of the impertinent. When I described his attitude as fantastic, I did so because I was certain that such an attitude would be taken up by no other conductor in the world."

The wrangle continued for a month. In the end Wood retired from it discomfited. Just in time to save the festival from foundering, the committee announced that, for the sake of his art and the festival's great tradition, Sir Henry had agreed to accept McCallum as leader and had withdrawn his threat of resignation.

* He evidently included in his reckoning the St. Helens Orchestral Society (1899) and the New Symphony Orchestra (1906), as well as the Beecham Symphony Orchestra and the LPO.

(5)

The LPO's formative years and Beecham's re-ordination at Covent Garden coincided with the spread of the great canker in Europe. Within Germany's borders and, to an extent, beyond them, music, like all other goods of heart and intellect, was ruthlessly cut back and perverted by Nazi doctrinaires. Certain singers and conductors heard at Covent Garden in the later 'thirties, especially during the German seasons, were dissentients from Hitler's régime, or had been proscribed by it, some on racial, others on political grounds, or had independently opted for self-exile. Certain others were loquacious or sly Nazi conformists. When the two factions took part in the same opera, as sometimes happened, the atmosphere backstage was strained and explosive.

For a long time Beecham's attitude towards Nazism was playful and lofty. To him the Nazis were something of a joke. As late as seven months before the outbreak of the war he described Hitler and Mussolini as great comedians, without whom life would be very dull indeed. His comradeship with Wilhelm Furtwängler, conductor-in-chief of the Berlin Philharmonic Orchestra, who began by resisting the Nazis and ended in compliance, survived all strains. Furtwängler conducted *Ring* cycles for him at Covent Garden. In turn he won immense ovations by guest-conducting Furtwängler's orchestra (as well as the State Opera) in Berlin.

Nor was Furtwängler the only bridge to Nazidom. At her own table in Grosvenor Square and at others where hostesses, some of them with great names, dipped their toes or waded ankle deep into world politics, Lady Cunard saw much of Joachim von Ribbentrop, the blustering popinjay who served Hitler as Ambassador in London from 1936 to 1938. So much did she see of him, indeed, that Lady Astor twitted him for the "bad company" he kept in England. Whom did she have in mind? inquired Ribbentrop. "Lady Cunard and Lady London-derry,"* replied Lady Astor. "But", said Ribbentrop, with wide, expostulating eyes, "they have always been extremely kind to me and my friends." Lady Cunard's kindness was sometimes of the probing and teasing kind. As hostess she had a way of baiting "my dear Am-bassador" with crucial questions. What, she would inquire, did Herr Hitler *truly* think about God? And why ("something we all want to know, dearest Excellency") did Herr Hitler dislike the Jews so? In obvious

* Wife of the 7th Marquis of Londonderry, Secretary of State for Air, 1931-35; later Leader of the House of Lords.

discomfort, Ribbentrop groped for replies and did not readily find them.

It was through Ribbentrop's offices that, in the early summer of 1936, Beecham received an invitation, which he accepted, to take the LPO to Germany for a brief concert tour, to be sponsored by the Nazi Government, the following November. In the negotiations that followed, Beecham's programme drafts for the tour were submitted to Ribbentrop's office. Among the fifteen or so items which Beecham proposed to play was one which bore the mark of the beast: Felix Mendelssohn-Bartholdy's Symphony No. 3 in A minor (the *Scotch*). Mendelssohn was a Christian by faith and a Jew by blood. For three years his music had been banned throughout Germany. According to the memoirs of Berta Geissmar, who had become Beecham's general secretary a few months earlier, one of Ribbentrop's aides hastened to the LPO offices and suggested that Beecham be "tactfully" requested to drop the symphony. Unwilling to jeopardise the tour by making an issue of the matter, Beecham complied.

Herself of Jewish stock (and Protestant upbringing), Dr. Geissmar had managed Furtwängler's affairs before she settled in England and joined Beecham. She had negotiated her transfer of residence with trepidation and obtained official Nazi endorsement of it at great expense. Innumerable precedents suggested that if ever she again set foot in Germany she would be arrested at the frontier by the Gestapo and have her passport confiscated. When, in his casual, airy way, Beecham instructed her to travel ahead of him and negotiate details of the tour in Berlin and seven other German cities, Dr Geissmar was much perturbed. Beecham waved her fears aside. She was, he assured her, free to visit Germany and move about there as often and as long as she pleased. There would be no trouble at all. "You see", he explained, "I had a talk on the subject yesterday with von Ribbentrop. Everything is arranged."

Ribbentrop's unwritten *laissez-passer* worked with bizarre smoothness. Not only did Dr. Geissmar cross the frontier unmolested. For her comings and goings in Berlin she was provided with an official motorcar bearing the swastika flag on its bonnet. Beecham's car bore both the swastika and an eagle mascot.

His eight concerts in Germany,* tumultuously successful, were

---

* Between November 13th and November 20th, 1936, he and the LPO performed in Berlin, Dresden, Leipzig, Munich, Stuttgart, Ludwigshafen, Frankfort and Cologne. His programmes included five items by British composers: the *Enigma* Variations (Elgar), *Summer Night on the River* and *On Hearing the First Cuckoo* . . . (Delius), *The Wasps* Overture (Vaughan Williams) and the *Triumph of Neptune* suite (Lord Berners). For the rest he played Rossini, Haydn, Berlioz, Handel, Mozart, Dvořák and Rimsky-Korsakov.

attended by massive official junketings. Towns were strung with
bunting and floodlit. Mayors orated at beery banquets to the orchestra
and their chief which were sometimes succeeded by revels into
the small hours. At least one morning rehearsal had to be cancelled
because of collective hangover. The inaugural concert in Berlin
was attended by Hitler and his entire Cabinet. The Führer, it was noted,
applauded everything with vigour. A few hours earlier he had received
Beecham at the Chancellery and informed him how important it was
that Britain and Germany should appreciate each other's artistic
attainments. For days the capital buzzed with gossip about the meeting. According to some, Beecham held the floor, voluble and brilliant.
(Five years later he remarked that in private conversation Hitler
struck him as "simple and unaffected".) According to others it was
Hitler who did the haranguing. Friedelind Wagner, granddaughter of
Richard Wagner, reported Beecham as saying on the morrow of his
interview, "Now I *know* what's wrong with Germany."

One thing, at least, was much to his taste in Germany: the congeries
of subsidised orchestras and opera houses. On his return to England he
loudly and repeatedly praised these institutions, without stressing—or
even acknowledging—that they were the handiwork mainly of pre-
Nazi régimes, including the much despised Weimar Republic. His
praise was characteristically interleaved with abuse of Britain, which
he judged to be musically backward, barbarous and, into the bargain,
chronically ill-governed.★ A visit to Sheffield revived his fury at the
festival authorities and prompted him to an ill-considered if implicit
comparison. The man who, five nights earlier, had been rapturously
recalled and loaded with laurel wreaths before an audience of 5,000
at the LPO's farewell concert in Cologne, said, "I have been playing in
civilised towns recently." For its future festivals, he contemptuously
added, Sheffield should book the Band of the Grenadier Guards or the
Besses o' th' Barn [a celebrated English brass ensemble]. Even if
the city had a hundred festivals, the LPO would never take part
again.

As the European shadows lengthened, Beecham's attitude, a compound of detachment and flippancy, gradually modified. In the early
summer of 1938 he told Dr Geissmar that he would accept no further
engagements in Germany. The inhuman acts of the Nazis, supinely
tolerated by the German people, had alienated even those sections of
English opinion which had hitherto been friendly to the "genuine"

★ The last note occurs in several pronouncements of the late 'thirties and early war years.
In the Spring of 1939 he toyed with the idea of entering politics as an Independent.

Germany. The sombre note was rare in Beecham's utterances. With it, for the first time, went a hint of weariness.

On a June night in 1939, he and his singers were cheered for ten minutes after a *Tristan* performance which ended an international season and heralded the end of an international epoch as well. In the conductor's room afterwards he said, "The public must be tired of me after all these years. What is more, I have been overworking myself." In his sixty-first year he was stoutish and white-bearded, nagged by foot pains and lumbago, inwardly battered by decades of fighting and shouting and contriving and orating with silver tongue in cheek. He had promised himself a year's complete rest from music. All was planned and prepared. He was to go abroad for sun-warmed leisure.

Then came September 3rd. The outbreak of war froze music in its tracks and put the company responsible for the London Philharmonic Orchestra into liquidation. This was no time for even a tired man to sit idly in the sun. Beecham postponed his year's respite and fought a rearguard action, by baton and word of mouth, for the LPO, which was now administered by a players' committee. Thanks to his and other efforts, the orchestra quickly took root again.

He did not leave England until the Spring of 1940. On May 9th he landed at New York from the Italian liner *Rex*. In London an accountant added up the LPO players' arrears. They came to £25,000. But other and heavier cares occupied men's minds. The Nazi armies had struck deep and were poised to strike deeper still. London was a hubbub of political reconstruction. To shipboard reporters in New York, Beecham oracularly commended David Lloyd George, old but dynamic, as the man who could lead Britain most surely to victory. Next day Winston Churchill came to power.

CHAPTER TWENTY-FOUR

MARGARET BETTY HUMBY

(1)

THE OLD SPARK rekindled. Weariness might never have been. During his four American years, Beecham criss-crossed the continent's length and breadth, making one foray into Mexico and several into Canada. In 1940 alone, taking into account his early tour of Australia (June to September),* he travelled 60,000 miles by sea and land. "One spends most of one's life in ships, trains and hotels, attending ladies' luncheons and performing other works of supererogation", he blandly complained. "Life has become a sort of *moto perpetuo*. Sometimes I forget which town I am in."

The orchestras he conducted on his travels were for the most part second-rate or worse—until the fury of his frown and the compulsion of his bark marvellously matured and vitalised them. At the ladies' luncheons one of his preferred topics was the English language as heard in American films. He spoke with thunder on his brow of "that piercing twang, that terrible, awful, high-pitched, metallic delivery." The lunching ladies—and their menfolk, too, when they read the newspapers next morning—gasped and fretted at diatribes which traversed many American trends and institutions, politics not excepted. Touchy citizens accused him of insulting the nation. Some went so far as to contend that he should be barred from the nation's auditoriums. "But why?" inquired Beecham, lifting his eyebrows in simulated surprise. "I am a peaceful, harmless man. I simply can't understand why people are always going for me. It's a positively pathological attitude. People see Beecham, and immediately their backs go up."

To young gifts and (as will presently be seen) down-at-heel talents he could be bountiful and avuncular. While in New York he was telephoned at the Ritz Hotel by a young Anglo-Saxon composer

---

* Soon after arriving in New York he had sailed for Sydney, arriving on June 11th. In that city and in Melbourne, Brisbane and Perth, between mid-July and the end of September, he conducted a dozen choral or orchestral concerts, obtaining brilliant results even, on occasion, with amateur or amateurish forces. His farewell pronouncements caused a blaze of resentment. Australians were "sublimely self-satisfied and complacent". A "stagnant population" of seven millions occupied a continent nearly the size of Europe. They lived in a fool's paradise, a "cuckoo-town of unreality". Their contribution to the war was incomparably less than that of Canada or New Zealand.

whose music had been recommended to him by certain connoisseur friends. "Let me see some of your music, my boy", he said.

"How much shall I let you have?"

"Oh, send me a suitcaseful."

A suitcase was duly packed and delivered. Two days later the young man called upon Beecham by appointment. He found him in a lavishly atavistic suite. The old masters and tasseled Tudor brocades which surrounded him were singularly like those among which he habitually lived in England. The murmur spread that he had brought his furniture across the Atlantic with him. Through the open door leading from the drawing room the young man saw him tug the suitcase from under his bed. Casually picking a symphonic score from the top of the heap, he settled in a high-backed chair which might have been carved for doges and began to turn its leaves, whistling an irrelevant tune the while. "Excellent work, my boy", he said, when half-way through the first movement. "I will produce this in Seattle, play it all through the mid-West and finally give it in New York." (He did nothing of the sort. A year later he produced a different symphony by the same young man. Characteristically, he never explained why he had changed his mind.)

The Ritz suite at this period swarmed with publishers, lawyers, fiddlers, assistant conductors and musical committee-men from all points of the compass. For every caller who expounded his business— or had it expounded to him—two or three others waited in the ante-chamber. One caller found Beecham drinking whisky with a trim, elderly woman whose manner had more than a touch of the *grande dame*. She was introduced as Lady Cunard.

"Emerald" had closed the Grosvenor Square house, which the Government requisitioned later for war purposes, at the beginning of 1940. Her wartime stay in America was briefer than Beecham's. For a while she bustled and held forth on the fate of nations at country house week-ends on Long Island and elsewhere. "Lady Cunard", wrote one of America's more acid commentators, "has certainly solved the problem of how to be a luxurious refugee."

Returning to an England under bombardment by the Luftwaffe and besieged by U-boats, she presently took a seventh-floor suite in a Park Lane hotel and, as far as wartime conditions allowed, indomitably resumed her function as hostess and oracle. Some of her judgments were brusque. When, in June 1944, somebody well-informed told her that the Nazis had begun to bombard London with "pilotless 'planes", she pronounced the thing impossible. The fact that people were ready to believe such rubbish, she said, only showed how stupid they became in wartime.

Lady Cunard had fallen from the Beecham orbit and from the heart of the Beecham legend. Four years later, in the same hotel, with two friends at her bedside, she died, a lonely old woman who had seen much that glittered tarnish over and turn to dust.

(2)

Meantime another companion had entered upon the scene: Margaret Betty Thomas, pianist, who preferred to be cited by her professional (and maiden) name, Betty Humby.

At the height of a sticky heat wave in June 1941, Miss Humby played in the Delius Pianoforte Concerto with Beecham at a Studio concert for the Columbia Broadcasting System in New York. Twinkling, comradely photographs were taken of them at a piano together. Several other joint appearances followed.

One of the most striking of these was a performance of Mozart's C major Concerto, K. 467, at the Carnegie Hall in March 1943. The orchestra, the New York City Symphony, was made up of unemployed musicians, most of them out of training, some of them apparently beyond it. (When its sponsor, Mayor La Guardia, asked Beecham if he would give the orchestra a helping hand, he had replied, "But of course. I like conducting any orchestra that will play the notes. You get the players to accomplish your purpose or you don't. Up to the present I have failed to encounter any orchestra that failed to accomplish mine.") Sandwiched between an evening recital by a star 'cellist and an afternoon concert by the renowned New York Philharmonic Orchestra under another English baton, John Barbirolli (now Sir John),[*] Beecham's programme began at an unpropitious hour, five-thirty p.m. Yet the hall was crammed with music-lovers mainly of the plain, unpretentious sort, who had paid as little as 28 c. for admission. In Tchaikovsky's *Francesca da Rimini* fantasy, Mozart's *Paris* Symphony and Sibelius's No. 7, Beecham transformed his troop of rags and tags and hopefuls into a tolerably sure and shining instrument. In a considered survey a week later *The New York Times* described his achievement as sensational.

About Miss Humby and her Mozart playing the note was hardly as rapturous. The critic Olin Downes complained that her over-ethereal pianissimos constantly made the melodic line fade out altogether.

[*] Twenty-six years earlier Barbirolli, then in his late 'teens, had played for Beecham among the 'cellos in the Drury Lane orchestra pit.

But Miss Humby's musicianship was only one aspect of her personality. Gossips began to put it about that Sir Thomas's interest in her was not exclusively professional. The gossips were right.

Daughter of a dental surgeon with a fashionable Mayfair practice, Betty Humby was born on April 8th, 1908, and discovered a taste for the piano some seven years later. She won a scholarship to the Royal Academy of Music at ten, a thing nobody had ever done before. At thirteen she had thirty pupils of her own. At sixteen she became a professor in one of London's more influential private schools of music. Along with the teaching grind went the excitement of concert work. By her middle twenties the former infant prodigy was a veteran of Wigmore Hall, Queen's Hall, B.B.C. studios and a score of provincial platforms. *The Times* did not greatly care for her late Beethoven, finding it superficial and overnuanced.

Fair, blue-eyed and pretty in a ringleted and rather conventional way, she had a more tenacious will and greater clarity of purpose that appeared on the surface. She came to Beecham's notice when in her late 'teens. Her Mozart playing in particular impressed him. Years later he was to say, "Bruno Walter once told me there were only two people who could play a Mozart concerto, and he was one of them. Wild horses will not drag the other name from me." Wild horses were not necessary. It was clear from the circumstances in which this cryptic judgment was made* that the name he and Walter had in mind was Betty Humby's.

During the winter of 1937-38 their names had been linked, though not conspicuously, in a series of Sunday night Mozart concerts at the Cambridge Theatre, London. As president of this endeavour, Beecham wrote a send-off article which commended Mozart's music as an antidote against the chaotic thought and action of a blatant age. "If I were a dictator", he blithely added, "I should make it compulsory for every member of the population between the ages of four and eighty to listen to Mozart for at least a quarter of an hour daily for the coming five years." This Mozart Series comprised nine concerts. Betty Humby was one among sixteen solo performers; merely that and (as it seemed from current advertisements) nothing more. From retrospective Beecham publicity, however,† it appears that these concerts

---

* The circumstances were as follow. Billed to play Mozart's A major Concerto, K. 488, with Beecham at a Drury Lane festival concert in May 1947, she withdrew from the programme owing to illness at forty-eight hours' notice. Beecham refused his manager's request to bring in a substitute pianist, maintaining in effect that, as a Mozart collaborator Betty Humby (by that time his wife), was irreplaceable.

† *The Royal Philharmonic Orchestra . . . First North American Tour 1950*, souvenir booklet.

and a subsequent series involved 300 artists, a total which presumably took in orchestral players and choral singers, and that they were all given under her "personal direction."

By this time she was long married and had a schoolboy son, Jeremy. Her husband, seventeen years older than she, was a vicar in West London, graduate of Keble College, a former East End curate and, for a spell during the Kaiser's War, temporary chaplain to H.M. forces.

.   .   .   .   .

In the autumn of 1940 she and Jeremy sailed for America, wartime evacuees. They landed in the east around the time that Beecham was landing from the Antipodes at Vancouver in the west. She made her American musical début in February of the following year. It was given out later that for some months Beecham had no knowledge of her presence in the U.S. One day his agent asked him if he would care to engage an able young English pianist, Betty Humby, for one of his 1941 concerts. "But I know Betty Humby", he is reported to have said.

Thus they came together: the "beloved companion, brave and beautiful, gracious and gay",* and the man whose conversation so fascinated her that, as she once said, "I could go on listening to Tom for ever." The reunion was momentous not only for their happiness but also for the contentment or otherwise of several who worked with or for them.

(3)

Boise, Idaho, is externally an agreeable place for anybody who is obliged to kill a long month there. Sitting among spur hills of a great mountain range, it is sunny, sheltered and richly wooded. There are relics and memories of gold strikes and gold-mining from the 1860s and later. On the banks of the Boise River stands a blockhouse where early settlers sought shelter from the Indians. The State Capitol boasts corinthian pillars in local sandstone. Its rotunda harbours a gilded equestrian statue of George Washington carved with crude tools from a yellow pine tree by a soldier whose only model was a postage stamp.

From Boise, on October 4th, 1942, the Associated Press circulated a message which named Sir Thomas Beecham, British conductor and (as he then was) director of the Seattle Symphony Orchestra. Sir Thomas, said A.P., had filed a suit to divorce Mrs. (sic) Utica Celestia Beecham, whom he married in London on July 26, 1903.

* The phrase is from the dedicatory page of Beecham's *Frederick Delius* (1959), completed after her death.

(Actually the marriage was on the 27th.) The message added: "The suit was filed in Idaho City, former mining town among the mountains. Sir Thomas said in the complaint that his wife 'early in their married life formed an aversion for the plaintiff'. He said she had not lived with him since 1909 and that she was extravagant, spending in one particular week an amount exceeding $500,000" (equivalent then to £125,000).

The crucial day in these proceedings was January 15th, 1943. On that day Beecham was in the pit of New York's Metropolitan Opera House, 3,000 miles away, conducting a dullish matinée performance of Charpentier's *Louise* for the national free milk fund. At the first rehearsal he had kept the singers waiting unconscionably on the roof-stage. Those who were not attuned to his habits expected some word of explanation, even of regret. When he arrived he treated them with the indifference of a satrap. The Louise was a former antagonist, Grace Moore. "I wondered", she noted afterwards, "whether Sir Thomas had overslept or whether he enjoyed giving himself special privileges." The rehearsal, nevertheless, went spiritedly. It amounted, in fact, to a genuine performance. The same could not be said of the matinée. Tempi were sluggish. There were bouts of off-pitch singing by Miss Moore.

At some point between Father's "Is supper ready?" and Louise's "Depuis le jour", the judge reached his decision. "Sir Thomas Beecham", said an A.P. despatch from Boise that afternoon, "obtained a divorce here today from Utica Celestia Beecham on the ground of extreme cruelty. The degree was granted by District Judge Charles F. Koelsch after the arrival of depositions taken in the case in London. Sir Thomas was not present. The conductor established residence in Idaho last summer preparatory to suing for divorce under the State's forty-two day residence requirement." It was added that in his complaint Beecham said he had received from Lady Beecham "only carping criticism in my chosen work" and that she "belittled the success which I continually attained".

Six weeks later newspaper readers learned that Mrs. Margaret Betty Thomas, née Humby, had obtained a divorce under the same legal jurisdiction. "Sir Thomas Beecham", they read, "was recently married to Betty Humby, a young English pianist, . . . it was revealed yesterday. Although neither Sir Thomas nor his bride would make any statement about their marriage, it was learned that the couple, who met for the first time in England fourteen years ago, were married in New York. It was the second marriage for both. . . . The new Lady

Beecham, whose former husband was the Rev. Thomas . . ., obtained her divorce in Boise, Idaho, a year ago."*

Legally this was not the end. The nuptial knot had to be retied with red tape. On the afternoon of September 7th, 1944, the Beechams went through a second marriage ceremony before Supreme Justice Samuel Null in his chambers at County Court House, New York. In the marriage licence issued by the City Clerk, the bride gave her age as thirty-six. The bridegroom was sixty-five. The witnesses were two attorneys from East Forty-fourth Street, Herbert M. Karp and Benjamin F. Foster. In a statement after the ceremony they said, "Sir Thomas's attorneys believed that, to assure compliance with technicalities of the English law, it was advisable that a second marriage ceremony be performed at this time."

Less than a week later they locked up their Manhattan apartment, with its baronial appointments and faint perpetual cigar fragrance. Voyaging in wartime convoy aboard a Dutch cargo boat, they lived in cramped quarters among motor trucks and crates of dried vegetables. The convoy ran into a hurricane which, testified Beecham, made the ship stand on her head. For seventeen days they had little sleep. Then Mersey-mouth and home. Beecham came ashore dishevelled. A reporter ran him to earth in a barber's shop.

"I always", he said, "come to Liverpool for a shave."

* *New York Herald Tribune*, February 24th, 1943.

CHAPTER TWENTY-FIVE

"I ALWAYS GET THE PLAYERS"

(1)

Beecham and his new wife were opulent nomads, for ever buying new houses or leases, carting tons of period furniture from county to county, debating in echoing, newly-carpeted rooms where this Florentine chest was to go, or that Zoffany be hung, whether the front hall was or wasn't the best place for the talismanic bronze of Delius's head, and so on. When they moved from one point to the next, they sometimes contrived, on a rising market, to transfer their lease or sell their bricks and mortar at a loss. In such matters Beecham was grandly careless; "no businessman", as the saying goes. Having installed themselves in some deftly chosen mansion or villa, they would impulsively pack their bags and camp luxuriously in hotel suites for weeks on end.

One of their first homes in London was at Circus Road, St. John's Wood. Beecham did most of his work in a long, sunflooded room with windows rather like those of a conservatory. His habit was to get up at five-thirty and study scores in the morning quiet. "I sit here", he used to tell his friends, "and wait until the staff decide to bring me a cup of coffee." When the coffee came he would light his first cigar and presently make his first telephone call of the day. More than once his orchestral manager or some personal assistant was awakened at six or seven a.m. by that curiously fatigued and floating drawl. "Mr. So-and-So", the voice would say, without any apology for the outrageous hour, "I have been wondering who is going to play the second horn to-night." Or (in the case of the personal assistant): "I am interested in six paintings which are coming up at Christie's today. I want you to buy them for me. Call at the office [that of his new orchestra, the Royal Philharmonic]. You will there find a catalogue marked marginally with the prices I am prepared to pay. The first of the six comes up at eleven o'clock." Reaching the saleroom in good time, a personal assistant who had been thus instructed found two of the paintings had already been knocked down. He bid successfully for the remaining four. Beecham gave one to Betty and three to friends as Christmas presents. He was almost as assiduous in the saleroom as his father had been, and indulged much the same taste for the 18th-century.

After Circus Road came Delves House, at Ringmer, on the Glyndebourne estate of John Christie, founder of the renowned Glyndebourne opera house. On Delves House the Beechams took a three-year lease. They lived there for perhaps six months. The house had a score rooms. With it went fourteen acres of lawn and gardens, two cottages, an ornamental pond, a well stocked piggery and a garage big enough for three Rolls-Royces. A mountain of furniture was brought out of store. New furniture was added. Men in baize aprons toiled for a week. The paintings alone would have stocked a small art gallery. Among them were a pair of Zoffanys, a big Constable landscape, at least one Reynolds, and a head-and-shoulders of David Garrick attributed to Gainsborough. Hanging was a long, fastidious labour. Followed by the Beechams, two men from the repository would carry something massive and gilt-framed from room to room.

"Now Mr. Hall", Beecham would say to the attendant expert, "let us see what it looks like on the wall facing the window."

After the painting had been experimentally hung and discussed for a minute or two, Betty would pronounce, "It's no good, Tom. It doesn't *belong* in this part of the house." Unhooking their burden, the repository men would resume their sweating trudge. It was three months before the paintings were hung to Betty's satisfaction.

When all the twenty rooms had been fitted and garnished, the question arose: to what end? Aptly sited and designed for week-end parties and routs (Lady Cunard in her prime would have queened it brilliantly there), Delves House existed in effect for two persons. The Beechams did no entertaining on the grand scale. Guests came in twos and ones. Betty Beecham was no Lady Cunard. She preferred simple and intimate social settings for her husband. Although such pleasures were hardly feasible in denuded postwar Britain, a crowded salon and a brilliant table in the Edwardian manner or that of the 'twenties would probably have shadowed her adoring, possessive spirit.

From Sussex the nomads moved back to St. John's Wood. The house they took in Grove End Road had six rooms, apart from servants' quarters. In came the pantechnicon loads from Delves. Betty did what she could to cram a quart into a pint pot. She would say to the removal foreman, "We'll have *that*" (a Chippendale writing desk, perhaps) "in the drawing room." "But", the foreman would object, "there ain't no bleedin' room left in the drawing room.

There's so much in the drawing room already that I can hardly open the bleedin' door to get in!" Even after some tons of splendour had been sent back to store, the Grove End Road house remained too cramped, as well as too urban, for a man of Beecham's burdens and commitments. On top of his concert schedules and the controversies which he zestfully kept on the boil,* he had begun to write his biography of Frederick Delius. The composer of *A Mass of Life* had died in 1934 after years of paralysis, blindness and paroxysmal agony, the outcome of syphilis contracted in the late 'nineties. Reportedly at his own wish (a puzzling one, given his outlook), the remains of the old sceptic and priest-hater had been brought from Grez and buried under an ancient yew tree in the quiet country churchyard of Limpsfield, Sussex. During the committal ceremony, Beecham, spruce and solemn, had conducted a section of the LPO in *On Hearing the First Cuckoo* and *Summer Night on the River*, among much else. Orating afterwards at the head of the grave he had affirmed his belief in that personal immortality which Delius had so tenaciously denied.

The biography had long been pondered. Masses of material had been collected. In his possession were hundreds of letters to and from Delius dating back to the 'eighties, which had been made over to him by Delius's widow. What he needed was some remote, untroubled retreat where he could get on with the business of turning these and other documents into a book.

The answer was, or seemed to be, Round Island. One reached Round Island, unless inimical seas were running—in which case one did not reach it at all—by motor launch from a point on the Dorsetshire coast in the region of Poole Harbour. The trip usually took half an hour. One made it either in the postman's launch, which brought in milk and groceries as well as mail, or in a launch with an independent pilot which went with the lease of the Round Island villa. In stormy weather visitors were liable to be cut off for days. On the return journey one could save time by coming ashore not at Poole Harbour but at a beach closer in; one caught advantageous trains to Waterloo after wading ankle deep through mud to a waiting hire-car.

* During these years he successively or simultaneously attacked the heads of the Hallé Concerts Society for deposing him during the war from the presidency of the Society (an episode which did them little credit); the upholders of State subsidies for overlooking that the RPO flourished happily without one; the London County Council for proposing to launch the Festival of Britain (1951) with inappropriate music under an alien conductor (Toscanini); the new Royal Festival Hall for looking "repellent, ugly and monstrous"; the directors of Covent Garden for every step they took and every word they uttered; and living composers in general for their inability to write tunes.

The villa was the only house on the island. One room in it was set apart and solemnly named the Delius Room. Here Beecham worked sporadically on files which classified the Delius letters in year-by-year groupings. When he had annotated a document he would drop it on the floor. Writing fluently with an old-fashioned pen, he shed his manuscript pages in the same way. At the end of the day his secretary would come along to pick up these strewments and sort them out. With interruptions for other business he worked thus for six spring and summer months. On his return to the mainland, he could not claim to have made much progress. *Frederick Delius* did not come out until some sixteen months before his death. He had been thinking, talking, researching, writing and re-writing it for most of thirty years. The task had been, as it were, a continuing obbligato to his founding and administering of two great orchestras. Some account must now be given of the second of these.

(2)

On his return to England in 1944, Beecham was vociferously welcomed by concert audiences. Yet his prestige was not as secure as it had been before the war. His leaving the country in 1940 and the legalistic contriving of his second marriage were found distasteful by some. Nor had his musical achievements while in exile been especially noteworthy. Of America's three leading orchestras, which he had often guest-conducted in peacetime with enormous *éclat*, the Boston Symphony and the Philadelphia Symphony were in other hands throughout the war. The third was the illustrious New York Philharmonic, Toscanini's former instrument. Of this he publicly asserted early in 1943 that it was "almost as bad" as a certain London Orchestra, presumably the LSO, when he first took it over. When, at last, in the early summer of 1944, he was offered a series with the Philharmonic, he swallowed any aversion he may have felt. In the vast Lewisohn Stadium out beyond Central Park, which drew audiences the size of a small town or mere shivering handfuls according to the weather, he conducted the Philharmonic in five programmes, three of which included concertos. With the pianist Artur Rubinstein in Rachmaninov's C minor he drew 18,000; with Kreisler in the Tchaikovsky Violin Concerto, 16,500; with Betty Humby in Saint-Saëns' G minor (No. 2), 6,000.

For the rest his orchestral assignments in the US were smallish beer. They took in Los Angeles, New Orleans, Salt Lake City, whose Philharmonic, he complained, "can only be called an orchestra by courtesy"; Seattle, where he succeeded one of his English juniors, Basil Cameron, who had conducted there for six years; and so on. At the Metropolitan Opera House in 1942 and 1943, one among several guest conductors from abroad, he had conducted a string of *Fausts*, *Carmens*, *Louises* and *Manons*, as well as his favourite coupling of *Le Coq d'Or* and *Phoebus and Pan*. Every time he appeared on the "Met" rostrum he was accused by the entire Press of the "awful crime of galvanising that ancient institution into something resembling animation." Such, textually, was his boast when back in England. Not that his revitalisings pleased every ear. Of his *Carmen* first night, Olin Downes wrote that for all his nerve-straining, pulling and hauling, the orchestra played villainously most of the time. His extremer *tempi* were such that the chorus hardly had time to breathe, articulate or act.

Altogether, it could not be said that Beecham came ashore at Liverpool in September 1944 trailing clouds of glory.

(3)

First there was a picking up of threads with the London Philharmonic. After his first packed and elating appearances with them, he was heard to observe, in the presence of LPO leaders and committeemen, that English orchestras were playing as badly as ever. "You can take that", he qualified, "with a pinch of salt—but not too large a pinch." It did not occur to him, apparently, that he might be rubbing the salt into open wounds.

As musicians the LPO players were stimulated and delighted to have him back. As husbands and fathers with bills to pay some of them remembered the £25,000-worth of pay arrears. There was a further disrupting factor. Up to 1939 the LPO, although nominally run by a private company, had been the unrestricted fief of its founder. Beecham not only conducted the LPO; he *was* the LPO. During his American years, however, the scene had radically changed. The LPO were now a self-governing "co-operative". If Beecham was to resume his old baton, he must do so as their salaried artistic director. To this end the directors offered him a contract which (as he analysed it), deprived him of freedom to select his players and choose his programmes; imposed upon him an assistant conductor whose duty it would be to conduct preliminary rehearsals; and gave the LPO prior claims on his services, with a proviso that all offers of engagements other than with the LPO (opera, radio and recording included) must be approved by the orchestra's chosen representative, who should have the right to decide whether or not such offers could be accepted. The contract proposed, in short, that the orchestra should be the head and the conductor the tail.

"I emphatically refuse", concluded Beecham, "to be wagged by any orchestra."

In the autumn of 1946 he struck drastically and swiftly. Without letting the LPO executive know what was afoot, he began to enrol a new orchestra. Taking a suite and a two-roomed office at the Waldorf Hotel, he told his orchestral manager, "I am going to found one more great orchestra to round off my career. The Royal Philharmonic Orchestra is going to be the greatest orchestra ever." For the LPO directors, when they came to hear of it, the new orchestra's name had a menacing ring. They soon learned that Beecham had negotiated a contract with the Royal Philharmonic Society whereby the RPO should replace the LPO at the Society's future concerts.

As had happened in 1909 and again in 1932, fixers went to work in the freelance pool and in other quarters. The news that Beecham was forming yet another orchestra was received with sardonic but indulgent smiles by players to whom he stood indebted. Their frame of mind was summed up by a leading brass player who, when tele-phoned by one of Beecham's agents, replied: "The old b——— owes me £1,000 down the years. But I want to play for him, man! You can count on me."

It took three and a half weeks to complete the orchestral list. During that time some of the 1939 debts were paid off. There was to be no cheeseparing. In an austere postwar community which seemed committeed in perpetuity to the State as prime mover in all things, the arts included, Beecham reasserted roundly and lavishly the prin-ciple of personal responsibility and initiative. In the background he had moneyed supporters and associates, including gramophone companies both here and in the US, with whom fat recording contracts had been negotiated. With its leader earning up to £100 a week and its principals in other departments £40 or £50, the RPO quickly ranked as the dearest orchestra in London, costing outside impre-sarios a minimum of £350 for a single concert, plus £250 as con-ductor's fee if Beecham was engaged with it.

The first rehearsal began at 2.30 p.m. in St. Pancras Town Hall only four days before the opening concert. Some of the players were newly out of the Forces. The second flute, indeed, had been de-mobilised at 12.30 p.m. that very day. Where had Beecham found the rest? He repudiated any suggestion that he had been poaching; none of his players, he insisted, came from pre-established orchestras. Inferentially, they came from the freelance pool. Recalling 1909 and 1932, he said, "People always tell me I shall not get the players. I always do. I have the finest players in England. They are so good that they refuse to play under anybody except me."

Four years later, by which time there had been changes in the personnel, Beecham's publicity claimed that the RPO was made up very largely of men who had played under his direction before the war. "In every department. . . .", it was added "are to be found not only the leaders but many of the rank and file of the orchestra of that day, to whom have been added a number of younger men of proved ability." Surprisingly—and mystifyingly—the programme of the opening concert, in the Davis Theatre, Croydon, on the afternoon of Sunday September 15th, 1946, carried no list of names.* Professional spotters identified the players, or some of them, as best they could across a vast, jammed auditorium, with the house lights dimmed so that Beecham might the better be seen as he lunged masterfully in a lilac "spot."

In the skimpy, print-rationed newspapers of the day, the RPO had a respectful welcome. But the old note of staggered rapture was missing. The general assessment was that, on Beecham standards, the RPO was good but might be better. At the final rehearsal Beecham had felt much the same. "It will be all right in a month's time", he had said. Then, with flashing eye and a characteristic down-thrust of the right fist: "But it's four times better than anything else you've ever heard!" The truth is that there were weaknesses and rawnesses in the string sections. Much weeding out was done during the next fortnight.

Within two years the RPO were established as one of the key orchestras of the world. In the autumn of 1950, he took them to America where, clamorously greeted, he conducted fifty-two concerts in forty-three cities in sixty-four days. Again the US was at his feet. The sweeping success of his tour rebuked the scattering of snipers and

* At the outset the principals and sub-principals were: Violins, John Pennington (leader) and B. Gipps; Second violins, D. Wolfstal and A. Ross; Violas, L. Rubens and A. Friedlander; 'Cellos, R. Clarke and K. Horitz; Double-basses, J. Silvester and S. Chesterman; Flutes, G. Jackson; Piccolo, B. Hanlon; Oboes, P. Newbury; Clarinets, R. Kell; Bassoons, A. Camden; Cor anglais, L. Brain; Horns, D. Brain; Trumpets, H. Barker; Trombones, W. Lover; Tuba, W. Scannel; Timpani, J. Bradshaw; Harp, J. Cockerill.

The opening programme was: Overture, *William Tell* (Rossini), Symphony in C, K. 435 (Mozart), *Over the Hills and Far Away* (Delius), *Romeo and Juliet* fantasy (Tchaikovsky) and suite from *Carmen* (Bizet).

detractors at home. The eclipse and frustrations of his wartime years had been expunged. At the beginning of his eighth decade, Beecham was again the unapproached and unquestioned king of the English musical scene, as well as one of the nation's chief symbols in foreign eyes.

CHAPTER TWENTY-SIX

THE AMBUSH

(1)

DEATH WHEN IT came was an ambush. There was to be no lingering sunset in the manner of a Delius tone-poem.

During the last decade, certain amiable obstinacies were strengthened. One of these had to do with getting to stations and catching trains. From Delves House to Lewes by road was, he erratically maintained, seven minutes flat; from Grove End Road to Paddington not more than four. These dogmas held good even in fog and snow. They involved his staff in waking nightmares. Moving one morning with stately shuffle from the Paddington booking hall towards a remote platform for the Shrewsbury train, he halted at the bookstall to cull newspapers and look over the latest paper-backs. He had one minute in hand. A messenger ran ahead and asked the guard to hold the train. In the end he had to be half lifted, half propelled into the guard's van. As the decade went on the shuffle became more painful. At times it degenerated into a wincing hobble. At seventy-six he underwent another foot operation. After the operation he went on shuffling as before.

Yet the iron of his nerve was untouched. His regard remained a bright skewer. His diatribes were rowdier than ever. (It is true that, through iteration, they had begun to lose impact; more people tended to discount or shrug them off.)

Every mail brought letters from aspirants who, to their own ears, were the Melbas and Carusos of the age. One specimen suffices to illustrate the general tone: "I am nineteen. I have a magnificent voice. My friends tell me I am beautiful. I must come and sing to you. I am the woman you are looking for." His private opinion as expressed to me was that, since the Kaiser's War, the European voice had declined everywhere but more particularly in England. Every year, nevertheless, he hopefully gave some fifty auditions at home and a comparable number abroad. Sometimes it was his whim to take the audition piano himself. His playing had undimmed gusto and was atrociously untidy.

With Betty at his side, voluble and advisory, he tirelessly roamed the earth in ships, trains and airliners, taking with him his baton cases and scores, his cigars and choice pipes and chessmen—and sometimes his orchestra. He appeared before packed, adoring multitudes now in Buenos Aires, now in Madrid, Rome, Lisbon, Vienna, Paris. A month or so later he would be scouring North America; we heard of him in Chicago, New Orleans, Washington, Seattle and half a dozen other concert rooms where his temper and tongue had long been as elating a drug as his music. But however crowded his travel schedule, however taxing the round of morning rehearsal and evening apotheosis, he never missed a stroke or dropped a stitch in the public debates which he initiated.

The most clamorous and protracted debate of all concerned Covent Garden. Against the State-aided régime there he stormed or sniped intemperately. His public references to the theatre's controlling Trust descended to scurrility.* His private references were, at their most heated, unprintable. The hard core of all this was a simple but highly debatable contention. If the Trust really meant to achieve their statutory aim, that of building up a *national* opera company, they must, he maintained, evacuate Covent Garden, which was suitable only for big continental voices, and concentrate upon light-calibre (as distinct from grand) opera in smaller theatres, where the Anglo-Saxon voice (very good of its kind but congenitally lightweight) would have a reasonable chance of reaching the back of the gallery.

The man who had ruled at Covent Garden with such relish and self-sufficiency throughout most of the 'thirties began, inconsequently, to cry the place down. Its name, he said, had acquired a spurious magic. Witchcraft was involved. The amateurs and so-called patrons who now ruled the operatic roost were so besotted thereby that no other theatre would or could serve their purpose. For himself, he had always been glad to give Covent Garden a wide berth and produce instead at the Shaftesbury, His Majesty's, Drury Lane—even at the Blackpool Opera House.

Into one of these tirades I inserted an objection. Surely the acoustics of Covent Garden were, as far as London went, unmatchable?

Grudgingly he admitted that the sound was good. But not as good as when he first conducted there. He talked learnedly of structural changes; of stout wooden pillars removed from either side of the proscenium, with deplorable acoustical results; and of experiments

---

* E.g., his speech to the Incorporated Society of Musicians, at Brighton, January 5th, 1949. In this he imputed incompetence or, a graver matter, interest to the Covent Garden directors, dismissed them as a "set of hapless ignoramuses and nitwits", said too much was going on that resembled a racket, and demanded an independent inquiry into the conduct of the theatre.

with the flight of sound, an erratic phenomenon, it seemed. When a singer sang a note at the audience, the sound went up to the right, hit the top gallery offside, travelled to the middle and halted before coming down to the stalls.

After this disquisition he paused. Then, with a bitter eye, he reverted to a matter which fretted him more nearly: the Trust's great sin of omission. In 1945, when setting up house, the directors and their advisers had never (was it to be believed?) consulted or approached him. "They never came near me!" In his day as an impresario he had given over a thousand performances of opera in English alone. To Covent Garden's benighted rulers this was evidently a matter of neither moment nor interest. The blaze went from his eye. His expression and the pitch of his voice were those of a hurt small boy; which proved more effectively than any amount of public rodomontade that the hurt went deep.

In 1951 there came an uneasy lull and a rapprochement. Returning to Covent Garden at the Trust's invitation after an absence of twelve years, he conducted six performances of *Die Meistersinger* with German singers mainly. The preliminaries were by no means frictionless. One morning he telephoned the theatre and asked how many chorus singers were being provided for the final scene.

"Eighty, Sir Thomas", replied a member of the musical staff.

"Eighty?" he shouted. "God Almighty, when I conducted *Meistersinger* at Covent Garden before the war, I always had 250 on the stage! Ring up all the singing teachers and academies and schools of music and tell them to send their pupils and students along as reinforcements."

In the event the chorus was augmented to 200.

Another dialogue involved playing time.

"Good morning, Sir Thomas. This is Covent Garden. We are sending round a *Meistersinger* score which indicates our cuts.

"There will be no cuts", said Beecham icily. "I am going to conduct *Die Meistersinger* in its entirety. *And* in German."

The first performance began at six p.m. and ended at a quarter to midnight. Tightening-up here and there subsequently docked the run by twenty minutes or more. The audiences yawned a little but roared excitedly every time the curtain came down. Beecham was not greatly moved. Five years later he characterised the performances as "inferior". The orchestra had been indifferent, the singers poor. This last was a grotesque epithet for casts which included Elisabeth Grümmer, Hans Hotter, Ludwig Weber and Benno Kusche. But by this time (1956) he was in the thick of his second main assault on the Covent Garden administration. Like his other attacks, this overreached itself and, far from serving any reformative purpose, confirmed the Covent Garden board in policies which, it must be conceded, have proved more fruitful than Beecham envisaged.

(2)

In most of his campaignings, as well as in the day-to-day running of a great orchestral and concert-promoting machine, he was intently counselled by Betty. When he telephoned this lieutenant or that before breakfast on the redrafting of some Delius programme, the booking of some new Constanze for a projected *Entführung*, or the temporary replacement of some orchestral sub-principal who had gone sick, the listener at the other end of the line soon became aware that he was talking in effect not to one person but two. He would be asked at the end of every sentence or two to wait a moment. The moments of waiting were filled with background consultations in which Betty's voice was plainly identifiable.

During conferences at home or in hotel suites, it was her pleasure to lie full length on a sofa, smoking cigarettes in a long holder, and offer "Tom" her opinions, often in brusque terms, on a dozen and one technical matters, whether invited or not. "Betty", it was commonly observed, "is always shoving her oar in." Differences of opinion between them sometimes blazed up into bawling matches which embarrassed newcomers to the circle but were soon perceived to be a sort of bravura double-act. Her influence with him was pervasive and acute. Word quickly spread among singers, instrumentalists and young composers that many of Beecham's decisions, especially those into which factors of personality entered, were his in name only. Who was taken up and petted, who discouraged and dropped, who beckoned back into the fold or kept for ever at bay: such acts and their timing stemmed (so it was concluded) as much from Betty as from Thomas. Many who abruptly fell out of favour ascribed their descent, rightly or wrongly, to the "gracious and gay" companion.

As she immersed herself more deeply in her husband's wider affairs, so did she withdraw from the concert platform. Whether they were put down to illness or mishap (e.g. a gashed hand), various of her concerto cancellations left the impression that her heart and ambition no longer lay in piano playing. A curious incident occurred as early as 1946. In the Davis Theatre, Croydon, she was rehearsing Mozart's C minor Concerto, K. 491, with her husband and the RPO for a concert the same night. Repeatedly she stumbled and lost her way.

Suddenly she stopped and exclaimed, "Tom, this piano's out of tune; it's bloody impossible!" Bursting into tears, she ran off the stage. Beecham casually strolled to the piano and played a couple of notes *fortissimo*. "What do you think?" he asked, with a circling glance and a wink of complicity at the orchestra. There were murmurs, sympathetic rather than sincere, of "Shocking!" and "Terrible!" The concerto was taken out of the programme and Schubert's *Unfinished* Symphony played instead. Lady Beecham, ran the official explanation, was suffering from influenza.

Illness dogged her into nursing homes and the operating theatre. Prettiness turned to pallor. A naturally vivacious manner became, at times, wayward or erratic. For the first time in his life Sir Thomas Beecham, it was noted, had intermittent cares of a kind that no degree of brilliance or genius could cancel or assuage. In moments of anxiety and trial, his bearing towards her was affable and patient, as devoted as a young lover's.

.   .   .   .

The summer of 1958 found them in Buenos Aires. He was billed for a glittering season at the Teatro Colón: *Otello, Carmen, Sansón y Dalila, La Flauta mágica* and *Fidelio*. Betty's health was by this time precarious. Three days before the *Flauta mágica* first night she suffered a heart attack. Beecham was at her bedside in their hotel when she died. He cancelled two rehearsals that day. Next morning a handful of friends, some of them singers from the opera, followed the bier to the chapel in the British Cemetery for a committal service. Cremation followed. It was given out that the ashes would be taken to England.

Condolences were conveyed to Beecham by a reporter. "I don't want sympathy, I don't want that guff", he roared. "I want to be alone." He found the antidote not in loneliness but in work. Resuming his rehearsal schedule, he continued the season without respite. On his last night the Colón thundered with affection. After the *Fidelio* finale the stage was pelted with flowers in his honour. In the orchestra pit players clustered around to grasp his hand. He had conducted for the last time in the theatre. What was his operatic aggregate? In mid-career he computed that from 1909 to 1920 alone he "gave" the British public 119 operas. My own count for these years is 95. If Beecham's reckoning is correct, it seems that throughout his career—i.e., from his début with Kelson Trueman's Imperial Grand Opera Company in 1902—he was associated, whether as conductor, artistic director or sponsor, with 203 operatic productions: an astonishing total for a man who spent so many of his professional hours in concert halls and recording studios.

During the closing years ovations thickened upon him. They came deeper from the throat and heart than anything he had known before. For his first appearance in London after the Buenos Aires season, the Festival Hall was crammed and radiant. As soon as the small, slippered figure appeared in the wings with the well-remembered (and slightly rumpled) dress coat and the far from immaculate white tie, the audience rose to its feet as one man and roared the kind of greeting which is usually reserved for warrior heroes on days of victory. Amid the cheerings and clappings and stampings he remained outwardly tranquil, with a hint in his eye of the old detachment and irony. The inner wound could only be divined. Stoical and silent about death, he expected others to be silent as well. When the silence was clumsily broken he could be ferociously macabre.

At a party to launch his biography of Delius (November 1959), he was accosted by a woman acquaintance who, through some freakish chance, had not heard of his bereavement. "How lovely to see you again, Sir Thomas" she gushed. "And how's Betty?" Without halting his shuffle across the reception carpet, he replied: "On tour." Pause. Then an afterthought: "With Vaughan Williams." The composer of the *London*, the *Pastoral* and seven other symphonies had died, aged eighty-six, a few weeks before Betty.

(3)

Two monologues of the last decade come back to me vividly. One of them dates from the year before Betty's death. He shouted it with eyes popping in self-whipped indignation. We were in his Mayfair hotel. He wore a green silk dressing-gown and white pyjamas which made concertinas round his ankles. Callers came and went. Everybody drank "pink ladies", a mixture, greatly favoured by the Beechams at that time, of grenadine, white of egg, gin and other pleasant things. The air was blue with cigar smoke.

The theme of his roaring bitterness was the failure of the British public, during the greater part of his career, to support him at the box office in preference to inferior foreign conductors. First came an exordium devoted to what he defined as England's two great failings: snobbery and homosexuality. The latter, he held, went on everywhere. "Everything is controlled by the sods. The country is riddled with homosexuals who are teaching the world how to behave—a spectacle of revolting hypocrisy." As to the twin vice:

"I struggled against English snobbery for thirty years. I gave concerts with my first London orchestra in 1906. Critics acclaimed me as a conductor of remarkable ability and individual outlook. Twenty years later another leading critic wote that I was one of the greatest musicians the orchestral world had ever seen. Nobody else in the country had noticed me. It took another ten years to make the slightest impression. I had no audience in London. My first concerts with the London Philharmonic Orchestra in 1932 were given to half-empty houses. That state of affairs lasted for another three years. Why? Because I was an Englishman! Until 1935, music was monopolised by such old humbugs as Mengelberg* and Toscanini. They gave third-rate performances. I and my orchestra gave first-rate ones, acknowledged as such in the United States and the world generally. It took me thirty years to arrive at this. It will take thirty years for anybody else to arrive at it. The talented young Englishmen of today will be doddering before it becomes evident in this country that they are equal to anything that comes from outside."

He paused and sent for another round of pink ladies. In what sense, I inquired, were Mengelberg and Toscanini humbugs?

In the sense, it seemed, that they sniffed up incense to which they were not entitled. "Toscanini", he said, "was a good conductor of Italian opera. But the Germans and the French never accepted him as an interpreter of their music. In this country he was accepted with slavish snobbery as a brilliant conductor of everything in sight. The same thing applied to Mengelberg. He was brought here in 1930 to show the London Symphony Orchestra how to play. He gave half a dozen concerts. That was enough. He retired unlamented from the scene. I have struggled against this prejudice and nonsense for half a century. All these damned foreign importations! Take Richter. He could conduct five works, no more. I was at a concert where he broke down in the *Peer Gynt* suite. Next morning I read 'Never has this great man asserted his dominance over the orchestra so completely'!"

Had he not, I asked, been responsible at Covent Garden for several "damned foreign importations" himself?

Yes, indeed, he was happy to say. He had brought in such guest conductors as Richard Strauss, Furtwängler, Schalk, Knappertsbusch and Clemens Krauss. "But", he thundered, "they don't bring in such people today. They bring in nobodies. The people I brought in were reputable conductors, not third-rate German opera house men,

---

* Willem Mengelberg (1871-1951), conductor during most of his career of the Concertgebouw Orchestra, Amsterdam.

répétiteurs, people nobody had ever heard of before. There are a dozen men in this country who can conduct every bit as well as these confounded interlopers, perhaps better. But we are not interested in our fellow countrymen. We are interested only in the picturesque foreigner with a spectacular name or romantic pseudonym and an unknown background. I'm going to drive these damned people from the country. I've suffered enough from their like."

     •   •   •   •   •

In September 1959, at the Lucerne Festival, he conducted not his own orchestra and the Beecham Choir but rival forces from London —the Philharmonia Choir and Orchestra—in a massively rescored version of *Messiah* which he had commissioned from his collaborator of forty years earlier, Sir Eugene Goossens. On a blue, burning afternoon he came down from their remote, mountainside hotel with his new wife, the third Lady Beecham (née Shirley Hudson)* for a choral rehearsal in the Lukaskirche directed by Wilhelm Pitz, the Bayreuth chorus master. I had a seat across the aisle from Beecham. After *All we like sheep* he turned and gave me an approving wink. It was a wonderful thing, I remarked tritely at the end, how intensely moving the *Messiah* music remained after thirty years' experience of it. He smiled a curiously sidelong, almost sly smile. "I've never been moved by *Messiah* in my life", he claimed. The smile changed to a frown of enthusiasm. Thumping the air with his fist, he added, "The importance of *Messiah* is that it is a work in the *grand* manner. It is one of the *grand* scores." Old-fashioned piety was put in its place, an obscure corner, it seemed.

The following night he took a general rehearsal in the Kunsthaus. As rescored by Goossens ("at my instigation", he insisted), Handel's music glowed, boomed and tinkled unprecedentedly. The brass and percussion writing often smacked of *Elgar* and *Die Meistersinger*, with tinctures here and there of Rimsky-Korsakov.

"What are the purists going to say about all this?" I asked.

"My dear boy", he answered, "I never think about the purists. They are a breed that has sprung up recently. If Handel and many other composers were left to the purists, with their parsimonious handfuls of strings and oboes, you would never hear any of them. The

* It became known nearly a fortnight after the event that Beecham had married Miss Hudson, formerly his secretary and now administrator of the Royal Philharmonic Orchestra, at a civil ceremony in Zürich Town Hall on August 10th. Miss Hudson was twenty-seven. She had worked at RPO headquarters, beginning on the telephone switchboard, for ten years.

thing to remember is that no man knows how these works were performed originally. I have thought about the problem for sixty years, much longer than the gentlemen who write strange monographs on the subject. They leave out of account the fact that Handel, who played the organ, clavichord or harpsichord in these performances, was the greatest *improvvisatore* of his day. Anybody who had the good fortune, as I had, to hear the improvisations of the greatest cathedral organists of the 19th century knows what extraordinary things the *improvvisatore* can do in 'filling-in'. There is no such filling-in by our purists. I have done purist versions of *Messiah* myself all over the world. Invariably the public walk out. And for a simple reason.

"Once people had heard the modern orchestra, the orchestra invented in the 19th century by Berlioz and Rossini (*not* by Beethoven), they refused to listen to the old orchestra any more. And now the modern orchestra has had its day. Its repertory is stale. It is dying. For over a century the orchestra lived on *new sound*, created by composers from generation to generation. Composers today are not creating new sound, any more than they are creating tunes and operas. (The last successful opera, by which I mean the last opera to remain in the international repertory, was Puccini's *Turandot*, which came out in 1926. All operas composed since have been fiascos in the sense that they do not go on being performed internationally.) These converging lines of decline lead to one conclusion. In twenty-five years' time there will not be an orchestra left in the world."

. . . . .

In a sweltering Kunsthaus three nights later he behaved frowardly. During the opening pages of *He trusted in God* he gave an angry shout, stopped beating time and brought the music to a standstill. The choir had sung accurately and spiritedly. They looked stony with unhappiness. After a second or two he started again without a word of explanation. At the end of *Lift up your heads* he caused further constraint by forcing an impromptu interval. Word passed from the rostrum along the line of soloists, who got up in bewilderment and drifted self-consciously into the wings. Backstage the choir were in a distraught, semi-mutinous state. Herr Pitz moved disconsolately from group to group, assuring them they were blameless.

When told of the singers' frame of mind, Beecham lifted his eyebrows and said in tones of innocent surprise: "But there has been an epidemic of dysentery. Singers were fainting, and I thought I had better pull up for a moment. I did not intend to criticise the choir in any way or in the slightest degree." It is true that two women singers had left the ranks for first-aid treatment during the performance. But nobody had fainted. And there had been no disturbance. One could only conclude that Beecham halted the chorus because he was dissatisfied with the overbrisk tempo at which he had started the movement.

The performance ended with tepid applause for Beecham and the soloists. Then Pitz came on to take a bow. The chorus gave him an ovation that almost turned into an anti-Beecham demonstration. In the middle of this the old man himself reappeared and appropriated the proceedings. Shaking hands with Herr Pitz, he waved the chorus to their feet again so that they could applaud Herr Pitz further, and finally walked off arm-in-arm with him amid vast applause. With perfect intuition and timing, he had turned a tricky and painful situation into a personal triumph.

(4)

His new marital state was as nomadic as the old. The American tours had become a settled annual routine. When in Europe he spent much time on the Riviera, or in Paris, or in Switzerland. His mobility was prompted in part by the tax inspector. Since it was impossible (he complained) to pay tax in three countries, he rationed himself perforce to seventy or eighty days a year in England, "a country where [on climatic grounds] it is impossible to live and nobody can afford to die." During his penultimate American tour he orated on taxation iniquities for three-quarters of an hour by transatlantic telephone from Chicago to one of his legal advisers in London. He ended with a reference to a group of persons much younger than himself with whom he was in conflict on certain financial matters. "Tell them", he boasted, "that I'm going to live for years. I'll see the boots off the lot of them." On the whole the doctors upheld this view. In his late seventies he was credited with the constitution of a hale fifty-year-old.

Events soon proved him vulnerable. Early in 1960 virus pneumonia interrupted his annual round of American auditoriums. Returning to England under doctor's orders, he prudently dropped a project to conduct five Covent Garden performances of Berlioz's *Les Troyens*, a work which he had vainly pined and planned to produce in that theatre for fifty years. By late April he was sufficiently recovered to conduct a concert at the Festival Hall. Ahead of him lay a heavily-loaded summer schedule. Ten performances of *Die Zauberflöte* were lined up at Glyndebourne Opera House. Before starting rehearsals there he must take a brief rest in Switzerland. Meantime there was one outstanding concert date in England. On Saturday May 7th he and the RPO arrived in Portsmouth.

First he lunched and wined his players in the town's handsomest banqueting hall. Wreathed in cigar smoke, the party left for rehearsal at the Guildhall. For fifteen minutes he toyed with a dozen or so bars of the evening's programme, polishing a phrase here, rebalancing a chord there. Then he put down his baton and said, "Now for the serious business of the day, gentlemen." The house lights were dimmed; a large-screen television set was switched on. Beecham and his men spent the rest of the afternoon with eyes glued to the 1960 Association Football Cup Final. As well as a connoisseur of soccer, Beecham was an assertive Lancastrian to the end. He bore the Wolves' three-goals-to-nil victory over Blackburn with jovial fortitude.

In the Guildhall that night he moulded familiar music with the old blandness and much of the old zest and fury. The concert ended as thousands had ended. The audience stamped and roared their joy and were loth to let him go. Who could have foreseen that this was the end of the journey; full-close to sixty sonorous and combative years? Thomas Beecham had conducted for the last time on any rostrum. Since they summarise a good half of his musical loyalties, the side of him that pursued and expounded "charm" and piquancy, it is well that the items of his Portsmouth programme should be listed here. They were: *Magic Flute* Overture, Mozart; Hadyn's Symphony No. 100 in G major (the *Military*); Suite, *Love in Bath* (Handel-Beecham), Schubert's Symphony No. 5 in B flat major; *On the River* from Delius's *Florida* Suite; and the Bacchanale from *Samson and Delilah* (Saint-Saëns).

.   .   .   .   .

There was a coda that lasted for ten months.

For his brief rest before Glyndebourne he travelled to Montreux. There he suffered a first attack of coronary thrombosis. The Glyndebourne engagements were cancelled. At the beginning of July he flew back to England. The rest of the year he spent in a nursing home. Early in 1961 it became known that he had made an almost complete recovery. Although weakened physically, he was mentally supple and alert. His head buzzed with recording projects. There was to be a gradual resumption of public concerts, too. To begin with these would be joint affairs, one half conducted by himself, the other half by Sir Malcolm Sargent. It was considered that a whole night on the rostrum might be too tiring for him.

Then came the second thrombosis attack. He died on March 8th, aged eighty-one, at his London flat, on the second floor of a vast Edwardian block in the Marylebone Road. To the west of his death-bed stood the Royal Academy of Music. Forty-seven years earlier he had witheringly lumped the R.A.M. with every other music school in the land as places which should superscribe their portals with: "Abandon hope, all ye who enter here." To the south, daylong and far into the night, sounded the faint grumble and ground bass of traffic between Paddington and King's Cross, stations from which he had taken a valiant young orchestra out on tour at a time when, to most ears, *Ein Heldenleben*—and even *Brigg Fair*—were harsh conundrums. To the north lay Regent's Park where, during their visits to London, Richard Wagner used to feed the ducks with bits of breakfast roll and Felix Mendelssohn-Bartholdy snowballed with the children of Ignaz Moscheles.

Two days later he was buried in a grave* remote from all such echoes and evocations. English music suddenly dwindled to what it was before 1906, a smallish and rather musty box. Not only that. Much glow and savour had gone from the English scene.

* At Brookwood Cemetery, Surrey.

THE END

INDEX

INDEX

Abbey Road, St. John's Wood, Beecham's flat in, 204
Ackroyd, G., 71
Ackté, Aino, 103-5, 134
Aeolian Hall, 131
Aga Khan, 183
Air raids (First World War), 157-8, 178-80
Albert, Eugen d', *Tiefland*, 106
Albert, Prince, 183
Albert Hall. *See* Royal Albert Hall
Aldwych Theatre, 93, 144, 153; Beecham Opera Company at, 164, 166, 172
Alexandra, Queen, 88, 101, 149
Allen, Sir Hugh, 201
Allinson, Adrian, 169, 173
Alvarez, Luis, 55
Andrews, Bernard, 213-14
Angelis, Hilda de, 55
Appletree Farm, Herts. (Sir Henry Wood's home), 213
Asquith, H. H., 103, 136, 174
Asquith, Margot, 136
Associated Press, 223-4
Astor, Lady, 215
Augusta-Victoria, Queen, 148
Austin, Frederic, 36, 45, 68, 125, 174
Australia, Beecham's tour in, 219

Balfour, A. J. (Earl), 130, 136, 170
Ballets Russes, 121-2, 131
Balling, Michael, 129
Bantock, Granville, 64-5
Barbirolli, Sir John, 221
Bariatinsky, Prince and Princess, 80, 112-14, 119
Barrett, Thomas J., 89
Bax, Arnold, 57, 65
Baylis, Donald, 127-8, 133, 137-9, 149, 151, 152, 158, 160, 165, 166, 172, 175, 177, 179, 180, 182
B.B.C., 197-8
Beard, Paul, 21, 202-3, 212, 213
Bechstein, Hans, 125
Bechstein (later Wigmore) Hall, 42, 45, 53, 115
Bedford, Duke of, 153
Beecham, Sir Adrian Welles (son), 62, 171
Beecham, Emily (sister), 15, 19, 23, 25-6, 29-33, 35, 41, 80
Beecham, Henry (brother), 185
Beecham, Sir Joseph (father): characteristics, 11; Mayor of St. Helens, 11; and his concert, 11-15; buys house (Ewanville) at Huyton, 20-1; and the Rev. Alfred Carter, 25-7; treatment

of his wife, 31-2; divorced, 32-3; threatens to disinherit Emily and Thomas, 33; continues wife's allowance, 34; reconciled to Thomas, 63, 71, 86-9; Thomas's feelings for, 82; finances operatic ventures, 89, 96, 108, 119, 134, 135; and Donald Baylis, 138; his Hampstead house, 140-1; his Grand Seasons of Russian Opera and Ballet, 141-7, 148-52, 154-5; baronetcy, and Order of St Stanislaus, 152; buys Covent Garden estate, 153-4, 170-1; death, 171; his estate, 171-2, 185
Beecham, Josephine (mother), 19, 31-4, 62
Beecham, Josephine ("Josie"; sister), 14-15
Beecham, Lady (*née* Shirley Hudson; third wife), 241
Beecham, Thomas (grandfather), 20, 23-4, 30, 62

BEECHAM, SIR THOMAS
LIFE
conducts at the Mayor's Concert, 13-18; birth, first music lessons, 19, 21-2; at private school, 21; holidays at Southport, and the Liverpool opera seasons, 22; at Rossall School, 22, 24; at Wadham College, Oxford, 24, 26-7; accompanies father to U.S.A., 25; holidays on the Continent, 25; enters father's firm, 27; founds St. Helens Orchestral Society, 27-8; engaged to Utica Welles, 29-31; difference with his father, and leaves home, 31; and his parents' separation, 33; at Roland Gardens, Kensington, 35; composes operas, 35; his music teachers, 35-7; and Joseph George Morley, 37; joint conductor in Imperial Grand Opera Company, 38-9; in Scott's madrigal group, 39-40; marries Utica Welles, 40-1; meets Puccini, 41-2; researches French composers, 42; first concert series with New Symphony Orchestra, 42-3; first public orchestral concert in London, 45-6, 48, 52; begins Thomas Beecham Orchestral Concerts, 53-6; and Delius, 56-61; sources of income, 62; lives at Mursley Hall, 62-3; his early protégés, 63-8; forms Beecham Symphony Orchestra, 69-73; his escapades, 73-4; and Elgar, 75-7; and Maud Christian Foster, 79-82; and Ethel Smyth, 82-6; reconciled to his father, 86-9; corespondent in Foster divorce case, 89-90,